The Good Guide to
Financial
Management

Professor Paul Palmer
Fiona Young
Neil Finlayson
Yogita Rajani

 UBS

Contents

Acknowledgements

Author's acknowledgements

We would like to thank the following for their contributions to this edition.

Graham Elliott at Withers for his extensive assistance on VAT (www.withersworldwide.com).

Greyham Dawes, Director at the Not-for-profit Unit, Crowe Clark Whitehill LLP, for his extensive contribution to Chapter 6: Charity accounts and financial management (www.crowecw.co.uk).

Pradeep Kachhala, Client Advisor to Charities at UBS for his contribution to Chapter 7 Section 3: Banking and borrowing.

Tony Austin, Chartered Accountant, tax consultant, for his contribution to the direct tax section in Chapter 8: Taxation (uk.linkedin.com/pub/tony-austin/8/a6a/126).

Dr Markas Gilmartin at Epoch for advice on investment and role of IFAs (www.epochwm.co.uk).

This edition would not be possible without the support of David Rowe of UBS and his team including Head of Charities, Andrew Wauchope (www.ubs.com/charities-uk).

We would also like to acknowledge the input of the various authors who contributed to the last three editions, much of whose work is still valid.

NCVO's acknowledgements

We would like to thank UBS for its on-going support of our financial management work, which produces valuable resources for the voluntary sector. Particular gratitude is due to UBS for its support of this update to *The Good Guide to Financial Management*.

Foreword

UBS is delighted to be able to sponsor what is, for many charities, the definitive guide to managing finance in the voluntary sector. *The Good Guide to Financial Management* gives both those who run charities and their trustees the tools to ensure that they are good stewards of its resources and that these are managed effectively to deliver the aims of the organisation efficiently.

This is as important as ever, at a time when charities can find their effectiveness under more scrutiny than ever before and when the pressure to deliver only increases. However, in dealing with these pressures, it is vital that charities have access to the right independent advice, and the guide provides clear answers to many of the questions facing charities on a daily basis. The authors have an impressive array of experience and expertise, and there is always a virtue in taking advice from people who have seen many of the potential problems at first hand.

As in all areas of the management of their affairs, charities are increasingly realising that they should expect more from their advisers (and indeed their investment managers). A 'one size fits all' or business-driven solution is not suitable for charities that increasingly need advisers who can work alongside them to achieve their important goals using all the resources at their disposal. Trust, open communication and developing a long-term working relationship with advisers is one of the distinguishing features of the sector and it should continue to be so. In this respect, the guide fills an important role in supporting such an approach and ensuring charities are able to set clear risk and return objectives.

At UBS we continue to support charities in achieving investment success through applying considerable resources and intellectual capital to the process of investment management whilst ensuring those of us who are involved with charities are also involved in charity.

It is only when one has faced issues as a charity trustee or school governor that one can truly understand the issues faced by others.

As a trustee myself, I very much appreciate the importance of *The Good Guide to Financial Management* in helping me understand and discharge my responsibilities, be it over 'opting up' or over our wider reserves policy. I hope you find it an equally valuable and helpful guide through the maze of regulation and best practice.

I would like to thank the NCVO trustees for asking UBS to sponsor this vital publication. We are proud of our partnership with NCVO and I hope you will contact us if, having read this guide, there is anything we can help you with.

Andrew Wauchope
Head of Charities
UBS AG
www.ubs.com/charities-uk

Introduction

This new edition of *The Good Guide to Financial Management* is, like previous editions, unashamedly about promoting best practice and is therefore full of prescriptive advice from experts, practitioners and research. I would like to thank my co-authors from the last edition: Fiona Young, who brings experience as both a finance director in a fundraising charity and subsequently a major grant maker, as well experience working on 'the other side' as an auditor to charities; and Neil Finlayson who acted as a professional reviewer and whose commitment to the sector, since I first met him as the audit manager to the charity I worked for in the mid 1980s, has never ceased. A fourth author joined us for this edition – Yogita Rajani is a director with UBS as a charities adviser on their investment team and brings a further dimension of experience.

Paul Palmer is Professor of Voluntary Sector Management at Cass Business School, City University, London and Consultant on Charities at UBS. Paul is a founder trustee of the Honorary Treasurers Forum and serves as a trustee on two grant-making charities. He also serves on the ethics panel of the Securities and Investment Institute and the Corporate Responsibility Advisory Group of the Institute of Chartered Accountants in England and Wales (ICAEW). In 2010/11 he project managed the Lord Mayor of London Integrity and Values Initiative.

Fiona Young MSc FCA DChA is Head of Resources at the Tudor Trust. Prior to this she was Director of Finance and Resources with Crisis UK and worked for a number of years at BDO as a senior charity manager. She co-authored the first three editions of *Preparing Charity Accounts*, published by ICAEW. She holds and has held a number of trusteeships, including CFG (until 2011) where she chaired the professional development group.

Neil Finlayson is Charities Partner at Kingston Smith Chartered Accountants and Guest Lecturer in Charity Auditing at Cass Business School, City University, London.

Yogita Rajani FCSI is Charities Advisor at UBS. She previously managed segregated, multi-asset global portfolios for UK charities and wealthy individuals at HSBC Private Bank and has over 12 years' investment industry experience. Yogita serves as a trustee at her local hospice and has recently completed the Cass Masters Course in Charity Accounting and Financial Management.

Structuring the organisation for financial strength

1.1
The governance debate

Governance was defined by the Cadbury Committee in 1992 as 'the system by which organisations are directed and controlled'. Institutions of every kind – government, public bodies, voluntary organisations and commercial companies – are under increasing pressure to be more transparent about what they do and more responsive to the people they serve. This has led to demands for higher standards of accountability, behaviour and performance.

This section looks briefly at the main developments in governance in the private, public and voluntary sectors. It will be of particular interest to the trustees of voluntary organisations, given the increasing professionalisation of the voluntary sector and the renewed emphasis being placed on the legal obligations of trustees. The 2007/08 global financial crisis and the failure of some UK institutions have continued to fuel the governance debate in recent years.

In any voluntary organisation, a precondition for financial strength is the clear definition of the roles and responsibilities of trustees, paid staff and volunteers. Without this clarity of roles, responsibility for income generation and expenditure will dissipate, along with any hope of control.

Corporate governance developments in the UK

In the 1990s there was a shift of attention away from how organisations were managed to how they were governed. This was partly the result of a series of prominent corporate failures and frauds in the late 1980s and 1990s. To prevent such failures happening again, a series of committees and codes have been introduced into corporate and public life – the first and most prominent being the 1992 Cadbury Committee on the Financial Aspects of Corporate Governance. Against the backdrop of prominent corporate failures such as Polly Peck and BCCI, the Cadbury Committee set out to address the low levels of confidence in company financial reporting and auditing, which have often been blamed for enabling executive directors' abuses to go undiscovered.

The Cadbury Report, however, goes beyond financial audit procedures to examine board structures and models of corporate governance. The committee developed a *Code of Best Practice in Corporate Governance*, which is based on principles of openness, integrity and accountability. The position of non-executive directors has also been strengthened by the establishment of audit committees that report directly to them.

The Hampel Report (1996) reviewed Cadbury and noted that few companies gave effectiveness opinions, concluding that this was because of the following points.

- Effectiveness was hard to define.
- It opened up the auditors and directors to unreasonable legal claims.
- It implied that controls could offer absolute assurance against misstatement or loss; in fact no system of control is proof against human error or deliberate override.

The Hampel Committee incorporated previous reports and produced the 'Combined Code', which requires public company directors to report on all internal controls, not just financial ones. The Turnbull committee in 1999 provided more detailed guidance in this area, linking governance to risk management and a system of internal control.

The Combined Code recognised the need to ensure a risk-based approach to developing sound business practices in order to protect the shareholders' interests. It stated that all companies needed clear systems of internal controls that were part of the normal management and governance processes of the organisation, embedded within the organisation's operations and not treated as a separate exercise undertaken to meet regulatory requirements.

The guidance also recommended that companies should be able to respond promptly to risks arising from both within and outside the company.

In November 2003 a new Combined Code was issued, which derived from a review of the role of non-executive directors by Derek Higgs and a review of audit committees by Robert Smith. These reviews were prompted by concerns that the principles on corporate governance outlined by Cadbury were not being adhered to and aimed to give clear guidance to boards on what was expected. Non-executive directors were expected to take an active role in their companies, for example, in relation to setting remuneration levels to executive management and providing an effective review to curb any management excesses, including undesirable behaviour and excessive risk taking. Smith focused on the role and effectiveness of audit committees, giving clear guidance on their role and composition, including their relationship with the board and with internal audit. In July 2004 the Financial Reporting Council set up a review of the Turnbull guidance led by Douglas Flint. As a result *Internal Control: Guidance for directors on the Combined Code* was published by the Financial Reporting Council in October 2005. The 2003 Combined Code was subsequently updated in 2006 and every two years thereafter.

In October 2008, the UK government commissioned Lord Turner to review the causes of the global financial crisis. The review included improvements needed on the effectiveness of internal risk management and corporate governance. Sir David Walker was then asked to review corporate governance in UK banks. His findings were published in November 2009 and he made a number of further recommendations. Key areas considered were:

- board size, composition and qualification
- functioning of the board and evaluation of performance
- the role of institutional shareholders – communication and engagement
- governance of risk
- remuneration.

The 2010 UK Corporate Governance Code incorporated the above findings and replaced the 2008 Combined Code. Four main new principles were introduced and addressed:

1. the chairperson's responsibility for leading the board

2. the need for directors to devote sufficient time

3. requirements for non executive directors to challenge constructively

4. the need for the board to have a balance of skills and experience.

The Combined Code explained that the board should be well balanced and consider its diversity, including gender mix. There was also a recommendation for directors to be re-elected annually.

Updates and current reviews

The 2010 UK Corporate Governance Code was revised in September 2012 and the main changes include the following points.

- If a company deviates away from the Code it needs to explain the rationale for this including any mitigating circumstances and when it does expect to comply.
- The annual report needs to include a statement on the diversity of the board. The board should consider the balance of skills, experience, independence and knowledge of the company on the board, including how it works together as a unit.
- FTSE 350 companies should put the external audit contract out to tender at least every 10 years.

In the future there is likely to be further guidance and focus around executive remuneration and women on boards. Draft legislation has been published to improve the quality of narrative reporting, which should contain information regarding company strategy, risk, remuneration and male and female diversity. These developments in private sector governance have had, and will continue to have, a major influence on how the public and voluntary sectors develop their own governance structures.

Developments in the public sector

The public sector response to corporate governance was in the Nolan Committee report, *A Report on Standards of Conduct in Local Government* (1996), in July 1997 and set out to consider an overall ethical framework for local government and how this framework might be adapted to different circumstances.

The code elaborated on the types of written agreements that should exist, including:

- the relationship statement
- job description and reciprocation
- reporting arrangements
- liability and responsibility statement.

The public sector has been deeply involved in the governance debate and fresh initiatives continue this involvement. In 2005 a new standard for the governance of public services was issued, which presented six core principles of good governance. Each principle was supported by principles that explained what was involved in putting good governance into practice.

1. Good governance means focusing on the organisation's purpose and outcomes for citizens and service users.

2. Good governance means performing effectively in clearly defined functions and roles.

3. Good governance means promoting values for the whole organisation and demonstrating the values of good governance through behaviour.

4. Good governance means taking informed transparent decisions and managing risk.

5. Good governance means developing the capacity and capability of the governing body to be effective.

6. Good governance means engaging stakeholders and making accountability real.

In 2007 the standard was reviewed in relation to how it had been used. It was proven to be fit for purpose, but the policy context had moved on, with new and emerging challenges such as an increasing emphasis on commissioning by local authorities and away from service provision and partnership and multi-agency working that involved public, private and voluntary organisations, making accountability less clear. New organisational structures such as employee-owned companies and social enterprises had also emerged.

The widespread structural changes, and the concerns over accountability arising from those changes, have resulted in new codes of conduct for central government and across public sectors, for example, the NHS, further education and police, seeking to establish good governance. At the same time, the push to make local authority services more economic and effective has introduced many private sector management practices into the public sector.

Developments in the voluntary sector

Section 177 of the Charities Act 2011 defines trustees as 'the persons having the general control and management of the administration of a charity'. In fulfilling this responsibility, trustees may delegate the management of the organisation's day-to-day affairs to an executive committee (a committee of paid staff in this instance) while they concentrate on governance. This delegation of duties does not, however, absolve trustees from being held accountable in law for the organisation's activities. Given these legal responsibilities, governance issues and practices are therefore particularly relevant to trustees.

The voluntary sector is facing a tough time against a backdrop of the deepest recession in the post-war period. Many voluntary organisations are facing a decline in a number of key income streams while experiencing an increase in demand for their services (partly due to public expenditure cuts) and rising costs.

The Charity Finance Group's March 2013 survey *Managing in the New Normal* highlighted that in 2012 as a result of the financial and fundraising challenges faced by the sector, 21 per cent of respondents had considered or were considering merger; 69 per cent had undertaken collaborative activity with others, most commonly in the form of joint programmes or service operations; 63 per cent were considering or planning to draw on reserves; 50 per cent had taken steps to reduce wages and salary costs. Of the 50 per cent that had cut salary costs, nearly one in three had restructured and a quarter had made redundancies. Furthermore, 55 per cent of those surveyed had increased trading or social enterprise activity since the start of the downturn.

NCVO's *UK Civil Society Almanac 2012* also described the changing nature of charitable status. First, the Finance Act 2010 introduced a new definition of charity for tax purposes and, in particular, rules requiring that the persons managing the charity must pass a 'fit and proper person' test in order to receive tax reliefs. Second, two sets of judicial proceedings turned the spotlight on the amount of public benefit that an organisation must provide in order to achieve and maintain its charitable status. It is important that the concept of charitable status matches the public's understanding in order to maintain the high levels of trust and confidence in the sector.

Good strategic leadership and strong governance is increasingly important to enable trustees to effectively manage the risks and opportunities in the current complex and challenging economic environment.

Good Governance: A code for the voluntary and community sector (The Code) was published in 2005 and updated in October 2010. The Code is endorsed by the Charity Commission and written by charity umbrella bodies, including ACEVO, NCVO, the Charity Trustee Network (CTN) and Institute of Chartered Secretaries and Administrators (ICSA).

The Code specifies six principles to enable an effective board to provide good governance and leadership. The new edition builds on guidance in the 2005 edition and includes advice on learning from the economic downturn and new thinking on governance.

The Code has encouraged sub sectors, such as student unions and sports associations, to produce their own tailored versions

The six principles state that an effective board will provide good governance and leadership by doing the following.

1. Understanding their role
- Avoiding inappropriate involvement in operational matters but taking responsibility for challenging and holding to account senior managers.

2. Ensuring delivery of organisational purpose
- Remaining alert to external and environmental factors that could result in the need to consider different ways of working.

3. Working effectively both as individuals and as a team
- Ensuring that the board invests sufficient time in developing positive working relationships among themselves and between the board and senior staff.
- Exercising effective control.
- Recognising the value of diversity as a means of identifying and managing risk.

5. Behaving with integrity
- Ensuring that the organisation's values and ethos are enshrined in its policies and practices.

6. Being open and accountable
- Demonstrating that the organisation learns from mistakes by handling complaints constructively as a valuable source of management information.

Full details of the code can be accessed at: www.governancecode.org.

Trustee annual reports and governance

The Charities Act 2011 requires all registered charities to prepare a Trustees Annual Report (TAR). Charities with an income greater than £250,000 must file their TAR with the Charities Commission where it is available to everyone who wants to know more about the charity.

Content of the trustees' annual report
The report should provide the following reference and administrative information about the charity, its trustees and advisers.

a) The name of the charity, which in the case of a registered charity means the name by which it is registered. Any other name by which a charity makes itself known should also be provided.

b) The charity registration number (in Scotland the Scottish Charity Number) and, if applicable, the company registration number.

c) The address of the principal office of the charity and in the case of a charitable company the address of its registered office.

d) The names of all of those who were the charity's trustees (Glossary GL 7) or a trustee for the charity (Glossary GL 59) on the date the report was approved. Where there are more than 50 charity trustees, the names of at least 50 of those trustees (including all the officers of the charity, e.g. chair, treasurer) should be provided. Where any charity trustee disclosed is a body corporate, the names of the directors of the body corporate on that date must be disclosed.

e) The name of any other person who served as a charity trustee (Glossary GL 7) or as a trustee for the charity (Glossary GL 59) in the financial year in question.

f) The name of any chief executive officer or other senior staff member(s) to whom day-to-day management of the charity is delegated by the charity trustees.

g) The names and addresses of any other relevant organisations or persons. This should include the names and addresses of those acting as bankers, solicitors, auditor (or independent examiner or reporting accountant) and investment or other principal advisers.

Source: The Charity Commission CC15b

It should be noted that the Charity Commission can give dispensation not to provide such details, for example, if a person would be deemed to be in danger. While the details identified in the SORP charity accounting standard are only applicable to larger charities, they are an example of best practice and should be followed by all voluntary organisations.

Quality standards

It is well established that there is a clear link between governance and quality assurance. A voluntary organisation's reason for existence is to deliver the best possible services to beneficiaries. However, sometimes it goes wrong. It has been suggested that this happens because voluntary organisations lack the bottom line of profit and have to rely on softer, less quantifiable and measurable performance monitors and goals. These issues also confront the public sector, and the search for value for money has often been linked to what have been termed the three Es, which can be defined for voluntary organisations as:

- **economic:** not spending 95p to raise £1 – essentially minimising waste
- **efficient:** getting the best use of what money is spent – a high output to input ratio
- **effective:** spending funds so as to achieve the organisation's objectives – getting things done.

The pursuit of quality and continuous improvement is not new to the voluntary sector: the commitment to deliver the best possible services to beneficiaries has been a major driving force for many years, and most voluntary organisations are highly motivated to deliver high standards of service. However, in the absence of the criteria used in the private sector – such as profit or return on investment – trustees, management and staff need other ways of measuring their performance. The following obstacles exist.

- Market or customer satisfaction is rarely a measure of quality – in the words of one charity representative: 'It is possible to give very bad advice very nicely.'
- Voluntary organisations often have a monopoly on providing certain services, therefore continued high demand is not necessarily an indicator of quality.

- Many end users are 'silent': for example, elderly people or people with mental health problems may not be able to make an informed view of quality.

For the last 10 years, voluntary organisations have been under pressure to show that they have achieved, and maintained, verifiable quality standards. This has increasingly been at the insistence of service purchasers, especially local authorities, or donors who fund activities. There has also been concern among the wider public about the probity and performance of the voluntary sector.

The Quality Standards Task Group was set up at NCVO in July 1997. After wide consultation, the Group recommended that the voluntary sector should do the following.

- **Establish quality principles:** to describe an organisation's fundamental beliefs that form the basis for its whole management ethos.
- **Commit to the concept and practice of continuous improvement:** to provide for the systematic and methodical enhancement of an organisation's capabilities and performance.

The proposed principles for the voluntary sector state that a quality voluntary organisation:

- strives for continuous improvement in all it does
- uses recognised standards or models as a means to continuous improvement and not as an end
- agrees requirements with stakeholders and endeavours to meet or exceed these the first time and every time
- promotes equality of opportunity through its internal and external conduct
- is accountable to stakeholders
- adds value to its end users and beneficiaries.

1.2
The trustee board

Given the huge range of requirements and best practice guidelines, an effective, well-structured trustee board of committed individuals is of paramount importance and the vital first step in ensuring an organisation's financial strength. In this section, we take a brief look at some of the issues to consider when recruiting trustees.

What are you looking for in a board member? Ideally you will want to find people whose skills, experience and personal qualities will complement those of your current board.

Thinking about any existing skills gaps could give you ideas about where to look and could help to improve the composition of your board. After carrying out a skills audit (see Appendix A of this chapter), the board needs to decide on a strategy to attract new trustees and to utilise the range of skills that are already available.

The board may wish to set up a nominating committee with the specific task of recruiting new trustees (as well as implementing board development/induction programmes). It is important to write a job description and person specification for trustees; these help the organisation to clarify the role of its trustees, support people thinking about becoming trustees and help those considering nominating others for trusteeship. It may also be useful to draw up a code of conduct, spelling out the relationship between trustees and the organisation; this can help to clarify expectations on both sides, making obligations plain to potential trustees. The code should state, for example, that expenses may be claimed and should give an honest estimate of the amount of support the organisation can give new trustees and the time commitment required of them.

Finding new trustees

Here are some ideas of where to look for potential trustees.

- Consider your volunteers, supporters, donors, service users/beneficiaries and colleagues in partner organisations or those involved in related areas of work.
- Organise an event that will enable people to learn about your organisation.
- Do any local firms have employee volunteering schemes? If not, you could encourage them to start one. Contact your local Chamber of Commerce for contact ideas.
- Use a newsworthy event to obtain media coverage.
- Advertise in national or local newspapers, professional journals, community centres or libraries.
- Try using a trustee brokerage service. These draw their potential trustees from a variety of different sources – retired people, professionals, business people, people from black and minority ethnic communities etc – and offer levels of service varying from basic introductions to full recruitment.

Inducting trustees

In order to be effective, trustees must be given all the information they need to understand the organisation – its aims, beneficiaries, the boundaries within which it operates – and their own role as trustees.

An induction pack should be compiled, containing information about the organisation and the role and responsibilities of trustees. Here are some suggestions about what it should include.

- A brief history of the organisation.
- The governing document.
- Standing orders.
- Roles and responsibilities of trustees, including trustee job descriptions.
- The annual report and accounts for the previous three years.
- Sets of recent board papers and minutes, including management accounts.
- Board and committee structures.
- Terms of reference for the board of trustees and all committees.
- Dates of forthcoming meetings.
- Names, addresses, email addresses, and telephone and fax numbers of trustees.
- Major policy documents.
- If staff are employed, the organisation's staff structure and the chief executive officer's job description.
- A manual (such as NCVO's *The Good Trustee Guide*).
- A self-assessment form to enable recruits to indicate their own support needs, for example, pairing, debriefing meetings.

An effective induction should not only prevent new trustees from becoming disillusioned and leaving, but should also mean that they quickly become a useful member of your board.

The Charities Act 2011 requires charities to disclose the induction programme of new trustees in their annual reports.

The governing structure

Recruits will need to know whether the main board of trustees has any sub-committees and, if so, what their terms of reference are. If the trustees have powers to delegate work to sub-committees, all decisions of those sub-committees should be reported to the full board of trustees, which must take ultimate responsibility for them. Recruits must also be told whether there are any advisory groups and how they fit into the governing structure and whether there are any additional working parties or ad-hoc committees.

The structure of the organisation

An organisation chart, together with a list of the names of key staff with their job titles and responsibilities, will provide a useful overview of the structure of the organisation. Staff are normally accountable through a line management structure to the chief executive, who is in turn answerable to the trustees. To avoid blurring these lines of accountability, trustees may need guidance on when it is appropriate to contact a member of staff directly and when they should go through the chair or chief executive.

Annual reports and accounts

Each year trustees should be given a copy of the organisation's annual report and accounts. They should keep these copies for at least three years.

Conflicts of interest

Conflicts of interest arise when the personal or professional interest of a board member is potentially at odds with the best interest of the organisation, for example, when a board member performs professional services for an organisation, or suggests that a friend or relative be considered for a staff position. These decisions are perfectly acceptable if the board makes them in an objective and informed manner and if they benefit the organisation. Even if they do not meet these criteria, such decisions are not usually illegal, but they are vulnerable to legal challenges and public misunderstanding.

A damaged reputation is the most likely result of a poorly managed conflict of interest. Because public confidence is so important to voluntary organisations, boards should take steps to avoid even the appearance of impropriety. These steps may include to following.

- Adopting a conflict of interest policy that prohibits or limits business transactions with board members and requires board members to disclose potential conflicts.
- Disclosing conflicts when they occur so that board members who are voting on a decision are aware that another member's interests are being affected.
- Requiring affected board members to withdraw from decisions that present a potential conflict.
- Establishing procedures, such as competitive bids, that ensure that the organisation is receiving best value in the transaction.

Connected persons

Section 118 of the Charities Act 2011 states that:

'Connected persons' are persons who at any time during the relevant accounting period, or the previous accounting period, are or were:

a) trustees of the charity

b) persons who hold or held the title to property or investments of the charity

c) donors of material assets to the charity (whether the gift was made on or after the establishment of the charity)

d) any child, parent, grandchild, grandparent, brother or sister of any person mentioned in a) to c)

e) any officer, employee or agent of the charity (which would include an organisation which provides management services)

f) the spouse of any person mentioned in a) to e)

g) any firm or institution controlled by any one or more persons mentioned in a) to f), or in which any such person is a partner

h) any corporate body in which any 'connected person' mentioned in a) to g) has a substantial interest, or in which two or more such persons taken together have a substantial interest.

'At least once a year the board should also review its own performance.'

Sample form

Conflicts of interest

As a trustee, you are required to act in the best interests of 'X' charity. However, inevitably, trustees have a wide range of interests in private, public and professional life and these interests might, on occasions, conflict, (ie director of supplier or consultant to charity). We are obliged to review any possible conflicts when preparing our annual report so ask you to supply the following details:

Has 'X' charity made any loans to you? No/Yes

Have you, or people connected with you through family, business or another charity, an interest in a contract or transaction with 'X' charity? No/Yes

Have you or any person connected with you derived any pecuniary benefit or gain from 'X' charity? No/Yes

Signed:
Date:

Self-assessment for the board

Evaluation is a central function of any board. The trustees must assess whether the organisation is carrying out its mission effectively. They should also carry out an annual evaluation of the chief executive. Unfortunately, many voluntary sector boards pay too little attention to these types of evaluation.

At least once a year the board should also review its own performance. Trustees should stand back and ask themselves what role the board is playing in the governance of the organisation and what its strengths and weaknesses have been, and use this evidence to plan for the years ahead.

This review can strengthen the board by:

- identifying the criteria for an effective board
- identifying important areas where improvement is needed
- measuring progress towards the goals set by the board
- shaping the future make-up and structure of the board
- building trust and enabling members to work more effectively as a team.

A self-evaluation by individual trustees is also helpful. This can: identify areas of strength and highlight weaknesses; support needs; and highlight those board programmes to which the trustee feels best able to contribute. This exercise can also lead a trustee to conclude that it is time for him or her to leave the board.

Another useful part of the learning process could be a one-to-one discussion with the chair of the organisation on the role a trustee has played on the board.

1.3
The financial management role of trustee boards

The financial management role of a trustee board is different to that of a commercial entity's board. Most voluntary organisations are financially accountable to a far greater number of stakeholders, because they are funded by a combination of tax concessions and money from the general public, local government and charitable trusts.

The goal of maximising shareholder value – which can be measured objectively – is not relevant to voluntary organisations. Instead, the whole trustee board (not just the treasurer) must demonstrate value for money and effectiveness, which by their nature are more subjective criteria.

This section of the guide examines the three main financial management functions of the board:

1. financial monitoring

2. financial procedures

3. financial management.

It examines typical weaknesses and introduces various techniques that will be studied in more detail in later sections.

Appendix B includes a checklist for identifying the financial governance issues that may affect a voluntary organisation. It will help emphasise the fact that financial management is the responsibility of the whole trustee board.

Financial monitoring

In practice, the financial monitoring carried out by boards may be typified by the following activities and motivations.

- The comparison of budgets for income and expenditure with actual results.
- The consideration of projected sources and levels of income and expenditure.
- The need to report to funders.
- The lack of any value added, instead seen as a compliance function.
- Information that is too detailed and conforming to accounting regulations.

- Completely reactive responses conditioned by when information is presented.

Ideally, however, financial monitoring should be characterised by the following features.

- The use of key financial ratio analysis (which can, for example, highlight financial stability).
- The inclusion of financial performance information against predetermined financial policies (for example, income reserves).
- A committee that is adequately empowered in its role by proper induction has an understanding of cost structures and understands its relationship with management.
- The provision of information that is understandable, timely and accurate.

Financial procedures

These procedures are designed to ensure the propriety and efficiency of the organisation's activities. They typically include policies for proper accounting, control and protection of the organisation's income, expenditure and assets.

By means of delegation, the board must ensure that financial procedures appropriate to the size and complexity of the organisation exist. This could be achieved by compiling and distributing a financial procedures manual and/or by responding to reports on areas of weakness by external auditors. Appendix C gives a typical financial procedures manual for a membership organisation; however, this will need to be tailored to the needs and structure of individual organisations.

'The importance of having the "right" trustees is increasingly evident.'

The external auditor may discover weaknesses in the internal control procedures that will affect the accounts. The auditor should report these weaknesses to the trustees.

The principal purposes of this report to management are to:

- enable the auditor to comment on the accounting records, systems and controls he or she has examined during the course of the audit, for example, weaknesses in credit control, the reconciliation of ledgers and the maintenance of grant approvals
- provide management and trustees with financial statistics that can be used to judge the performance of a charity, for example, the number of weeks' expenditure in reserves or total staff costs expressed as a ratio of total resources expended
- communicate any matter that might affect future audits, for example, new accounting standards
- recommend what changes need to be made to systems in situations where there are no other compensatory controls.

The auditor must ensure that the recommended changes have been made.

Financial management procedures

These procedures cover a wider area of decision making than the purely financial ones: they are the procedures that help management to decide overall strategy and make the best use of resources. Examples might include the decision to outsource an area of operations, such as catering or payroll. Too often, however, the board lacks the expertise to carry out these procedures, or is reluctant to 'step on the chief executive's toes'.

As a result, financial management is often seen as a luxury, since the funding does not allow for it. If done at all, it tends to be restricted to budget construction, with little or no consideration of resource inputs, outputs and outcomes.

This guide will enable more informed decision making by management and a greater financial management role for trustee boards.

The financial team and the role of the treasurer

The financial management team for a voluntary organisation might comprise the honorary treasurer, a chief finance officer, internal audit function (for the larger charity), external auditors/accountants, investment advisers and bankers. Each is a specialist function in its own right, and together they ensure that the organisation is managed efficiently and effectively.

In 2003 a group of honorary treasurers began meeting at the Cass Business School as part of an initiative by the Centre for Charity Effectiveness based at the Business School. In 2005, assisted by business school charity students, they produced a definitive guide on the treasurer's role in a charity that was published by NCVO in 2006. Appendix D contains a synopsis of a job description and person specification for a typical treasurer's post.

Conclusion

This chapter has examined how the governance debate is resulting in changes that will help voluntary organisations to clarify relationships between the executive management and the non-executive trustee board and to establish codes of conduct that are value based.

The importance of having the 'right' trustees is increasingly evident as more emphasis is being placed on the proper induction, training and assessment of trustee boards. All this strengthens the role of trustee boards, enabling them to contribute in a way that adds value to the aims of the organisation. What remains is to provide trustee boards with the financial management skills that will allow them to examine objectively, and perhaps critically, the issues presented to them by management. Armed with these techniques, trustee boards can help to ensure that charitable objectives are met in a way that is demonstrably efficient and effective in the eyes of all key stakeholders.

Checklist

Answer the following questions before checking the answers in the text.

1. How is value for money defined?

2. What should a voluntary organisation be able to demonstrate?

3. What are the two principal financial differences between a commercial organisation and a voluntary organisation?

4. What are the ideal financial monitoring characteristics of a voluntary board?

5. List five key controls that should be contained within a financial procedures manual.

Action points for your organisation

'Audit' your organisation by checking to see if you have:

- a clear procedure for the election, times served and retirement of board members
- undertaken an assessment of the requirements and type of skills you want the management committee to have
- a procedure to record conflicts of interest that may arise for board members
- undertaken regular self-assessment of the organisation: is it carrying out its mission effectively?; have you appraised the chief executive's performance or reviewed the boards performance (strengths and weaknesses)?
- timely and effective management information to assist with control
- a financial procedures manual – does it have clear rules on the authorisation of expenditure, cheque-signing authority etc?
- a board that is proactive in financial management with a plan for longer-term objectives
- a job description for the honorary treasurer or terms of reference for the finance committee
- an annual 'management letter' from the external auditors.

Case studies and exercises

Managing conflicts of interest

From time to time every board faces a period of conflict. Sometimes these conflicts are between individual board members, sometimes they are between factions within the board and sometimes they are between the board and the staff. The first thing to note is that conflict is not inherently bad; some tension can be productive. Indeed, many community organisations function as a forum in which conflict can be resolved.

However, there is a difference between healthy conflict, where differences of opinion are expressed and debated, and unhealthy conflict, which simply hinders the organisation from fulfilling its mission.

These case studies illustrate the different kinds of conflict that may arise and the lessons that can be learned from them.

1 Conflicts between the board and staff

Case study

A chief executive of a thriving community centre had been in post for many years.

She had extensive management experience and had recently taken a higher degree in management. The trustees, by contrast, were largely unwaged local people, including a large proportion of young mothers and retired people. Few had much experience of modern management, and the chief executive consequently held them in contempt. In her eyes, they did not 'add value'. For their part, they found the endless papers the chief executive presented on topics such as performance indicators, strategic planning, benchmarking, quality standards and appraisal systems almost incomprehensible. The trustees' solution was to recruit an able chair who was familiar with the current management and governance agenda and could consequently begin to wrest control of the organisation back from the chief executive.

The lessons

The management committee and the chief executive must work together, if not in partnership then at least in a mutually beneficial way. Each must respect the role of the other, which means that the chief executive must respect the governance role of the trustees. Even though they may not have the professional and business skills a manager needs, they are still the custodians of the charity. It is easy enough for a high-powered chief executive to marginalise a management committee of ordinary people, but a skilful chief executive draws on the skills the management committee does possess, and empowers them to do better by providing sympathetic trustee development programmes, encouraging trustees to seek outside professional advice and presenting information clearly and concisely, if necessary through presentations and question and answer sessions. By contrast, a marginalised trustee board may feel they have no alternative but to recruit a chair tough enough to take back control of the organisation from a domineering chief executive.

Case study

The newly recruited chief executive of a small counselling organisation had previously been a senior manager in a large statutory agency. He had been accustomed to regular structured supervision, the informal support provided by colleagues and calling in experts from elsewhere in the agency to help with difficult cases. He soon began to feel isolated in his new post, and blamed the trustees for failing to provide adequate support.

The lessons

The chief executive is at the top of the management ladder, no matter how small the organisation. The role therefore calls for leadership and an acceptance that the line management provided in a large bureaucracy is neither appropriate nor possible.

Trying to force the trustees (or the chair) to take on a line management role will overburden them – it is, after all, an unpaid, part-time job – and could generate yet more conflict: the chairs of small voluntary organisations are not necessarily familiar with the concept of supervision as practised in large statutory agencies.

The chief executive can reasonably expect the trustees to set out the strategy and direction of the organisation in policies and plans. The chair and chief executive should aim to develop a good working relationship – in practice that will mean contact at least once a week, probably by phone or email.

Chief executives who feel they need more support than the trustees can give should explore other avenues, such as peer networks and action learning sets. Part of their new leadership role is to show initiative.

2 Conflict with an individual board member

Case study

A new trustee who had previously been a volunteer has been upsetting people by coming into the office unannounced, bossing staff around, countermanding the director's orders, demanding confidential information and generally meddling in day-to-day affairs.

The lessons

This is a classic example of someone who is confused about which hat they are wearing. The chief executive should organise a development session for the board and do a 'hats' exercise, based on the leadership tool developed by Edward de Bono, which encourages people to be more productive. They should be reminded that trustees must act jointly – they have no power individually except that which is specifically given to them by the board or potential trustees. This will help to avoid conflicts of interest that may bring the organisation into disrepute, and should enable members to recognise when apparently unrelated individuals standing for election form a faction.

General principles

Ensure that new trustees and staff are properly selected and adequately inducted.

Make sure that the boundaries between different roles are clearly defined and clearly understood by everyone.

Put the organisation's interests first. Staff, volunteers and trustees work together to help the organisation fulfil its mission; the only justification for prolonging conflict is where the long-term benefits will outweigh the short-term disruption.

Consider the values that inform your organisation. Trustees and staff may have competing or incompatible values.

Consider Nolan's Seven Principles of Public Life.

1. Selflessness

2. Openness

3. Integrity

4. Honesty

5. Objectivity

6. Leadership

7. Accountability

Case studies exercises

These exercises can be used by trustees as part of a management development programme, for example, in a role play.

1 Founder issues

'Mind Craft' trust was founded five years ago by a senior art therapist, John Thurstrom, who was concerned that the artistic output of people who had mental health problems was not being displayed in commercial art galleries. John, himself an artist, set up the charity to be a 'clearing house' and advocate between artists who had mental health problems and the commercial art galleries that sell their work. John formed a committee of trustees, made up of direct friends and their friends, which included prominent artists who did not have mental health problems, a leading gallery owner and respective partners in top firms of accountants and solicitors. John was the chair of the trust, which had no paid staff.

John continued to work as an art therapist but after two years explained to his fellow trustees that the charity was not going to get anywhere unless there was some full-time staff. John was due for a year-long paid sabbatical – to write a book – and proposed to his fellow trustees that he would also spend more time on developing the trust. During the year John's energy and enthusiasm transformed the trust, which obtained some contracts with commercial art galleries, receiving a commission of 25 per cent on the sale of each picture as a fee. It also received a substantial donation from a wealthy individual and a grant from a trust. At the end of the first year the trust's income was £250,000 with five staff in London (in John's house) and a network of volunteer agents/staff spread throughout the country.

John proposed to his fellow trustees that he should continue working for the trust and had arranged a further 12-month unpaid sabbatical from his employers. The trustees agreed that he should continue in this role and remain as 'executive chairman'.

The solicitor trustee advised that she would write to the Charity Commission telling them of this decision and seeking their approval, as John would be paid. The trust continued to grow, doubling its income by the end of the year. John then proposed to the trustees that he should step down and the trust should appoint a chief executive. 'After all,' he said, 'I still have my book to write.' A chief executive was subsequently appointed who in-turn appointed new staff and a new London head office was acquired. Six months into the job at a meeting of the trustees, the chief executive explained that the organisation's business plan, which had been drawn up by John, was totally unrealistic. Growth of income to £1m was unsustainable as it was based upon verbal, unconfirmed promises and expectations. Staff and volunteers were exhausted and some artists were complaining about the 25 per cent commission the trust took. One artist had contacted *The Guardian*, which had sent a reporter who said that commercial agents' normal fees were 10 per cent. John replied that the very nature of a voluntary organisation was to be pioneering and adventurous or it would never succeed. Second, the higher commission fee was based on promoting the trust and its vision. The chief executive's view was that it would have been a good idea to tell the artists. The vision was fine but business sense also had to be applied.

Following the meeting the chief executive submitted his resignation with 'immediate effect'. The trustees met and John explained that he had negotiated a further leave of absence and would again 'manage the organisation' until the current problems were resolved.

Questions

1. What are your observations on the governance of the organisation?

2. What different actions could the trustees have taken?

3. What actions should the trustees take now?

2 The treasurer's role

People concerned with the use of chemicals in food production had founded the Association for Agricultural Advancement in the early 20th century. The Association had grown to over 10,000 members at the start of the 21st century but membership had since declined to 7,000 members by the beginning of 2010. The trustees met six times a year and consisted of 45 members who were elected from a variety of different professional interests. For much of the 20th century the Association's income had come from membership fees and examination fees from its qualification in nutritional management. In 2005 the Association found that its qualification had been superseded by university qualifications and that income from registration and examination fees, which had once been 70 per cent of the income, was now closer to 40 per cent, around £400,000 in 2010 and still declining at the rate of 10 per cent per year. The association produced a quarterly journal and held lectures for its members, whose fees had not increased since 2005, partly to stem the loss in membership. This had only been partially successful as membership continued to decline by 250 per year. Fees were £85 per annum. However, the annual expenditure exceeded the annual income and the substantial reserves of £700,000 that the Association had built up in earlier years were being drawn down quite quickly. Some good news and potential for the association was the interest in organic food. Two of the trustees were experts in this area and they had proposed a new qualification.

The trustees had appointed a new chief executive and director of finance in 2010. To support them and to 'manage the crisis' a new committee structure had been agreed at the annual general meeting, which had abolished all the former committees and replaced them with a smaller executive committee that met monthly. The full trustee meeting was to be half-yearly. The new honorary treasurer, chair and deputy chair formed the executive committee with the chief executive and finance director. The new committee set about their roles with enthusiasm, particularly the honorary treasurer who regularly visited the organisation. With the finance director they reviewed financial procedures and introduced cost-cutting measures. Over half the staff in the education department that administered the qualification had been made redundant at a one-off cost of £150,000 leaving an on-going annual expenditure for the year 2012 of £1.2m.

At the next trustee meeting, the member who edited the journal complained that writers for the journal who received a fee of £50 per annum had either not been paid or found that tax had been deducted. She explained that her job was becoming impossible as people were upset by such 'shabby treatment' and were refusing to write for the journal. One member pointed out that the journal was now the only 'benefit' members received. A former chairman, now retired, who came down from Scotland to the meetings in London claimed that his expenses had not been paid because his tea receipt for 95p had not been attached.

Three months later he was still waiting for payment despite sending it back saying that the society could have the 95p. He went on to say that the fare was in excess of £100, which he had personally incurred, and that as a pensioner this was money he could ill afford.

The honorary treasurer replied that the association was in financial crisis and that all expenditure had to be monitored. He personally checked all expense claims. The writers for the journal had not been paid, as they had not sent in proper invoices or a letter from their tax offices that confirmed that they were self-employed for tax purposes. He had taken advice from the auditors on freelance staff and they had advised him that tax had to be deducted.

One member explained that he had not realised how desperate the situation had become. They asked how long the association had to survive and whether they were protected from personal liability if the organisation was to become insolvent. Another member said the treasurer deserved everyone's support for his hard work. One of the experts in organic food asked if there had been any progress made on the new qualification. Heated discussions followed before the questions of 'How long have we got?' and 'What plans are there to get us out of this problem?' were put to the chair. As the chair turned to the chief executive, the treasurer interjected, 'I am working on these figures at the moment and it would be inappropriate to answer this question until the executive committee has discussed them.'

Questions

1. Estimate the current financial situation of the Association and how long it has got before reserves are exhausted (assuming cost inflation of 3 per cent per annum on expenditure, but no increase in exam fees or membership subscriptions).

2. Is the treasurer correct in his advice on the payment to the writers?

3. Is the treasurer's conduct and current role appropriate?

4. Critically evaluate the current management of the organisation and make suggestions as to how they could improve it.

Answers

These draft answers are designed as discussion points. As with all case studies, there is no definitive answer. However, from the financial management and governance perspective, they illustrate points of best practice.

1 Founder issues

1. There is potential confusion between John's role as chair, founder and employee. The trustees sought Charity Commission permission for his paid role. If they agree to him taking over they will have to do so again unless the constitution has been changed.

2. Founders who then become chief executives and move back to being chairs have a potential conflict with a new chief executive. The other trustees could have appointed a different chair to John to avoid such conflicts. Imposing a business plan as ambitious as this one on a new chief executive would inevitably lead to conflict. The trustees should have recognised that a potential conflict would arise. They should have provided a mechanism to review the business plan that would have depersonalised the review. For example, the honorary treasurer could have chaired and presented the revised business plan.

3. The organisation's vision has clearly not been communicated and the organisation's accountability to its beneficiaries is confused. While corruption is probably not an issue, the potential for exploiting the users is real. Equally, poor communication could lead to embarrassing publicity. Has the charity made clear in its literature and contracts with artists that it charges a higher commission? Why does it charge that amount and has it got the commitment of its supporters to this policy? John is clearly highly committed to the organisation but now needs to take a step back. The trustees, if they agree to John's offer of managing the organisation, again need to have a clear exit route for John and a succession plan.

2 The treasurer's role

1. The Association has an annual income this year of:

Fees £85 x 7000 exams	£595,000
	£400,000
Total income	**£995,000**
Expenditure	£1,200,000
Redundancy	£150,000
Deficit	£355,000
Reserves	£700,000
Balance on reserves	£345,000
Next year	
Fees £85 x 6750	£573,750
Exams £400,000 less 10%	£360,000
Total income	**£933,750**
Expenditure (3% inflation increase)	£1,236,000
Forecast deficit	£302,250
Reserves brought forward	£345,000
Balance on reserve	£42,750

The society has just over two years of reserves without changing its expenditure pattern or allowing for interest on its balances.

2. Unless there is clear evidence that the writers are self-employed or they have signed the appropriate declaration form, tax should be deducted. However, if tax is to be deducted this should be communicated to the writers before they carry out any work.

3. The treasurer has become confused and is acting more like a financial controller than the honorary treasurer. What is the job of the finance director? The honorary treasurer has become too involved in day-to-day matters instead of taking a strategic vision and facilitation role.

4. The Association has clearly not thought through its governance.

- There are petty disputes, for example, withholding payment while sorting out 95p.
- Only meeting half yearly will lead to divisions and hostility at a time when trustees should be pulling together.
- Not giving or having the financial information to hand and sharing it, given the nature of charity trusteeship as a joint liability, is counterproductive.
- The executives are not different to their fellow trustees. While having 45 trustees making decisions is too many, changing suddenly to three trustees has gone to the other extreme and communication is clearly breaking down.
- The Association has adopted a 'knee jerk' reaction to its problem and turned it into a crisis. It needs to take a strategic view of its future. It has some time and opportunities to develop a new income stream. By making the staff redundant it has lost the capacity to take advantage of this opportunity.

Appendix A:
Sample skills and audit questionnaire

Name:

_____

Date:

_____

1. What kind of expertise do you consider you
bring to the Board?

☐ Administration campaigning

☐ Change management/restructuring

☐ Consultancy

☐ Customer care development

☐ Disability

☐ Equal opportunities

☐ Financial fundraising

☐ General governance

☐ History of the sector

☐ Human resources/training

☐ Information technology

☐ Legal

☐ Management/management systems

☐ Marketing media/PR networks/alliances

☐ Policy implementation

☐ Research

☐ Risk management

☐ Strategic planning and training

Comments:

2. What other experience or skills do you feel you offer?

_____

_____

_____

_____

_____

_____

3. Are there any particular areas of 'X' charity's work in
which you would like to be involved?

_____

_____

_____

_____

_____

_____

_____

Thank you

Appendix B:
Financial governance framework

1. Does your charity have a clearly defined organisational structure, and has this been effectively communicated throughout the charity?

2. Does it incorporate all levels within the charity, not just senior management?

3. Do you know what the greatest threats, both internal and external, to your charity are?

4. Has any kind of risk analysis or risk awareness programme been conducted within the charity?

5. Does the charity have a planning cycle that fits with its overall objectives?

6. Does that planning cycle require departments or functions to evaluate the previous year's performance against plans?

7. Are explanations provided where planned objectives have not been met?

8. Do employees understand the significance of controls and what they are designed to ensure?

9. Do written procedures exist for all key areas of the charity's business?

10. Aside from internal audit, are the results of any other independent, objective reviews disseminated throughout the charity?

11. Are the trustees assured of the effectiveness of any controls, plans or procedures in place? If so, how?

12. Is there a process for reporting discrepancies to the trustees? If so, what form does it take?

Appendix C:
Suggested contents of a financial procedures manual

Trustees' financial responsibilities

- The executive committee
- The annual plan
- Approval of the budget
- Reserves policy
- Conflicts of interest
- Staff financial responsibilities
- Controls on income
- Grants
- Legacies
- Publication sales
- Decentralised sales invoicing
- Credit control
- Bad debts

Controls on expenditure

- Estimates and tendering
- Purchase orders and invoices
- Bank mandates and cheque signatories
- Credit cards
- Petty cash

Controls on the financial assets

- Reconciling cash book to bank
- Reconciling purchase ledger
- Reconciling sales ledger
- Reconciling stock accounts
- Reconciling publications stock
- VAT
- Inland Revenue
- Reconciling payroll control
- Treasury management
- Investment portfolio

Exercising budgetary control

- Virement

Controls on human resources

- Staff complement
- Staff salaries
- Staff regrading
- Extra responsibility allowance
- Starters and leavers
- Contracts of employment
- Travel and subsistence
- The probity book
- Season ticket loans

Controls on physical assets

- Computer equipment
- Computer software and data

Appendix D:
Job description for treasurer

This specimen job description and person specification for a treasurer can be adapted to meet an organisation's particular needs. It is also advisable to provide job descriptions for trustees and honorary officers. In addition to clarifying roles, these descriptions are useful for people thinking about becoming trustees or honorary officers, and for those who are considering nominating others. Comprehensive advice prepared by the Honorary Treasurer's Forum has been published by NCVO at: www.ncvo-vol.org.uk.

Job title: Treasurer of [name of organisation]

The role of a treasurer is to maintain an overview of the organisation's affairs to ensure that it is financially viable and that proper financial records and procedures are maintained. The responsibilities of the treasurer will include the following tasks.

- Overseeing, approving and presenting budgets, accounts and financial statements.
- Making sure that the financial resources of the organisation meet its present and future needs.
- Ensuring that the charity has an appropriate reserves policy.
- Preparing and presenting financial reports to the board.
- Ensuring that appropriate accounting procedures and controls are in place.
- Liaising with any paid staff and volunteers about financial matters.
- Advising on the financial implications of the organisation's strategic plans.
- Ensuring that the charity has an appropriate investment policy.
- Ensuring that there is no conflict between any investment held and the aims and objects of the charity.

- Monitoring the organisation's investment activity and ensuring its consistency with the organisation's policies and legal responsibilities.
- Ensuring that the accounts are prepared and disclosed in the form required by funders and the relevant statutory bodies: for example, the Charity Commission and/or the Registrar of Companies.
- If an audit is required, ensuring that the accounts are audited in the manner required, and any recommendations of the auditors implemented.
- Keeping the board informed about its financial duties and responsibilities.
- Contributing to the fundraising strategy of the organisation.
- Making a formal presentation of the accounts at the annual general meeting and drawing attention to important points in a coherent and comprehensible way.
- Sitting on appraisal, recruitment and disciplinary panels as required.

Person specification

In addition to the qualities needed by all trustees, the treasurer should ideally also possess the following skills and experience.

- Financial qualifications and experience.
- Some experience of charity finance, fundraising and pension schemes.
- The skills to analyse proposals and examine their financial consequences.
- A readiness to make unpopular recommendations to the board.
- A willingness to be available to staff for advice and enquiries on an ad-hoc basis.

Financing the mission

2.1
Defining your mission

All voluntary organisations must first define precisely why they exist and how they plan to fulfil their mission. Only when this has been done can discussions on preparing a budget begin.

This chapter begins by examining the conflict that often exists between those responsible for carrying out the charitable mission and those responsible for ensuring the financial stability of the organisation. It then introduces techniques to improve strategic planning.

Voluntary organisations usually exist because they have a mission: for example, to cure the sick, to advance a profession, to discover new technologies, to educate the public.

Meeting financial goals is essential to fulfilling this mission, but it is not the top priority. Managers must ask a 'chicken and egg' question: which comes first, the programmes to fulfil the mission or the income (earned and voluntary) to finance the programmes?

It is important to recognise that aspirations and financial mission and its resources are related, and that it is management's task to coordinate the two.

The planning process for voluntary organisations is complex, as they must not only accomplish their mission, but also meet their financial goals. An organisation's mission and its financial goals can be viewed as parallel objectives that complement each other. Certainly, vigorous demand for the services of an organisation is an indication of success. However, if financial management is neglected, it will not be long before the whole organisation begins to run on a deficit budget. Once in this situation, the organisation will find it hard to secure extra funding. Similarly, the provision of services for which there is no need – irrespective of the level of finance – will not enable the organisation to accomplish its mission, and can, conversely, result in 'mission drift'.

2.2
The necessity of planning

Voluntary organisations need to plan effectively. For too many organisations, however, this process merely consists of adding a percentage to last year's budgets, which can only be valid in a world where nothing ever changes. For most voluntary organisations, planning is usually short term, typically in one- to three-year cycles, corresponding to funding. This planning also tends to happen in a vacuum, cut off from what is happening in the outside world.

The short-term nature of most funding and the uncertainty caused by constant change are often given as reasons not to plan. However, they are very good reasons why voluntary organisations should plan in a robust way.

Although it is beyond the scope of this guide to give detailed guidelines on strategic planning (comprehensive signposting is given at the end of this book), this chapter will provide a general outline that sets the context for the later sections on financial planning.

For any organisation, planning is a continuous process that seeks, in essence, to describe:

- what the organisation aims to achieve
- where it currently stands in relation to those aims
- what future actions will be required to achieve those aims
- how the organisation will know when it has achieved them.

2.3
The language of planning

The mission

This is a brief statement of an organisation's purpose and values; it is the reason why it exists. The mission says little about what an organisation will do, or how or when it will do it. Missions should be a long-term statement of intent deriving from the vision that originally inspired the organisation.

Example 1: The Toxoplasmosis Trust (now called Tommy's)
Our vision is to reduce substantially the incidence and effect of toxoplasmosis (an infection harmful to the unborn child) and ultimately to eradicate congenital toxoplasmosis in the UK.

Example 2: Weston Spirit
Weston Spirit works in the inner city areas of Britain offering young people, who may be experiencing feelings of isolation and hopelessness, a real alternative to problems such as unemployment, drug use, alcohol misuse, homelessness and abuse.

Strategic goals

These set out the direction of the organisation; they are a statement of its priorities in the medium to long term. Everything the organisation does should be related back to a strategic goal.

Example 1: The Toxoplasmosis Trust
- To raise awareness of toxoplasmosis.
- To support people affected by toxoplasmosis.
- To campaign to raise the profile of toxoplasmosis amongst government, health carers and the public.
- To ensure better prevention and management of toxoplasmosis.

Example 2: Weston Spirit
- Have a presence in each major city in the UK.
- Influence policy formulation by and within major organisations and institutions affecting young people.
- Network with other organisations providing high quality youth work.
- Increase our annual membership numbers.

The operational objectives

These are detailed, costed and timed plans of what the organisation will do to meet each strategic goal. They set out a work plan for the organisation, typically over a 12-month period.

Example 1: The Toxoplasmosis Trust
- Organise four pilot study days on toxoplasmosis for midwives around the country.
- Develop a midwives' education pack.
- Send out a toxoplasmosis newsletter to local and hospital laboratories.
- Develop a new fact sheet for parents of children with retinochoroiditis.

2.4
The process of planning

What is, or will be, our strategic position?

To answer this question, a voluntary organisation must gather information. It needs to identify the factors that will influence its results, both in terms of outputs and outcomes. Analysing the external environment is important because opportunities may be missed and threats overlooked until too late.

Despite its importance, this analysis of the external environment tends, in practice, to be constrained by two factors.

1. In many voluntary organisations, urgent immediate demands, such as meeting income targets and controlling expenditure, leave little time for important, but longer-term, strategic planning analysis.

2. Too little is known about how complex external factors affect voluntary organisations.

The effects of these constraints are decreasing, however, as more and more 'professionals' take part in the governance and management of voluntary organisations.

External review

Here are some brief examples of how external factors can affect voluntary organisations.

- **Economy:** economic growth, or lack of it, affects the disposable income of individuals and donor companies. In times of uncertainty, donors may be less willing to commit to regular donations.
- **Government:** the voluntary sector, particularly social welfare organisations, will be considerably affected if more community care services are transferred to the independent sector.
- **Society:** there is evidence of a shift of public confidence away from traditional institutions, such as political parties, and towards more voluntary forms of association.
- **Technology:** the increasing flexibility of people's work patterns will affect their ability to volunteer their time.

In short, analysing the external environment in which a voluntary organisation works should make it possible to identify opportunities or threats. For example, levels of economic activity, together with society's attitudes towards volunteering, may affect the organisation's income and other resources, and thus its ability to deliver the desired level of services.

Internal review

As mentioned earlier, an internal review should also be carried out as part of the information-gathering process. The aim of this review is to identify weaknesses that must be addressed and strengths that are not being exploited. A list of the areas that should be covered in a review is given below, followed by a description of the tools that can be used to conduct the review.

Leadership
- Trustee board characteristics and balance
- Trustee board focus: core activities and other decision-making systems
- Skills experience and balance
- Management training

Culture
- Power groupings
- Power sources: authority, control over resources, ability
- Social norms
- Attitudes

Structure
- Reporting lines
- Level of integration
- Resources balance
- Information systems

Functional analysis
- Programme services
- Community development
- Information, training and education
- Fundraising
- Finance and administration

Control systems
- Planning systems
- Budget systems
- Performance appraisal
- Internal audit (where appropriate)

Tools to use for internal review

Management audit
This sets out to assess the effectiveness of the trustee board, management team and organisational structure in achieving charitable objectives. It will look at leadership, culture and structure to identify existing and potential weaknesses and recommend ways to rectify them.

Ratio analysis
Key ratios – such as liquidity, fundraising performance, cost ratios and trading profitability (for trading groups) – can, when analysed over time and compared with those of other voluntary organisations offering comparable services, provide a valuable indication of trends and highlight key relationships.

Contribution analysis
This identifies the absolute or percentage amount that a particular programme contributes to the general overheads (after deducting direct programme costs from any earned or unearned income for that programme). The aim is to ensure that each programme makes a contribution to these overheads.

Ratios and contribution are explored in more depth in Chapter 5.

The position audit

Combining the results of the review of the external environment with those of the internal review and comparing them with the organisation's strategic goals, makes it possible to carry out a 'position audit'. This shows:

- where the organisation currently stands in relation to its goals, by identifying what opportunities or threats exist externally
- what internal strengths need to be exploited
- what internal weaknesses need to be addressed.

This assessment will help to identify the strategic choices open to the organisation. These may include answering the following questions.

- Should the organisation grow, stay the same or reduce its size, or is a recovery programme necessary?
- Should the organisation remain within its existing market, expand into different geographical locations or enter entirely new markets?
- Does the organisation need to modify the services it provides or develop new ones, or can it maintain the existing portfolio of services?
- Should the organisation become a more specialist, or more general, provider of services?

Choosing a course of action

Once the choices available to the organisation have been identified, there will need to be an evaluation, since it is unlikely that all options will be feasible with the available resources. The choices could be evaluated in terms of their acceptability, suitability and feasibility.

- The criterion for acceptability would be whether the chosen strategy fits in well with existing resources, competencies and culture.
- The criterion for suitability would be whether the chosen strategy maximises the strengths or reduces the weaknesses of the organisation, and whether it seizes the opportunities or averts the threats offered by the external environment.

'Once the organisation's strategic goals have been identified, they must be translated into day-to-day activities.'

- Testing for feasibility requires the following questions to be asked.

  - Is the leadership suitable?
  - Is the culture capable?
  - Is the organisational structure appropriate?
  - Are the functional policies appropriate?
  - Are the resources available?
  - Is this strategy an improvement on not changing at all?
  - Are there procedures for implementation and monitoring?

Each chosen strategy needs to satisfy all these points. If it fails on any, the organisation must assess whether remedial action is possible.

Preparing day-to-day plans

Once the organisation's strategic goals have been identified, they must be translated into day-to-day activities. The Toxoplasmosis Trust, for example, identifies its strategic goals as:

1. to raise awareness of toxoplasmosis

2. to support people affected by toxoplasmosis

3. to campaign to raise the profile of toxoplasmosis amongst government, health carers and the public

4. to ensure better prevention and management of toxoplasmosis.

Based on these four goals, a set of **operational objectives, or action plans, was** formulated.

1. organising four pilot study days on toxoplasmosis for midwives around the country

2. developing a midwives' education pack

3. sending out a toxoplasmosis newsletter to local and hospital laboratories

4. developing a new fact sheet for parents of children with retinochoroiditis.

For each of these operational objectives, a detailed plan needs to be drafted. These plan should ideally be SMART:

- **S**pecific (detailed)
- **M**easurable (both financially and otherwise)
- **A**ttainable
- **R**ealistic
- **T**imed.

For example, the objective 'developing a midwives' education pack' might be broken down further into the following tasks.

1. Identify major issues, medical and otherwise, of which midwives need to be aware.

2. Identify main contributors to the educational pack.

3. Prepare draft and check accuracy of content and design.

4. Conduct a limited testing with readers'/users' panel.

5. Print.

6. Market and promote pack to midwives through hospitals.

The persons responsible for each of these tasks, and the time allotted, should be identified, to provide a basis for performance appraisal.

2.5
Programme resource assessment

This chapter has emphasised that mission-orientated goals and financial goals are interdependent and highlighted the importance of acceptability in terms of fit (with existing strategies), resources (both financial and otherwise), competence (ability and skills) and culture (leadership style).

Any changes that give a new strategic direction to charitable programmes require a parallel adjustment to the financial resources devoted to that programme. This section will look at the financial adjustments needed when expansion (or contraction) of services is planned.

Figure 2.1 shows the kind of connections that should be made between mission orientated goals and financial goals.

It may be useful to consider a situation where a voluntary organisation is faced with the need to reduce expenditure. The finance committee might prepare a list of possible solutions, with committee members marking each solution as V for viable or U for unacceptable, as shown in figure 2.2.

Figure 2.1

Goal to accomplish mission	Financial resource
Feed more children to relieve the suffering of the poor.	Get donations of food from supermarkets.
Double the congregation to spread the church's spiritual message.	Market the church through weekly gospel programmes on the public radio.
Publish more training manuals to better educate our league members.	Recruit skilled writers to update and expand manuals.

Figure 2.2

Rating	V or U
Research public perception of accomplishments; interview recipients of services to evaluate their needs and ideas.	
Establish a development officer to increase contributor base.	
Raise membership rates, service fees, publication prices.	
Charge for services currently offered for free.	
Eliminate programmes or downsize staff.	
Merge with or take over another organisation.	
Sell off under-utilised assets.	
Improve marketing, publish magazine, sponsor public events.	
Reallocate resources to realign strengths and weaknesses.	
Establish new measurement systems to evaluate performance.	

2.6
Organisation resource analysis

Another part of the planning process is a critical look at the organisation's wider financial situation, which provides an opportunity to evaluate its long-term financial stability. The key ratio and financial indicators from the annual financial statements (which are discussed in Chapter 5) can be used for this.

Depending on the results of this analysis, the voluntary organisation might adopt certain steps to improve its financial situation. An example is given in the form of a model balance sheet of a church in figure 2.3. At first sight, the church's financial situation may seem healthy. It has £108,510 of unrestricted net assets on its balance sheet, total assets of £390,000 and only £281,490 of debt. This indicates that the church has accumulated assets well in excess of the money it owes.

However, a closer examination of the balance sheet reveals that the church does not have the money to pay the bills that will soon be due. Compare the liquid assets of £20,000 – that is, the assets currently available to pay bills – with the current liabilities of £81,490. In other words, the debts becoming due in the next year are four times the current assets.

The first glance at the bottom line of a financial statement can also be misleading. The church's unrestricted net assets of more than £100,000 might seem reasonable for an organisation of its size. However, it is noticeable that the fund balance consists of non-cash assets – the church's equipment and buildings.

Because these assets are used every day, they cannot be sold to pay bills. In this condition, the church is vulnerable – a delay of a few weeks in funding can cause havoc as creditors become increasingly demanding, cheques bounce and overdue taxes begin to cause embarrassment.

Once the church's management recognise the financial problem, however, they can devise solutions. Over the next two or three years the church might focus on financial goals A, B, C and D in figure 2.4. To enable these goals to be realised, the church must also take steps to balance its mission and financial goals.

The church would have to introduce formal financial planning. First, it would prepare a budget for the coming year, following the guidelines in Chapter 3.

Next, it would convert the budget into a monthly cash flow projection. The church's financial managers would review the accounting systems to ensure that accurate and up-to-date information is available to assess the financial position at any give time. Finally, the church might consider using ratio analysis (see Chapter 5) to improve its current funding position.

Figure 2.3 Holy Spirit Church summary balance sheet

	£		£
Building	250,000	Long term debt	200,000
Equipment and furnishing	120,000	Current liabilities	81,490
Current (liquid) assets	20,000		
Total assets	390,000	Total liabilities	281,490
Net assets	108,510	Unrestricted funds	108,510

Figure 2.4

Priority level 1–10	Macro	Resource goal
	A	Establish working capital base.
	B	Maintain three (or more) months' operating cash balance (improve cash flow).
	C	Retire debt or reduce accounts payable.
	D	Seek endowment funding to provide income to offset annual fluctuations in grant funding.
	E	Buy or build permanent facilities.
	F	Establish branches.
	G	Conduct marketing campaign.
	H	Raise salaries or increase personnel.
	I	Improve employee benefits, eg pensions.
	J	Hire chief financial officer to improve financial reporting, planning and management.

Conclusion

Voluntary organisations should be clear about why they exist and how they will fulfil their mission. A voluntary organisation's mission and its financial goals complement each other and should not be in competition. Planning is an essential tool in understanding and delivering the mission. Internal and environmental analysis are important techniques in understanding the strategic role of the organisation.

Checklist

Answer the following questions before checking the answers in the text.

1. Draw the financial planning cycle.

2. What are the stages of planning?

3. Outline the four aspects of understanding a strategic position.

4. What are the factors that need to be examined when evaluating an organisation?

5. What additional questions need to be asked of a chosen strategy?

6. Describe the proposed planning quality principles for a voluntary organisation.

Action points for your organisation

Audit your organisation by checking to see if it has:

- a mission statement that is relevant and understood throughout the organisation and by its stakeholders
- a strategic plan, with goals and objectives
- a planning process that corresponds to the quality framework
- action plans with clear responsibilities
- performance measurements linked to the action plans
- a management committee, which undertakes regular performance and organisational resource assessment.

Case studies and exercises

1 Language Line

This case study demonstrates the usefulness of an environmental analysis.

Background

Language Line was set up to provide a telephone interpreting service in seven minority ethnic languages. Remarkably, as director Marc Kiddle observed, 'Although similar services were long established in Australia, the United States and Holland, this was the first telephone interpreting service in Britain. It was, then, truly innovative.' At the outset, however, Language Line did not know of the existence of any similar services and so had nowhere to turn for advice or experience.

The initial objective was to offer the service to health organisations in the Tower Hamlets area of London, with plans to extend the scheme to other users and areas. The project received initial support for a pilot from a government task force, British Telecom and a charitable trust. The pilot was judged a success, and a year later it was decided to conduct research to establish whether the project could find alternative sources of income when the initial grants ended. An analysis of how interested potential users might be was therefore needed.

Types of information

Five main types of information should be collected as part of an environmental analysis.

1. Information about the needs and opinions of current and potential users of the services of your organisation. The views of past users of the service will also be valuable in assessing your strengths and weaknesses.

2. Information on important trends and influences in the organisation's environment.

3. The criteria used by grant makers and other funders in deciding whether to support funding applications.

4. Existing patterns of service in areas of activity you wish to become involved in.

5. The activities of organisations with similar services to those of your own.

The director of Language Line and its five permanent interpreters knew that there had been a steady increase in demand from existing users. They believed, from discussions with local officials, that the separation of purchaser and provider roles resulting from reforms of the health service was leading to a new emphasis on access to services for minority language speakers. They also knew that there were other concentrations of minority language speakers who made demands on the statutory services – such as the police force and health service – that might also become users.

In other areas, however, staff were largely in the dark. The service had been provided free: would new customers be willing to pay for the service?

What were the decision-making procedures? Staff were unaware of any direct competitors and did not know how successful their limited public relations activity had been in creating awareness of Language Line.

On the basis of this assessment of the information gaps, the project decided that it needed to acquire information on the following issues.

- Existing provision of interpreting services for minority language speakers (if any) by potential purchasers.
- Plans of potential purchasers for improvements in interpreting services.
- The decision-making procedures of potential new users.
- The awareness potential users had of Language Line and their interest in its services.

The information collection methods used can also vary according to whether the environmental analysis is external or internal (see figure 2.5).

Figure 2.5

Internal sources	External – secondary	External – primary
Analysis and discussion	Publications	User surveys
Information on service usage	Material from other organisations, eg annual reports	Discussion or focus groups
Published information		Visits to other organisations
Contacts and networking	Library searches	Exhibitions

Language Line used the following sources.

- **External:** review of census data to pinpoint geographical areas with highest concentration of minority language speakers.
- **Internal:** telephone questionnaire to local authorities, health authorities and police stations in the target area.

Interpreting and presenting the information

In presenting the findings of your environmental analysis, you need to:

- demonstrate a clear understanding of the needs and expectations of different groups of current and potential users of your organisation's services
- identify the opportunities for, and threats to, your organisation as a result of developments in its environment
- summarise the management actions you intend to take to maximise the opportunities, and minimise the threats, you have identified.

2 Understanding business language

This exercise removes the jargon from business terms.

Happy Homes has two properties, which provide short-term residential accommodation for disabled people in the Bristol city area thereby allowing those who care for them to have a holiday. The finance director said, 'We plan to raise more money to allow us to build more homes – we expect to borrow at a good rate, which will enable us to give more people who look after their relatives a break. After all, we've promised our supporters a 10 per cent increase in places available and we do not want to break our word.'

- Identify the organisational, business and functional strategies in the above quotation.

Suggested answer

The organisational objective is to expand its service to support people who care for others. The organisational strategy is the decision that this will be achieved by building new homes rather than, say, diversifying into day support. The business strategy suggests that this would be best achieved by building new properties rather than extending current properties. The operational strategy involves the decision to invest in new properties (the service function), which is to be financed by loan finance (the finance function) rather than seeking funds from government or the public.

3 Understanding business planning

You have recently been appointed as the finance and administration director of an ethnic minority national membership based organisation, which coordinates local groups. The organisation has an income from various sources of £1.2m. The chief executive has been asked by the management committee to organise its first business planning exercise following a critical report on the organisation by a major funder, and they ask for your help.

• Prepare a briefing note for the chief executive and the three other senior managers outlining the topics that should be covered in the business planning process and advising them on who should be included in the business planning team.

Answer

The briefing note should cover the following points.

1. The reason or rationale for having a business plan, for example, to set down effective criteria for improving the organisation's performance through a process of planning and evaluation.

2. The objectives of a plan.

3. The main components of a business plan, normally:

a) the organisation's mission, including the extent to which the organisation's values have changed over time and how this should be reflected in what the organisation does

b) internal and external appraisal

c) environmental assumptions

d) clear objectives, ideally quantified

e) strategy (including marketing)

f) budgets

g) performance measures to demonstrate efficiency and effectiveness of the organisation

h) feedback system.

4. The staff involvement in the process.

All the organisation's senior managers and the management committee should be involved in the business planning process, not only to approve it, but also to own the strategy. While the senior managers will develop the business plan, everyone in the organisation will be involved and therefore will know what is expected of them. This will mean that a hierarchy of objectives and delegated responsibilities from the management committee to operational staff will exist. A failure to involve operational staff and management committee members will result in confusion and a loss of direction.

4 Appraising the external environment

The Emergency Support Service (ESS) is faced with a changing environment. It was founded following local government reorganisation to provide volunteers for social services. In the past ESS was funded entirely by national government on a grants basis. The grant was increased in line with inflation every year.

The last government believed a central incremental grant encouraged inefficiency. The government introduced a tapering reduction in the grant of £1m per year (the ESS budget was then £6m) and required ESS to instead tender to individual local authorities for its services on a contract basis. Local authority contracts were increasingly being awarded to local voluntary organisations, particularly in Scotland and Wales, or other national charity competitors who undercut ESS prices. In addition ESS was faced with a general freeze on government spending in accordance with the new government's commitment to keep within borrowing limits and the previous government's expenditure plans. ESS has a budgeted contingency reserve of one year's current expenditure and has a remaining 20-year lease on its London headquarters.

• Appraise the situation of the ESS and recommend appropriate strategies to deal with its problems.

Answers

Situation appraisal

ESS is not in a good position. It has seen its reliable source of income disappear and is now exposed to new and growing competition in a static market. ESS has moved from having one 'customer'– central government, to having some 400 new customers throughout the country. Viewed as a 'London English' organisation, it is unlikely to have developed regional structures, marketing skills or commercial acumen. It probably lacks a proper costing system.

Strategic plan

This would have to take the following factors into account.

a) The competitive environment is hostile, with a static market and geographical problems; new competitors exist and barriers to them have been abolished. It is not all bad news, however, as ESS is now free to consider tendering to health authorities.

b) The political environment is unlikely to restore the ESS central grant. Government spending plans indicate that there will be an increase in public sector spending – particularly in the health sector – but not yet. It is not feasible for ESS, with limited reserves and assets, to undertake a sort of holding operation in the expectation that funding and new markets will increase.

c) The economic environment predicts low levels of inflation, except in London where ESS is based and where wage inflation has outstripped national levels reflecting the higher cost of living. Low levels of inflation also indicate that contract funds are unlikely to increase. Local and health authorities will seek to maximize the lowest economic cost. For the voluntary sector economy, the increase in funding to the sector has come from government or trading activities. Donations from the public and businesses have been static. ESS has no expertise in raising funds from the general public or corporations.

d) The competitive environment is not likely to diminish, with national and local competitors. ESS has major problems with its geographical position in dealing with the devolving of power to Scotland and Wales.

3 The organisation structure and culture of the ESS

a) ESS had been reliant on just one source of finance in a very cosy relationship. This has not prepared it for the rigours of the new contract environment. ESS probably has few marketing skills as it has never had to tender for contracts. Trustees would have been appointed for their 'name' and prestige in government or the voluntary sector. As the organisation has never really had a marketing objective, it does not have the experience in its paid staff or trustees to re-orientate itself. At the same time, it still has contact with government and a tapering arrangement, which might enable it to 'buy' more time to equip itself with those skills.

b) It is possible that the services provided by ESS were organised according to central government specifications. Local government is free to decide on its own service provision and may not have the same priorities. Having been a monopoly supplier with a distinct culture of one type of service delivery, this may not be relevant for all local authorities.

c) The one grant a year has meant that the accounting system has not previously priced contracts. It could be that the organisation has no real idea of how much a particular service costs and what the contribution to organisational overheads should be. Losing contracts on price to other national competitors would indicate that there is something wrong with the way ESS prices. On the other hand, it may be that other competitors are larger and so benefit from economies of scale or that ESS is inefficient and lacks proper project management skills.

Strategic options available to ESS

a) Expand into the health service market. This may not be easy, as ESS has no relationships or background with health authorities. Existing service suppliers will be hostile to ESS.

b) Develop new services. This is easier said than done, as ESS has been a single service organisation. Does it have the skills to develop new services and are these services that local and health authorities would need?

c) Develop a more aggressive pricing policy – it still has a government grant covering some core costs.

d) Change the accounting system for more accurate and relevant cost information.

e) Make itself more efficient by rationalisation.

f) A long-term strategic option would be to assess the need for volunteers, particularly in caring for people who wish to stay in their own homes rather than go into residential care. ESS could set itself up as a specialist operator in keeping people at home and charge wealthier people a fee.

g) The competitive static market, with increasing costs, might lead to ESS considering sharing its resources with other voluntary organisations. Alternatively it may have skills in training and supporting volunteers that it could provide to smaller voluntary organisations. ESS could set up joint ventures with other voluntary organisations.

If ESS, having reviewed its options, fails to come up with a viable plan, or the plans it develops require resources that the organisation does not have, then it should, in the interests of all its stakeholders, consider merging with another voluntary organisation. This would preserve jobs and the commitment and skills of volunteers

5 Fundraising appraisal

This exercise looks at using appraisal techniques to evaluate fundraising.

Veterans Benevolent Fund (VBF) is a national charity established to help veterans of all ranks from the armed forces and merchant navy suffering illness and disability as a result of active service.

For some men and women, their involvement in actions throughout the world can result in psychiatric conditions, post-traumatic stress and physical disability requiring long-term support. Drug and alcohol problems have also become greater over the last 20 years. VBF has a national network of welfare officers as well as residential and therapy centres to ensure that the best care and support possible is available.

The residential centres provide a safe environment for those needing specialist help, together with remedial and therapeutic treatment in the therapy centres. Welfare officers support those people wishing to remain within their own homes and communities.

VBF participates in lobbying government to improve the support services provided to these men and women, particularly in mental health provision and pensions. The Fund also works with other agencies to provide study teams looking into specialist areas of care or mental health issues.

Clients are referred from agencies, such as the War Pensions Welfare Service, the Regimental Associations, the Royal British Legion, the NHS and social services. The age range of the current veterans being supported by VBF is from early 20s to 70s.

Current position

Legislation introduced the need to refurbish the residential accommodation and refurbishing one of the three residential centres has now been completed. The remaining two centres now need refurbishment and it is hoped the work will commence once funds have been secured.

Recently, there has been a fundamental change in the method of support, moving from long-term admissions to an increasing number of clients requiring short-term respite admissions thus allowing them to remain in their own homes and communities.

This significant change, and the increasing demand for support for those with anger, self-esteem, drug and alcohol-related problems within the therapy centres, has demanded additional resources. One of the therapy centres has been upgraded and the others must follow if the support demand is to be met, including the urgent need for additional staff.

Welfare officers and their teams around the country are the first port of call for clients and their families, the referring agencies and the carers. These welfare teams have now reached the point where there is an urgent need for additional staff to ensure the clients and their families can cope with the difficulties caused by the traumas, illness and disabilities.

VBF's income has remained level over the past three years but must now increase in order to provide the resources needed for refurbishment of the residential accommodation, the therapy centres and additional staff. It does, however, own all the properties and has six months' expenditure in reserve.

The new director of fundraising and PR has been informed that the funds received from one of the three service charities (service charity 3) will cease to support VBF next year, while the other two have given notice that they will need to reduce their donations by 10 per cent and 5 per cent respectively.

Social services has stated that the contribution per residential client will remain at the current level for the next two years and the health authority has indicated that there could be an increase per client in the coming year.

As for many benevolent funds, legacy income has been a mainstay for VBF, but it has seen a substantial drop in the current year. Donations from individuals represent only about 3 per cent of the total voluntary income.

Events have provided an increase in income from the previous year, but this has been due to the fact that there was a major overseas trek, which may not be repeated in the coming year. Christmas card sales grew in the last year, increasing net contribution by 10 per cent on the previous year.

There has been some success in attracting media interest in the work of VBF and it is hoped that this will have the two-fold effect of increasing income and lobbying power. The trustees have expressed the hope that the PR activity will increase in the coming year.

The chief executive and the trustees are aware that in order to satisfy the resources required by VBF, there is an urgent need to review the fundraising and have begun to look at the income and expenditure for the year to December 2012. Figure 2.6 shows the breakdown.

Questions

The chief executive and the trustees have asked you, as the new director of fundraising and PR, as a matter of urgency to assess the effectiveness of the fundraising programme and how to increase the income to allow VBF's requirements to be met.

1. Analyse the current income and provide an assessment of the areas of weakness and major threat-making recommendations to minimise the effects of these.

2. Explain the actions you would propose to develop a strategy to increase the income to meet the future needs and development plans of the VBF.

Suggested answers

1. Weaknesses and the major threats.

- **Individual donations:** only 3 per cent of the total. Research into donor profile would give an indication of strength or weakness of the donor base in terms of sustainability. Could look at potential donor areas in terms of service personnel and families. Direct mail campaign needs to be researched to increase this area of funding.
- **Legacies:** drop this year could indicate a trend. Ageing population, economic climate and work patterns could affect the future of legacy gifts. House prices are increasing, but often needed for the care and support of elderly. The trend of skipping inheritance – to grandchildren and great grandchildren. Using the house to supplement income. Look into the legacy campaign if there is one and the message.
- **Trusts:** second largest contributor to the voluntary income – change in guidelines could substantially affect the unrestricted income. Need to develop the relationships with the major trusts.
- **Service charities:** affected by the economic climate so may be experiencing drop in their income – therefore grants will be limited. Discussion with the charities would elicit their reasons for the withdrawal of funds.
- **No corporate donations:** this is a major weakness with no indication of whether there have been any attempts to fundraise in this area. It would be wise to look at the industries where there is a real synergy.

51

Figure 2.6 VBF's income and expenditure for year to December 2012

Breakdown of income of the fundraising department for year to December 2012			
	Unrestricted £000	Restricted £000	Total £000
Voluntary income			
Individual	78		78
Trusts	650	143	793
Events	80		80
Legacies	660	222	882
Christmas cards and goods	7		7
Service charity 1	250		250
Service charity 2	175		175
Service charity 3	200		200
Statutory income			
Social services	908		908
Health authority	1816		1816
Total fundraising income	4,824	365	5,189
Investment income			
Investments	211		211
Net gains on disposal of assets	3		3
Total VBF income	**5,038**	**365**	**5,403**

Breakdown of expenditure for the VBF for year to December 2012				
	Staff costs £000	Other direct costs £000	Other £000	Total allocated costs £000
Fundraising	227	332	23	582
Residential treatment and care	2,820	634	230	3,684
Welfare services	790	97	141	1.028
Management and administration	152	14		166
Refurbishment and repairs		186		186
Total VBF expenditure	**3,989**	**1,263**	**394**	**5,646**

- **Statutory income:** social services and health authority funds – could be fees or contract work – changes in policy within the areas could be responsible for the reduction or level playing of the income. Vulnerable to the changes in legislation and direction so need to have other resources available to meet the potential deficit.
- **Lottery:** there appears to have been no attempt to raise money from this source. Big Lottery Fund might well be a source particularly where dealing with the community – needs to be investigated.
- **Community fundraising:** look at the activities within the areas of the welfare officers in order to maximise the publicity about the cause and the work undertaken by VBF – look into some of the events and activities in the local communities to provide support if appropriate.
- **Trading:** Christmas cards and goods probably take up too much time – limit this to just Christmas cards – perhaps sending them out to a wider network as the donors increase.
- **Events:** the trek was successful – the reason for not doing it again is the over stretched market – is this really the case? Research needed. Could the service personnel be encouraged to undertake more – local to the areas of support.

2. Fundraising strategy should be part of the whole overall strategy and not set apart. It is essential that there are good lines of communication between all departments to ensure that the fundraising has a clear perspective on what is needed, not only for the coming year but within the years of the overall strategy. It is also important that the targets set for the fundraising are not expenditure driven but rather a carefully executed budget process. This will allow the fundraising strategy to build on past relationships and meet the needs of the organisation as a whole for the coming year and for the next three years. The strategy should include the following.

- Capital campaign for the refurbishment of the residential and therapy centres – small but could be regional.
- After researching the legacy breakdown – develop a modern legacy campaign.

- Continue with the trust fundraising – developing relationships with warm trusts and at the same time research new potential donors – not a scattergun approach.
- Service charities – meet to discuss the relationship and the potential action for the future. The outcome will dictate how to proceed to ensure that the targets are met.
- Research into potential corporate donors – looking at industries with a synergy with the organisation.
- Develop a campaign to attract new individual donors. The organisation would lend itself to direct mail, but research is needed into the possibility of contacting serving personnel initially in order to increase the income. At the same time research the possibility of a donor recruitment campaign.
- Working with the service delivery departments – look at the statutory funding in order to establish where there could be deficits in the future and plan for replacement resources.
- Research the potential for a Lottery application.
- Research the potential for a major events programme involving serving personnel and families of those receiving support.
- Develop a media campaign that would raise the profile of the organisation.
- Community fundraising – local events to help with the refurbishment.

Budgeting

3.1
Budget planning

After the organisation has examined its priorities and refined its mission in accordance with the financial resources available, the budget can be prepared. The budget is a tool for allocating resources and implementing strategic plans. It charts a way of allocating and maximising the use of resources and, ideally, identifies financial problems that could arise in the coming year.

The budget provides indicators for evaluating employee performance and gives the staff goals to reach and steps to achieve them.

The scope and size of the voluntary organisation's programmes and asset base will dictate the complexity of its budgets.

As a financial measure of the voluntary organisation's goals, a budget compiles the next year's programmes in some detail, based upon certain assumptions, for example, how many students the voluntary organisation expects to enrol; how much it plans to spend on saving which endangered species; the amount of money it plans to raise; or the number of new fee-paying members that will join. It is, in effect, the financial representation of the organisation's plans.

It is important to distinguish between the portion of the budget that can be readily calculated and that which has to be estimated. The budget planner needs both scepticism and optimism. The process necessarily involves uncertainty; decisions are made about a future that the organisation cannot control. Should the financial planner assume that existing programmes will continue? Which (if any) programmes are essential? Before developing the budget, the planners must make the specific policy decisions outlined here.

Balancing

As a first step, the organisation must decide whether the budget is to be balanced, ie with income matching expenditure. An organisation that needs to build up working capital might want to project a budget imbalance of revenue over expenses (a surplus). Alternatively, a deficit budget may be acceptable if it arises from investment in future restructuring, for example. However, the organisation will, in most cases, cease to be viable if there are recurring operating deficits. One exception may be where a policy decision has been made to rely on income from investments, for example, to finance deficits incurred on charitable programmes. (Obviously the question of the level of organisation reserves required to fulfil the plan must also be addressed at this stage.)

An effective budget also balances programme priorities: the organisation's capabilities and resources are allocated to impact on the maximum number of beneficiaries.

There might be other, more detailed parameters affecting the budget, particularly when budgeting and forecasting is devolved to individual programme or project managers, for example:

- no additional posts unless fully funded (for example, by external project funding)
- 2.5 per cent growth in non-salaried expenditure, to account for inflation
- any new programmes must be fully funded (both in terms of direct and indirect costs).

'As a first step the organisation must decide whether the budget is to be balanced.'

Timing

Budgets (and the plans from which they are created) must be completed by a deadline that allows ample time for planning in advance of the period to which the budget applies. The lead time required for grant requests and multi-year projects also makes it imperative that the budget process is properly timed. Realistic target dates for the completion of planning should be established for all involved to follow.

Evolution

A budget is not a static document, but needs to be updated in accordance with new situations and to reflect new information as it becomes available.

Many voluntary organisations continue to compare current financial information with the originally approved budget, and provide footnotes explaining the circumstances that have caused the results to be better or worse than originally expected. The original budget will continue to provide valuable information for trustees, but would be ineffective for monitoring purposes. It is therefore good practice to review budgets on a monthly basis, and reforecast when necessary.

Ownership and accountability

A budget developed, monitored and revised in the accounts office is of little value to the programme staff. The people expected to accomplish the programmes, and the financial goals expressed in the budget, must be actively involved in the budgeting process. Unless the people who actually carry out the activities actively participate, a budget's usefulness is diminished and it is far less likely to be met.

Zero basis versus incremental budgeting

Those responsible for budgeting may adopt either a zero-based system or an incremental methodology for preparing the budget for the coming year.

In **zero-based budgeting** the financial planners start from a zero base, assuming that no programme is necessary and no money need be spent. To be accepted, the programmes will have to be proven worthwhile, as well as financially sound, after an evaluation of all elements of revenue and spending. Each programme is examined in order to justify its existence, and is compared with alternative programmes. Priorities are established and each cost centre is challenged to prove its necessity. This can make programme managers feel threatened, so budget setters should exercise sensitivity when using the zero-based method.

An **incremental budget,** on the other hand, treats existing programmes and departments as already approved, subject only to increases or decreases in the financial resources allocated. The organisation's historical costs are the base from which budget planning starts. The focus of the budgeting process is on the changes anticipated from last year's figures; the planning process has already been completed and the programme priorities established. However, there are dangers in using last year's figures. Basing the budget on these figures can, if not properly challenged, introduce an element of 'creeping' costs year on year. For example, each year the organisation may take 'last year plus 5 per cent' as its figure and fail to query the basis for the decision. In this way, an arbitrary decision in a given year can continue unchallenged for a decade. Also, basing the budget on the actual results can encourage the practice of spending up to the budget in the last few months, to prevent future cuts. Despite these dangers, incremental budgeting is often less time consuming than the zero-based method, and is also felt to be less threatening to programme managers.

'For a budget to be effective, it is important that the possible disadvantages are considered and addressed.'

Types of budget

Before the budget process begins, the organisation should decide which type of budget is best suited to its planning and monitoring needs. The basic budget is a comprehensive look at the entire organisation's projections of income or financial support and its expected expenditures. An endless number of supplementary budgets can be created to meet specific planning and assessment needs. The options might include at least the following items.

- Annual, quarterly and/or monthly projections of income and expenditure for the entire organisation, as well as for each of its departments and branches.
- Receipts and payments budget.
- Revenue projections by type, such as contributors or student tuition.
- Individual project, department, branch or other cost centre projections.
- Service delivery costs by patient, by student, by member or other client.
- Capital additions (buildings or equipment acquisition).
- Investment income (and/or total return).
- Cash flow (short and long term).
- Fundraising event revenue and expenses.
- Retail shop sales.
- Personnel projections.

Advantages and disadvantages

In addition to its value in allocating resources and implementing strategic plans, the budget can produce a wide range of other beneficial results. Programme personnel directly involved in carrying out activities can use it to measure their accomplishments numerically and to respond to unexpected changes. Management can use it to evaluate staff performance. However, like any tool, the budget can produce good or bad results, depending on the skill and diligence with which it is used.

The chief advantages of effective budgeting include the following.

- A thoroughly planned and implemented budget increases the likelihood of a voluntary organisation being financially successful.
- A budget translates abstract goals into determinable bites: it sets performance goals.
- The planning and preparation of a budget forces the organisation to look at itself, set priorities and narrow its choices.
- A budget facilitates coordination and cooperation between the various programmes and financial departments.
- Periodic comparisons between the budget and actual financial performance can signal trouble and allow time for an appropriate response.
- A budget measures how far financial performance meets an organisation's expectations.

For a budget to be effective, it is important that the possible disadvantages are considered and addressed. These may include the following.

- The presence of controls may stifle creativity.
- Because there are so many unknowns at the time when the budget is prepared, the natural tendency is to emphasise cost control.
- A budget based on historical information alone cannot always keep up with a rapidly changing environment.
- Non-financial staff do not often participate in the budgeting process, resulting in operational blueprints that have been approved without the input of programme staff (who should be involved where possible).
- A budget is not always easy to implement and may not always be accepted as useful by the management staff.

Who participates in budgeting?

A budget cannot guarantee its own success: it is no substitute for responsible management. Almost everyone involved with a voluntary organisation may appropriately participate in planning its budget – at the very least, the top administrators, programme heads and board members or trustees. A budget should be a compilation of information from all the senior programme and administrative personnel, who have in turn taken account of contributions from the people with whom they work. No one person should be responsible for preparing the budget, although the organisation's accounts department should compile and monitor it.

How far down the organisational ladder the leaders solicit contributions will depend on the organisation's circumstances, structure and resources, but the further the better in ensuring accuracy of information and a true sense of ownership.

The ideal budget is highly participatory, involving input from all the programme staff and volunteers who work to accomplish the organisation's goals.

There will also be a broad range of interested stakeholders, including funders and supporters. Outside funders can sometimes exert considerable influence on the budget – they may want to know if the organisation plans to provide services that are already provided by another organisation in the community or they may try to influence grant recipients to conduct programmes that accomplish the funder's goals.

A budget imposed from the top down dampens the enthusiasm of staff and can hamper the realisation of the organisation's goals. During the budget process there will naturally be compromise and trade-off. If staff participate from the outset, they may be more willing to accept alterations not initiated by them. It may also make them more understanding about changes, including budget cuts that affect them personally. The participation of the board, officers, staff and volunteers in the process of setting goals enhances the organisation's chances of achieving those goals. Preparing the budget should motivate personnel and inspire the organisation's performance.

Scheduling the budget process

Ideally, budgeting is a continuous process that repeats itself cyclically and is based on the organisation's long-range plan. This requires sufficient time for the budget plans to be fully developed.

Preparation of the budget should ideally begin six months before the beginning of the period to which the budget applies, for example, an organisation whose financial year ends on 31 March should start preparing the budget for the next financial year by September of the current financial year. This allows enough time to gather reliable forecasting information and to go through an orderly approval process.

The steps to follow are shown in figure 3.1.

Figure 3.1

Step 1	Perform strategic planning
Step 2	Identify programmes and activities to accomplish goals
Step 3	Describe method of actualising the goals
Step 4	Quantify revenue and expenditures based upon forecasts and programme services accomplishments
Step 5	Compile reports comparing budget to actual

Use of budgets

Budgets can be used for a variety of purposes, but this guide focuses on how they can form part of funding applications, project appraisal and project monitoring.

When budgets are used as part of funding applications, their format and construction will be guided by the funder's requirements. Typically, a funder will require costs to be split between capital and revenue items and, where applicable, over the term of the project life (maximum three years). There are likely to be restrictions on the percentage (if any) of apportioned overheads that will be funded.

Changing budgets mid-year

No budget, no matter how carefully prepared, ever comes to pass in its original form. Some voluntary organisations may find a 'living' budget, that regularly changes throughout the year as circumstances change, to be preferable to a fixed and unchanging budget, as long as the 'bottom line' remains the same.

The reasons that could require the budget to change are endless. Budgets often prove inaccurate because of inadequate information or circumstances beyond the organisation's control – a grant renewal is unexpectedly cut back or denied; a major funder defaults on a pledge; a natural disaster compounds the demand for aid to the public; a member of staff leaves, causing disruption.

The issue when unforeseen changes occur is whether the approved budget should be altered or updated to reflect the changing conditions. Alternatively, the monthly management reports can use footnotes to explain significant variances from the approved budget. The attributes of a 'living' or constantly changing budget are compared with a static budget in figure 3.2.

A good solution can be to update the budget on a regular basis (allowing a flexible budget) but to return a separate column showing original forecasts. This can be very helpful in organisational learning and in preparing plans for the following year.

Figure 3.2

Static budget	Living or flexible budget
Compares dreams at a point in time to reality of current situation	Presents realistic statistics in view of changing circumstances or conditions
No time spent on revisions	Requires continual updating – time intensive
Can waste funds on programme to be discontinued or found to be ineffective	Constant maximisation of resources
Allows unreasonable expectations	Positive context for accomplishment

3.2
Preparing forecasts

Voluntary organisations face particular problems in forecasting their income flow, particularly those supported by contributions and grants. Voluntary donations depend upon the giver's support for the organisation's mission, but the public's concern about a particular social problem – for example, HIV/Aids – may wane. Other intangible factors, such as changes in legislation, can compound the difficulty of making projections.

A service-providing voluntary organisation, such as a school or a professional association, may have a slightly easier task in forecasting future income. People will pay for services if they feel that they are useful. As long as the services are of high quality and meet the needs of users, the organisation can reasonably assume that they will continue to pay for them.

The forecaster first studies current income and spending and asks if they can be sustained at present levels.

- If unusual events have occurred in the past year or two, are they likely to recur?
- Otherwise, is it reasonable to expect an increase in revenue?
- What increase does the organisation expect as the result of an action taken in the past, such as last year's setting up of a development department?
- What increases in revenue might result if a new marketing scheme is added to the expense side of the budget?

Donations and membership

Forecasting the income from voluntary contributions and membership fees becomes easier as an organisation matures. In these circumstances, the best guide to predicting the future is the organisation's own history and, in particular, tables showing several years of revenue. Some voluntary organisations enjoy considerable goodwill generated during years of operation, but new or young organisations may need to be more cautious about forecasting the success of their development plans. However, even for mature organisations, changes in the external environment can have a considerable impact on membership and donations.

Using information about donors generated internally (for example, their age, frequency of giving, average amount of gift) in conjunction with an examination of significant trends in the voluntary sector economy can greatly enhance the reliability of forecasts.

According to NCVO's *UK Civil Society Almanac*, the main factors affecting this type of income are as follows.

- Voluntary income is often described as 'free' income, as it is not tied to a particular outcome; increasingly, however, donors seem more inclined to give if there is a specific project.
- Organisations that appeal to the philanthropic motives of individuals are heavily dependent on the trust that has been developed.
- Public confidence in all types of public institutions continues to decline, which is likely to affect levels of giving.
- There is increasing competition, not only among voluntary organisations, but also with other types of activity, for the disposable income of individuals.

Findings from the UK Giving Survey 2012, commissioned by NCVO and the Charities Aid Foundation (CAF), show that over 2011/12 the UK public gave £9.3bn to charity. Compared with 2010/11 this is a decrease of £1.7bn (15 per cent) in cash terms and a decrease of £2.3bn (20 per cent) in real terms. This has manifested itself in three ways.

1. A drop in the number of people giving.

2. A drop in the size of donations given.

3. The compounding effect of donations in real terms was significantly reduced.

Figure 3.3 shows the main characteristics of voluntary income in a SWOT analysis.

Earned income

Service delivery fees

An organisation's age is also significant when forecasting revenue. A mature organisation will know the average number of student places, research reports or other services delivered in the past few years. The needs of these services, and any policy decisions about their delivery, will already have been reviewed as part of the strategic planning process. The financial planner's job may simply be to express these strategic goals in a financial format, for example, the number of people to be served and the expected price. In some cases, however, this price may not reflect the full cost of the service; a subsidy may have to come from voluntary income and/or investment income.

Grants and contracts

Predicting whether grants from local authorities, charitable trusts and business sponsors will be renewed is full of uncertainty. Have the local authority's funding priorities changed? Has the value of the charitable trust's assets fallen, reducing the amount available for grants?

Corporate sponsorship is usually tied to the sponsor's profit level, which is usually unknown at budget preparation time. Furthermore, research funding often has to be based on incomplete data, which makes prediction equally impossible.

If an organisation's operating overheads or administrative costs are paid for out of grants, very cautious forecasting is needed. Think about the consequences if the grant that funds half the executive director's salary is not renewed. If there is a strong possibility of grants not being renewed, a flexible or evolving budget (as discussed in the previous section) may be sensible; the budget should also specify alternative courses of action.

Figure 3.3 SWOT analysis – voluntary income

Strengths	'Free'	'Projectisation'	Weaknesses
	Altruism	Direct action	
	Philanthropy	Trust and confidence	
	Charity	Voluntary income	
	Discretionary disposable income	Competition	
	Feasibility study		
Opportunities	Target innovation	Free-riding	Threats

Source: NCVO

Conditions of employment for staff members funded by a grant (and the corresponding expenses budget) should recognise the possibility that the funds may cease.

A SWOT analysis showing the main characteristics of earned income is given in figure 3.4.

Some points to bear in mind when developing an earned income stream are listed here.

- If an organisation enters into a variety of service contracts, there is a risk that it might lose sight of its mission and become financially dependent on contracts.
- Contracts for services, such as providing health care, often lead to significant growth in infrastructure.
- Losing a contract can have a devastating effect on service delivery organisations, as they typically employ a large number of staff.
- There is considerable competition in certain areas of earned income activities, such as health care, particularly when for-profit companies are also providing the same services.

Investment income

The caution required when forecasting investment income depends upon what proportion of its income the organisation expects to derive from investments – for many voluntary groups, this will be modest. However, for an endowed grant-making trust, which gets all its income from investment, this forecast is vital in establishing funding levels for the coming year.

Forecasting becomes particularly difficult for organisations with long-term investment funds. If the funds are administered by a professional investment manager, he or she should provide projections of investment income.

A SWOT analysis showing the main characteristics of investment income is given in figure 3.5.

Figure 3.4 SWOT analysis – earned income

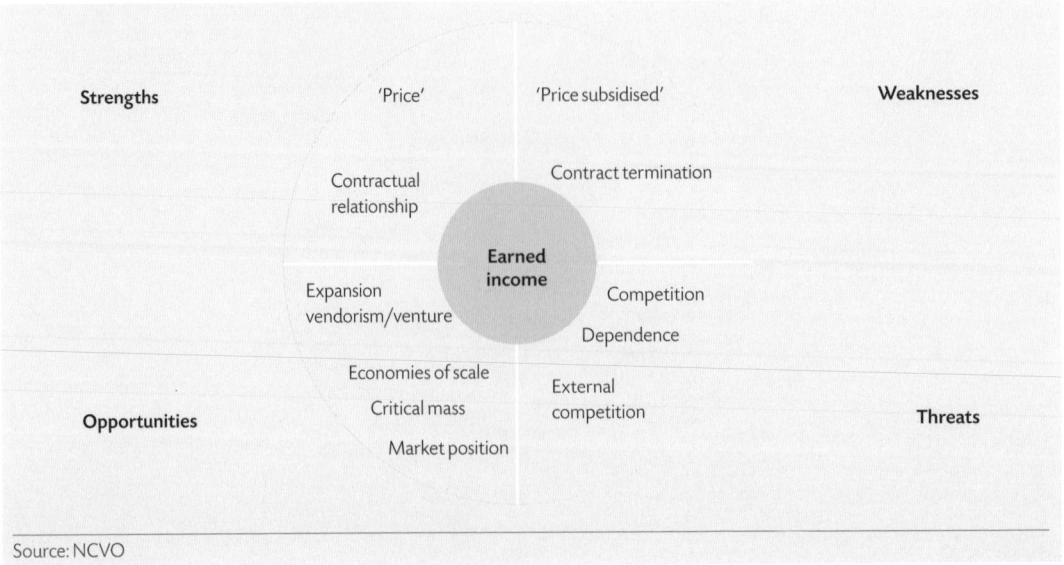

Source: NCVO

Expenses

Most voluntary organisations can predict their expenditure with some certainty, as they have more control over expenditure than income, for example, the cost of salaries and the lease/mortgage on premises will be relatively stable. Historical expenses are therefore the basis for the expenditure budget, subject to adjustments for inflation, for example, last year's figures plus 3 per cent.

One major challenge in forecasting costs is to identify those that are unpredictable, for example, a disaster relief agency may know how much it costs to clothe and house flood victims, but it cannot know when the storms will occur. Again, historical records may be useful.

Demand for an organisation's services is often difficult to predict, so it is essential to acknowledge this uncertainty and submit a flexible budget. The prudent budget planner uses the best possible information to hand, but submits forecasts that are subject to change.

Another option is to distinguish clearly between costs that are controllable and those that are uncontrollable.

If expected costs are too high, the financial planner must consider cheaper alternatives. For example, a voluntary organisation may need skilled people to supervise a specialised project, but the salary such people would expect might skew the organisation's overall pay scale. In such a situation, the organisation has several options.

- Outsource the job to another organisation.
- Hire skilled people on a part-time or hourly basis to run the project and train in-house staff.
- Eliminate the project, reduce its size or run it jointly with another voluntary organisation.

Figure 3.5 SWOT analysis – investment income

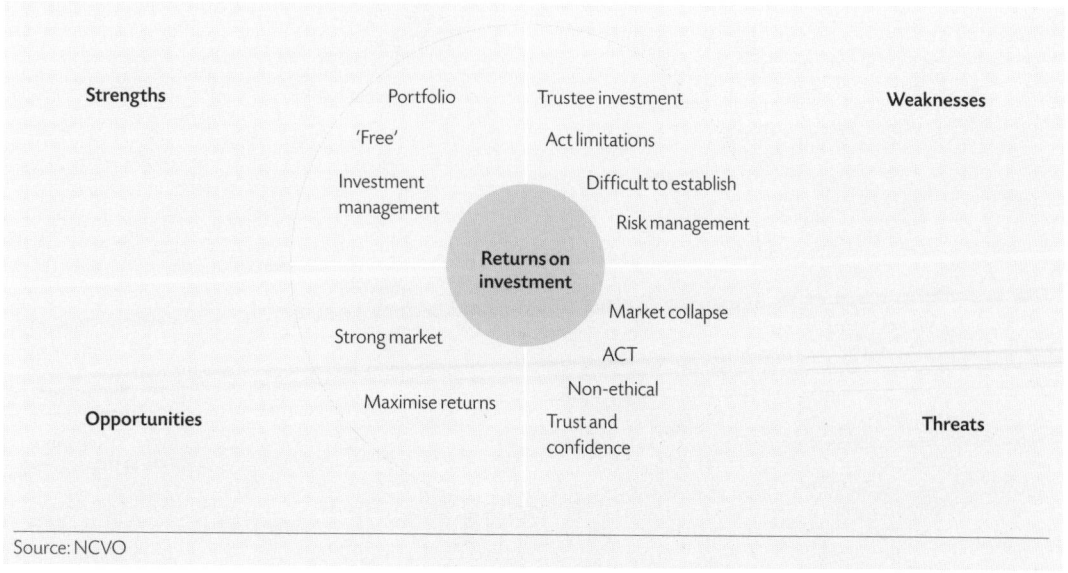

Source: NCVO

Phasing the budget

When preparing an income and expenditure budget for a project, it is important to identify when in a 12-month period the income and expenditure items are likely to arise. For example, costs such as insurance and rates are not incurred regularly throughout the period. Similarly, grants might be paid quarterly in advance or in arrears, and income from events will arise just before an event.

This phasing of the budget is important, because without it, useful comparisons between actual and budgeted income and expenditure will not be possible.

Statistical operational data

A voluntary organisation must regularly gather statistics and information relevant to the budgeting and planning process. Each organisation needs a method of measuring its own effectiveness: are its goals being met? What are the results of its efforts? Successes and failures, and weaknesses and strengths, should be regularly evaluated and the results used as a basis for making decisions. The sophistication and scope of the self-assessment process will vary according to the organisation, but to be effective, not only the performance of the organisation itself, but also that of staff, volunteers, managers and trustees, should be measured.

3.3
Structuring the budget

A voluntary organisation should have a structure that will ensure the efficient fulfilment of its strategic aims; in practice, this means setting up departments, or appointing project managers, with the responsibility for providing products or services. In most voluntary organisations, budgetary control and budget reports reflect the hierarchy of the organisation. The reporting – from the project manager responsible for delivering services to the board of trustees responsible for the financial health of the whole organisation – will be less detailed the higher up the organisation it goes.

Model budgets and budget monitoring

At board of trustees level, the concern will be to ensure that the organisation meets its financial goals: for example, to achieve a balanced budget of income and expenditure to the end of the year or to plan for a surplus. A further concern will be to ensure that the organisation has sufficient incoming cash resources to meet its obligations as they fall due.

The income and expenditure budget shown in figure 3.6 has the totals for rows A to D and a balance shown in row E. Staff costs have been separately disclosed because for many voluntary organisations they represent up to 60 per cent of total expenditure and thus warrant careful monitoring. Total running costs (C) will include both direct costs of projects and an element of organisation-wide costs.

The budgeted surplus or deficit should correspond to the target identified at the initial planning stages.

The headings for each of the columns are explained below.

- **Full year budget (1):** this represents the original budget or plan, which the organisation's staff and management would have started to compile six months before the start of the year, and would have been approved by the board approximately two months before the start of the year.
- **This month actual (2), this month budget (3), variance (4):** these columns taken together represent the difference from the original budget or plan for the current month as identified by the variance column. This set of figures allows for the examination of current month activities in income and expenditure terms.

- **Year to date actual (5), year to date budget (6), variance (7):** taken together, these columns represent the accumulated difference from the original plan or budget, as identified by the variance column. They enable the examination of six-month figures for income and expenditure, and therefore serve as a guide to the feasibility of the year-end financial goals.
- **Last forecast (8), this forecast (9), variance to last forecast (10):** these columns allow amendments to be made to the original budget, to reflect changing circumstances since it was approved. The variance to budget (11) column enables the effect of changing assumptions on the original plan or budget to be monitored.

The six-month income and expenditure budget for the Environ Alliance Trust delivers key messages that should concern the trustee board.

- The original budget planned for a surplus of £23,122 (column 1) to be taken to reserves. At the end of the six-month period the organisation is forecast to make a reduced surplus of £14,255 (column 9).
- The reduction occurs because the current forecast for total income to the end of the year is £511,777, compared with the original budget of £547,270.
- In response to the revised income forecast, the organisation has been cutting non-salary costs, as is evident in the reduction of the running costs budget from the original £256,655 to £226,258.

'The cash flow forecast is produced by reference to the income and expenditure budgets.'

- The trustee board should examine the possibility that income will further decline and the effect this might have on the work programme of the charity.
- The trustee board should investigate the reasons why income has declined. Have earned income targets been met? Has a grant application fallen through?

Cash flow forecasts

The cash flow forecast is a crucial document for trustees. Any organisation that runs out of cash will collapse, no matter how worthy its objectives. The cash flow forecast, or cash budget, is primarily used to ensure that the organisation has sufficient incoming resources to meet its obligations as they fall due. The example presented in figure 3.7 is a six-month forecast with the accumulated results to August rolled up into the first column, and a separate column for September. The cash flow forecast is produced by reference to the income and expenditure budgets, which serve as a basis for adjusting the individual entries to reflect amounts accrued or prepaid for each month. For example, since membership subscriptions are invoiced on a monthly basis, the amounts shown in the income and expenditure account will reflect the total invoiced for membership in a particular month. However, the amount shown in the cash flow statement reflects the actual receipt of cash credited to the bank for membership subscriptions in the month. Management will know from previous experience what proportion of subscriptions invoiced in any month will be paid in the following and subsequent months.

The six-month cash flow forecast for the Environ Alliance Trust delivers certain key messages that should concern the trustee board.

- From month to month there is a net cash outflow from the organisation averaging £5,000, which is currently being met from the accumulated balance at the bank.
- Although this net cash outflow may be sustainable in the short term, the trustee board must consider whether additional finance should be sought or must examine the feasibility of reducing the cash outflow by making additional savings.
- The 'project charges' row in both the cash inflow and cash outflow sections recognises that projects that cannot be directly attributed should be charged for general overheads. Since these charges are internal movements of cash, there is no impact on the cash flow of the voluntary organisation.
- It is important to appreciate that the cash flow statement will be different from the income and expenditure figures. The cash flow statement represents movements in cash held at the bank, whilst the income and expenditure statements reflect amounts that are due to the organisation (income) and amounts payable by the organisation (expenditure).

Figure 3.6 Total income and expenditure budget for Environ Alliance Trust

September 2013 Description	Full year Budget (1)	This month Actual (2)	This month Budget (3)	Variance (4) (3)−(2)
Total income (A)	547,270	31,331	27,418	3,913
Total staff costs (B)	267,493	21,047	21,828	781
Total running costs (C)	267,493	8,581	16,995	8,414
Total expenditure (D) (B) + (C)	524,148	29,628	38,823	9,195
Surplus (deficit) (E) (A) − (D)	23,122	1,703	(11,415)	13,108

• The cash flow statement will also need to include the effects of value added tax (VAT). This may result in a cash outflow (representing payments to Customs) or a cash inflow (representing a refund from Customs). The impact of VAT on the organisation will depend upon its business activities (see Chapter 8).

The trustee board should ask the following key questions of management.

• If income projections decline further, what effect will this have on the organisation's ability to carry on with its projects?
• Are there any contingency plans to safeguard the project (for example, borrowing or bridging-type loans)?
• Is it feasible to launch an immediate fundraising appeal?

To answer the above questions, the trustee board may need to be supplied with more detailed budget sheets on which each department's income and expenditure will be monitored.

As mentioned above, the trustee board may wish to seek further explanations of the income and expenditure position of Environ Alliance Trust, and for this purpose should be provided with the detailed departmental breakdown (figure 3.8). This report would be provided as a matter of course to the director and departmental managers.

The format of the report remains the same, making it easier to prepare. The main highlights from this report are listed here.

• The chief executive's office, research and policy, and services departments currently run on a deficit budget, being financed through membership subscriptions. This may be based on management's policy of allowing members' subscriptions to pay for policy and research activity and members' services. However, as is evident from the detailed report, such an arrangement requires careful cost management, as it may not be possible to pass on increasing costs to members through increased subscriptions.
• The income from the research and services department is significantly below that budgeted at the end of six months. The variances in column 7 under year-to-date income clearly show this. There may be many reasons for this decline in income, for example, the original budget was not phased for income and therefore meaningless variances are being generated; income generation activities have not been undertaken; or loss of funding has resulted in the shortfall.

Year to date Actual (5)	Year to date Budget (6)	Variance (7) (6) – (5)	Last forecast (8)	This forecast (9)	Variance to last F/C (10)	Variance to budget (11) (1) – (9)
188,761	234,130	(45,369)	519,838	511,777	(8,061)	(35,493)
111,966	110,775	(1,191)	269,498	271,264	(1,766)	(3,771)
65,835	100,820	34,985	231,741	226,158	5,483	30,397
177,801	211,595	33,794	501,239	497,522	3,717	26,626
10,960	22,535	(11,575)	18,599	14,255	(4,344)	(6,867)

- It is important to recognise that, when profiling the budget, the budget holder will need to consider the timing of when income and expenditure may arise within the year. Although it is reasonable to assume that certain expenses, such as rent, are incurred evenly over 12 months, this is not always the case; for other items, the budget holder will need to consider when in the year a particular activity will give rise to income being earned or expenditure incurred. In the absence of such profiling, large variances can occur, rendering the budget practically useless as a management tool.

- In response to the identified shortfall in income, Environ Alliance Trust has made significant savings in the running costs of both the research and services departments, as demonstrated by the variances identified in column 7 under running costs (row C).

Figure 3.7 Environ Alliance Trust cash flow forecast 2013

	Year to August Actuals	September Actuals	October Budget	November Budget
Receipts				
Membership subscriptions	34,560	10,588	12,500	12,500
Grant income	30,000	2,500	0	0
Publications	11,024	1,051	920	920
Conferences	13,762	936	1,188	1,938
Fees and other income	55,316	14,675	3,500	5,000
Project charges	0		0	0
Cash inflow	144,662	29,750	18,108	20,358
Payments				
Staff costs	92,250	17,235	17,218	17,237
Premises costs	6,669	1,350	1,500	1,205
Publication costs	4,877	1,565	1,220	3,000
Conference costs	6,358	1,458	1,500	2,500
Other running costs	32,974	6,859	5,000	5,000
Project charges	0	0	0	0
Cash outflow	143,128	28,467	26,438	28,942
Net cash inflow/(outflow)	1,534	1,283	(8,330)	(8,584)
Bank balances at beginning of period	42,344	43,878	45,161	36,831
Bank balances at end of period	43,878	45,161	36,831	28,247

- As a result of the identified shortfall in income, Environ Alliance Trust has decided to reforecast its total income, as is shown by the latest forecast figures for income (column 9). Column 11 reveals the total effect of these revisions on the original budget: total income is now forecast at £511,777, compared with the original budget of £547,270, a variance of £35,493.

- Because of the revised total income figures, Environ Alliance Trust had decided to defer or cancel programmes and expenditure in the research and services departments.

December Budget	January Budget	February Budget	March Budget	Total Budget
12,500	12,500	12,500	12,500	120,148
2,500	0	0	2,500	37,500
1,990	2,500	920	1,070	20,395
1,988	1,838	1,738	1,988	25,376
5,000	5,000	5,000	5,000	98,491
0	0	0	0	0
23,978	21,838	20,158	23,058	301,910
17,237	17,166	17,166	17,167	212,676
1,205	1,205	1,305	1,305	15,744
1,000	1,000	1,000	2,000	15,662
2,500	2,000	1,500	1,500	19,316
5,000	5,000	5,000	5,000	69,833
0	0	0	0	0
26,942	26,371	25,971	26,972	333,231
(2,964)	(4,533)	(5,813)	(3,914)	(31,321)
28,247	25,283	20,750	14,937	42,344
25,283	20,750	14,937	11,023	11,023

Figure 3.8 Detailed departmental breakdown for Environ Alliance Trust

Description	Full year Budget (1)		This month Actual (2)	This month Budget (3)	Variance (4) (3) – (2)	Year to date Actual (5)
Income						
Chief executive	100		0	83	(83)	210
Research and policy	101,050		3,668	5,391	(1,723)	25,948
Services development	129,690		1,685	4,556	(2,871)	18,206
Membership	120,000		11,998	8,698	3,300	60,209
Non-team	196,430		13,980	8,690	5,290	84,188
Total income (A)	**547,270**		**31,331**	**27,418**	**3,913**	**188,761**
Expenditure						
Chief executive	45,000		3,700	3,750	50	18,750
Research and policy	72,758		6,239	6,062	(177)	33,405
Services development	122,887		8,915	9,779	864	47,878
Membership	11,173		878	931	53	4,398
Non-team	15,675		1,315	1,306	(9)	7,535
Total staff costs (B)	**267,493**		**21,047**	**21,828**	**781**	**111,966**
Chief executive	5,930		2,150	494	(1,656)	4,126
Research and policy	71,991		1,249	5,471	4,222	13,527
Services development	112,051		1,899	5,857	3,958	19,080
Membership	36,308		1,252	2,173	921	14,452
Non-team	30,375		2,031	3,000	969	14,650
Total running costs (B)	**256,655**		**8,581**	**16,995**	**8,414**	**65,835**
Chief executive	(50,830)	(1)	(5,850)	(4,161)	(1,689)	(22,666)
Research and policy	(43,699)	(1)	(3,820)	(6,142)	2,322	(20,984)
Services development	(105,248)	(1)	(9,129)	(11,080)	1,951	(48,752)
Membership	72,519	(1)	9,868	5,594	4,274	41,359
Non-team	150,380	(1)	10,634	4,384	6,250	62,003
Surplus/deficit (A) – (B) – (C)	**23,122**		**1,703**	**(11,405)**	**13,108**	**10,960**

Year to date Budget (6)	Variance (7) (6) – (5)		Last Forecast (8)	This Forecast (9)	Variance to last forecast (10) (8) – (9)		Variance to budget (11) (1) – (9)
415	(205)		100	100	0		0
46,677	(20,729)	(2)	97,655	93,912	(3,743)		(7,138)
41,638	(23,432)	(2)	104,783	99,785	(4,998)		(29,905)
57,730	2,479		121,000	121,000	0		1,000
87,670	(3,482)		196,300	196,980	680		550
234,130	(45,369)		519,838	511,777	(8,061)		(35,493)
18,700	(50)		45,000	45,000	0		0
31,628	(1,777)		77,610	77,011	599		(4,253)
49,260	1,382		120,532	121,940	(1,408)		947
4,656	258		10,681	10,638	43		535
6,531	(1,004)		15,675	16,675	(1,000)		(1,000)
110,775	(1,191)		269,498	271,264	(1,766)		(3,771)
2,471	(1,655)		5,930	7,930	(2,000)		(2,000)
29,035	15,508	(3)	67,080	62,731	4,349	(5)	9,260
42,665	23,585	(3)	91,394	88,060	3,334	(5)	23,991
13,993	(459)		36,962	37,162	(200)		(854)
12,656	(1,994)		30,375	30,375	0		0
100,820	34,985		231,741	226,258	5,483		30,397
(20,756)	(1,910)		(50,830)	(52,830)	(2,000)		(2,000)
(13,986)	(6,998)		(47,035)	(45,830)	1,205		(2,131)
(50,287)	1,535		(107,143)	(110,215)	(3,072)		(4,967)
39,081	2,278		73,357	73,200	(157)		681
68,483	(6,480)		150,250	149,930	(320)		(450)
22,535	(11,575)		18,599	14,255	(4,344)		(8,867)

Budgets and budgetary control

When used properly, budgets can enable effective financial control of a voluntary organisation. Since they often reflect the organisational structure and are typically assigned to departments, projects and individuals, budgets are a way of assigning specific responsibility for the resources that have been allocated according to a plan of activities. It should be possible to trace back each of these activities to the strategic aim it seeks to meet. In this way, the organisation can move from its high level strategic aims to identifying objectives and drawing up detailed activity plans that have been costed and approved in the form of a budget.

Budgetary control is the practice of holding departments, projects and individuals to account for allocated resources, by comparing actual results for income and expenditure against the costed plan of activities. Budgets and budgetary control can affect the way people behave; many studies have shown that departmental or programme managers seek to safeguard the level of spending allocated to them. Meeting the budget targets often becomes the primary objective for individual employees, a tendency that is reinforced if that individual's performance and reward are determined by whether the targets have been met. Empire building and manipulating the budget in order to meet targets can rapidly become the norm. This causes the link between strategic aims and actual activity to become blurred, if not lost, and at worst budgets are used to measure organisational performance; the fulfilment of charitable aims ceases to be the primary measure of performance.

To guard against this loss of direction, the management of a voluntary organisation needs to monitor and measure its outcomes and the impact it has on society (according to its strategic aims), as well as its financial performance – this is clearly evidenced by the adoption of impact reporting in many charities.

The management committee and board of trustees need to be informed about the organisation's financial health and its effectiveness in meeting its strategic aims. As mentioned in Chapter 2, programme aims and financial goals are interdependent, and success in one cannot be achieved at the expense of the other.

To be able to provide this more balanced reporting, the voluntary organisation needs to monitor and measure performance over a broader range of criteria than simply the financial.

3.4
Communicating financial information

The responsibility for compiling financial reports often falls on the finance officer or finance department, who are charged with maintaining financial data and manipulating it in a variety of ways to produce reports. These reports set out to inform a wide range of stakeholders, including project managers, the organisation's management and trustee board, funders and regulatory bodies. The design and content of these reports should be determined by the needs of the audience; it is not enough to follow blindly a predetermined template. The internal audience would usually be presented with management accounts consisting of income and expenditure and cash flow reports, whereas for external audiences – such as funders and the Charity Commission – the form and content will often be prescribed beforehand.

For many people in voluntary organisations, 'management accounts' mean reams of paper covered in numbers that are produced by the accounts department and ignored by everyone else. Management accounts are, however, vital for running an organisation effectively – so what should be done to make them more accessible?

The information provided must be relevant

Management accounts must contain the financial information that the reader actually needs to plan and control the financial resources for which he or she is accountable. The finance officer who is preparing the management accounts must, therefore, be aware of the issues that affect the organisation in general and the reader in particular.

Understanding the organisation's cash flow may be much more important than income and expenditure. How often are balance sheets used, and have restricted funds been used according to the donor's wishes?

The information must be up to date

There is a trade-off between accuracy and speed: the more accurate the information, the longer it will take to produce. Management needs to understand the organisation well enough to determine at what point accuracy ceases to affect the decision being made.

The information must be accurate

Inaccurate information is worse than no information at all. Accuracy here means not only eliminating data handling errors – miscodings, wrong entries, incorrect totals or transfers of figures – but also ensuring that nothing is omitted.

The accounts must be intelligible

However timely and accurate the accounts may be, they are of no use if they do not inform the reader. Management accounts frequently contain too many numbers presented in a discouraging format. The finance officer must be clear about who the audience are and what information they need to make the decisions expected of them.

The accounts must be available

Users should have access to management accounts at the times when they need them. This is unlikely to coincide with predetermined deadlines for monthly reporting. For many organisations, however, this flexibility may be impossible, particularly if the accounts are held on a manual system. However, it should remain an objective for organisations with computer accounting systems to allow non-accounting staff 'read only' access to information.

The accounts must describe what is actually going on

What do readers understand 'actual' to mean? Expenditure and payments are not the same thing, but do they realise that? What the user of management accounts sees in the 'actuals' column will depend on the method of accounting for transactions that is adopted. If users are not clear about which transactions are included, they can seriously misinterpret the true financial position.

Using a cash accounting policy, an amount will appear in the actuals column only once a payment has been made, for example, once a cheque has been written. This might be some time after the legal liability has been incurred and well after a commitment has been made to spend the funds. If management accounts only reflect the commitment once the liability has been met, the risk of overstating 'free' funds is considerable.

A first step in rectifying the above position is to move to an accruals accounting policy, by accruing liabilities when they are incurred rather than recognising them only when they are met. This means, for example, charging invoice values as expenditure and coding payments to creditor balances.

Figures are useless in isolation. To make sense of them, a user needs to compare them with suitable other comparators. Some useful comparisons of results might be:

- the five most successful UK charity results, suitably adjusted
- your best ever performance
- any commercial organisations listed as an example of best practice in the Inside UK Enterprise scheme
- your closest competitor
- your equivalent organisation overseas.

Who owns the management accounts?

Because budgets are produced by the accounts department, that department is often seen as owning them. Users need to feel that they are the owners of management accounts, rather than passive recipients. This question of ownership can be resolved by addressing the following issues.

- **Involvement:** the more the user can influence the management accounts, the more likely they are to value them as a decision-making aid. This does, however, require the user to have commitment and the relevant skills. Involvement is more likely when:

  – operating or programme staff (those involved in spending the money) prepare the budgets
  – programme staff have a detailed understanding of the organisation's priorities
  – programme staff contribute to the design of reports, albeit within the statutory framework
  – the inputting of data – such as invoice details – is performed by programme staff instead of accounts clerks
  – users are able to get reports whenever they need them.

- **Transparency:** organisations should recognise that information is a resource that should be made freely available to all staff (but without compromising privacy). In this way, both good and bad news can be communicated.

- **Accountability:** those who make decisions about the use of the charity's financial resources should be held accountable for those decisions. Accountability can be achieved by requiring the users of management accounts to:

  – prepare budgets using a zero-based approach, where the user has to justify the resources needed
  – explain variances that arise, so that problem areas are identified and action taken
  – reforecast year-end results as the year progresses, so that programme staff are encouraged to think about whether they are on track
  – revise budgets if the resource requirement for the programmes has changed.

- **Trust:** users of management accounts should feel that they are trusted to manage the resources for which they are accountable. This can be difficult, as it requires the accounts department to strike a balance between wise stewardship of the charity's financial resources and obtrusive policing. In practice, trust means:

  – examining the levels of authority that users exercise, and perhaps increasing them in order to give the users the discretion to spend resources
  – managing expectations by stressing that the budget is a plan based on assumptions that may not hold true – it is not to be used for disciplinary purposes.

3.5
Budgets and IT solutions

For years, voluntary organisations of all sizes have used spreadsheet applications to prepare management accounts. It is no surprise, therefore, that Excel is the tool most commonly used by accountants. Information technology (IT) is used to produce budgets because of its speed and convenience, but a successful budgeting system is a lot more than just a spreadsheet. This section gives guidelines on how to organise, design and implement budgetary control using spreadsheet applications. They will help organisations to use IT solutions that genuinely assist management rather than hinder it. Larger organisations should be aware that there comes a point when a spreadsheet solution is outgrown and they should look to the myriad of specific budgeting and planning tools that are on the market.

Pre-planning

A budgetary control system has a number of different elements that will vary from organisation to organisation. A straightforward system might be for departmental/project budgets consolidated to an organisational level, with the ability to track these against actuals month, for the year-to-date, and for the same period last year. For anything other than the simplest application, there are key stages to developing a spreadsheet model that should be followed.

System design

Before entering data into the spreadsheet, think carefully about the design of the system. Talk to the people who might need to extract information from the system when it is complete. It can be difficult to change the format of a spreadsheet-based budget after it has been created. At this stage, the level of detail required should be decided and the best design of the system identified to achieve this. Users should be familiar with some of the more advance features of a spreadsheet including multi-dimensional capabilities and macros. If in-house skills do not exist in this area, users should consider some training.

Thought should be given to any interfaces required for external systems such as the accounting application itself. Do you, for example, want to import data into the spreadsheet from the finance package or vice versa? If individuals are completing their own departmental budget, can you give them their own forms to complete, which you can automatically consolidate into the system?

Model specification

Next, it is usually worth laying out the more detailed system specification. Look at what information will be kept on which sheets, what data will be stored in separate files, use of tables etc. Thought should be given to any security requirements to ensure sensitive data, such as salaries, is not accessible by unauthorised users.

System backups should also be checked to make sure there is a resilient fall back for the work you are doing.

If you have several people working on the application, make sure they all have the appropriate version of the spreadsheet you are using.

Documentation

Thought should be given to the amount of documentation you wish to prepare on the system. Make sure there is sufficient material so that if the system designer is away someone else can understand how it is put together. Make sure you provide documentation for users to help them use the application.

Spreadsheet development

This is the point at which the actual building of the system begins. Too many people ignore the preceding stages and jump straight into spreadsheet development. This usually results in needlessly complex models that take longer than necessary to develop, based on assumptions that were not part of the original brief.

Testing

Even after thorough planning and careful spreadsheet development, it is a good idea to test all components of a system. This can be done by entering several sets of data and checking the logic; historical data with known results is useful for this purpose.

Implementation

The effort required for implementation will vary according to the complexity of the system, the number of people who will use it and whether training or on-going support will be needed.

3.6
Digitising the accounts

Most voluntary organisations have digitised their accounts or are considering doing so. The benefits are typically saving staff time, obtaining more detailed or more accurate information, and producing reports and answering queries more quickly.

It is usually clear when an accounting system is failing to meet the needs of an organisation, or when the resources it is consuming seem out of proportion with the results. In some cases, improving the existing manual system may be all that is needed. However, every organisation is different; here are some suggested criteria that you might consider when deciding whether to digitise.

- Is your annual income or expenditure more than £100,000?
- Do you have several different projects that need separate accounting?
- Do you handle a large number of similar transactions?

If the organisation is small, with a simple financial structure, it should be possible to design an effective manual system for the main accounting records.

However, within such a manual system there may be areas of work involving a large number of repetitive transactions – such as subscriptions – that would be quicker using a computer.

When to start

A potentially good time to change systems is at the end of the financial year. Unfortunately, this means that the busy period, when annual accounts are being prepared, will coincide with any teething troubles in the computer system, although potential problems can be minimised by careful planning and preparation.

Planning should begin well in advance: for a smallish organisation, typically three to six months before the start of the changeover. These early discussions should include a review of the additional resources needed to install the new system, for example, will it be necessary to bring in outside expertise and/or temporary assistance?

Are there any sources of funding, or free expertise or assistance, for this investment? At this early stage it can be useful to visit similar voluntary organisations in order to learn from their experiences.

What to avoid

Here are some guidelines on what not to do.

- Use 'informal' systems – those that allow entries to be changed at a later stage without a clear record being kept of the amendment.
- Expect staff without adequate training, supervision or control to enter complex data reliably.
- Become over sophisticated, for example, by trying to provide excessively detailed analysis or automating procedures that would be better as manual tasks.
- Allow one enthusiastic employee or volunteer to set up a system that only he or she can understand.

Choosing a package

It is often the case that a computer package that lends itself to a project-based system would be most useful, as that reflects the structure (and funding pattern) of many voluntary organisations.

There is a trade-off in choice of package between cost, ease of use and the range and sophistication of features that are offered. Make sure you evaluate any proposed solution to ensure it meets your needs. Talk to similar charities and see what they use to get an idea of what might work for you. Choose a supplier with care, ideally based on good references from your contacts.

Try and see if you can pilot the product before you buy it to make sure it meets your key requirements. Talk to your accountants to get their views on the proposed solution.

Setting up

In the computer package, income and expenditure headings will be represented by codes (a chart of accounts) that will enable you to analyse income and expenditure.

This needs careful thought, as no two charts of accounts will be the same, but a few general tips may help.

- Work backwards from the reports you want to produce to determine the most convenient structure and sequence of accounts.
- Use different levels of analysis as appropriate, perhaps using a separate code for each individual's training costs, but one code for, say, postage.
- Leave generous gaps between codes to allow for new developments.

Who needs training?

Almost everyone in the organisation, and perhaps a few people outside, should be made aware of the new system. Those with the main training needs will be the people who prepare information for inputting – whoever looks after the petty cash, for example – or people who receive output information, such as the members of the committee who read the final reports.

Checklist

Answer the following questions before checking the answers in the text.

1. What are the key decisions that have to take place in budget planning?

2. Describe the differences between a fixed and flexible budget.

3. What is the purpose of preparing a cash budget?

4. How does variance analysis work?

5. List the key action points to consider when planning to digitise the accounts.

Action points for your organisation

Audit your organisation to see if it has:

- a budget manual
- a cash budget
- a flexible budgeting system, particularly for budgetary control reports
- appropriate forecasting techniques
- an IT strategy.

Case study and exercises

Giltim Union

This case study provides a comprehensive examination of a budgeting system.

Specifically, it allows the reader to:

- evaluate the Giltim budget reporting system in terms of design, speed, frequency, clarity and overall effectiveness for region, division and head office
- criticise the design of the report
- establish how well the budget system motivates regional secretaries to achieve union objectives
- consider how senior management could make the system more effective.

Top management approach to reporting

The general secretary and controller of Giltim insisted on a rapid and efficient system of reporting monthly operations. They believed in up-to-date reports to enable timely action by head office, division and regional secretaries. However, they believed that regional secretaries should not wait until the month end to deal with critical problems, but should deal with them on a daily basis. Regional reports were reviewed on an 'exception' basis, comparing actual performance against budget. This was felt to be good for morale, and regional secretaries were expected to explain overspending but not underspending.

Monthly flash reports

On the third business day after the month end, each region faxed key figures for income, gross surplus and net surplus to division and head office, together with the variances from budget. A summary of these figures was studied the next day by senior management, who were concerned about critical variances.

Monthly detailed reports

On the eighth working day the regional operating summary and supporting reports were due at divisional head office. These were consolidated to show the results by region and division, then distributed the next day to senior management.

In addition, at the beginning of each month regional secretaries were expected to submit current reforecasts of anticipated performance for the month and year-end. Such reforecasts enabled head office to shape financial plans and to get regional secretaries to look at their programmes on a yearly as well as a day-to-day basis.

Dealing with regional problems

When a potential problem became apparent, daily reports on it were required for the division and head office.

A specialist team was sometimes sent to the region concerned to make recommendations. It was up to the regional secretary to accept or reject these, but it was generally expected that they would accept such 'advice' gracefully.

Income decline

If a decline in income became evident early in the year, and the regional secretary could convince senior management that the change was permanent, the regional budget could be revised to reflect the new circumstances. However, if income fell below the predicted level towards the year-end, no revision was allowed.

Regional secretaries were expected to go back over the budget with their staff to see where cost reductions could be made that would do the least harm. Specifically, they were expected to consider what could be either eliminated or postponed until next year.

Branch and region coordination
Whenever problems arose between regions and branches, local managers were expected to solve the problems themselves. Members' needs always came first. However, if the local programme involved a major regional expense out of line with the budget, this was decided upon by division or head office.

Motivation of regional secretaries
Regional secretaries and all of their staff were motivated to meet surplus targets through promotion and pressures from division and head office. In addition, each month the regions were ranked competitively for recruitment efficiency, and the results were published widely throughout the union. Inter-region competitions with prizes were also conducted for special cost-reduction programmes, improvements in methods etc. Regions were encouraged to stress quality and delivery to meet competitive pressures. All regional workers knew that, to survive in the competitive market, Giltim had to produce high-quality services on time and at reasonable cost.

Conclusions
Regional secretaries and other staff were not particularly happy under the system, but they worked hard to achieve targets and were generally successful, despite changes in the market conditions.

Schedule of monthly regional report
- **Regional operating summary:** income, costs, other income and expense. Actual against budget for the month and year to date. Percentage analysis on sales and assets employed.
- **Income analysis:** income by membership bands. Actual, budget and variance analysis for the month and year to date.
- **Regional variance:** cost of material, labour and variable expense. Actual budget and variance analysis.
- **Recruitment and sales.**
- **Regional fixed expense:** regional expense other than variable and special expense. Actual, budget and variance analysis.

- **Special costs and surplus:** special items under the control of the regional secretary, including sale of scrap, methods improvement, standard revisions, cost-reduction programmes etc. Actual, budget and variance analysis.
- **Regional investment:** stock, capital projects, debtors included in computation of assets employed by the region. Actual, budget, variance and ageing analysis.

Evaluation of reporting system
- **Design:** reports include actual and target data. Head office requires reforecasting of activity that deviates from budget. Highlight on excess spending over budget, but no importance attached to under-spending. Concentrates on problem areas with special reports. Report sample is badly designed.
- **Speed:** flash reporting in three days and full reporting to head office in eight days provides timely data for management. Probably achieved by cutoff of activities before the month end and efficient data processing.
- **Frequency:** excellent – monthly data on regular operations, weekly or daily for critical problems.
- **Clarity:** poor layout and lack of graphical presentation.
- **Effectiveness:** highly effective for head office control of activity against budget. Provides control data to focus manager on target achievement and critical problems. Probably over-emphasises short-term meeting of the budget at the expense of long-term performance.

Performance of region and design of report
It was difficult to evaluate the performance of Region No 1 from this report as 'year-to-date' figures were not provided. However, evaluation of March's performance raised many questions that needed investigation, which would need to be answered before meaningful conclusion and effective action could be taken.

- Recruitment income is seriously below target: is this a national trend or a regional failure?
- Variable cost of recruitment and sales controlled: is this due to office efficiency?
- Fixed costs seriously above target: why?
- Operating income well below target both in amount and percentage: is this due to failure of income?

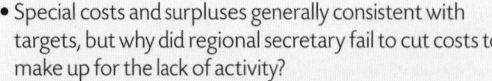

- Special costs and surpluses generally consistent with targets, but why did regional secretary fail to cut costs to make up for the lack of activity?
- Region income well below target and return on assets employed unacceptable.

The following improvements to the design of the report are suggested.

- Eliminate 'last month' and 'last year' columns, since the budget is the real target.
- Show only actual data for the month and the year to date with variance from the budget (not the budget itself).
- Eliminate all data below £1,000 to reduce the digits to significant items only; reports should not be too dense.
- Design each report page as a complete entity supported by detail on subsequent sheets.
- Design report with graphics sections to emphasise signals.

Figure 3.9 Giltim Union: No 1 region operating statement, March

	This month Actual £	Last month Budget £	Last month Actual £	Last year Actual £
Recruitment income	170,168	294,325	162,271	289,979
Other income	47,132	16,000	37,420	13,111
Total income	**217,300**	**310,325**	**199,691**	**303,090**
Variable costs	142,217	187,500	137,821	192,175
Gross margin	75,083	122,825	61,870	110,915
Fixed costs	41,211	36,400	38,174	41,118
Operating income	**33,872**	**86,425**	**23,696**	**69,798**
Operating income as a % of gross income	15.59%	27.85%	11.87%	23.03%
Special costs (surplus):				
Method improvements	−17,426	−21,300	−28,322	−12,174
Standard revisions	24,174	9,400	7,416	6,811
Price variances	−12,111	−6,000	3,567	4,667
Miscellaneous	−8,126	−6,000	−30,100	−22,179
Total	**−13,490**	**−23,900**	**−47,438**	**−22,875**
Region surplus	47,362	110,325	71,134	92,672
Assets employed	1,816,411	1,874,426	1,742,112	1,052,112
% return	2.61%	5.89%	4.08%	8.81%

Source: School of Social Entrepreneurs

Motivation of managers

1. System provides highly centralised control by head office and is probably defensive.

2. Extensive interaction in setting the targets probably conditions managers to accept them. Personal contact with head office staff and visit by controller most helpful.

3. Unreasonable to expect regional secretaries to meet surplus budget if recruitment falls off, but quite possible for them to feel bound to do so and to believe that they can and do achieve budget.

4. Regional secretaries probably underspend on maintenance, research, training etc, in the early months of the year until income levels indicate that they can 'afford' to spend up to the budget cost levels.

5. Regional secretaries motivated to achieve target by:

   - budget preparation process
   - senior management interest in and follow-up of reporting
   - salaries and bonuses
   - competition between regions
   - staff assistance and daily reports on critical problems
   - requirements to continually reforecast any expected performance below target
   - budget effect on personal promotion in the Union.

6. Tendency to achieve short-term targets with some loss of long-term potential. However, this loss may not be significant.

7. Long-term planning retained by head office and divisional management (the latter is fairly powerless). Little motivation to think beyond current year at region level. Poor development of regional secretary's potential.

8. Fairly dynamic environment created by the constructive friction between region, head office and division.

9. May achieve a lower level of long-term performance, but all staff are not merely cost orientated but out-turn orientated too.

10. System meets senior management objective of surplus now. Puts surplus responsibility close to operations that achieve surplus. Related to the specific industry sector features of delivery, quality and efficient cost control.

Changes recommended

1. Consider the technical, human and organisational problems that any change would have to overcome. Managers may prefer 'the devil they know', and may therefore be reluctant to accept any new system.

2. Consider all the alternatives and their implications.

   - Make division out-turn orientated, ie, positively seeking opportunities to generate income as a contribution to costs (regions become only cost orientated).
   - All-budget revision when income falls off (managers more motivated to justify revisions than to achieve out-turn budgets).

3. Proposals

   - Try to assign income and surplus responsibility to one manager in one centre.
   - If this is not possible, introduce some flexibility in budget revision when income falls off substantially.
   - Expand budget system for a three-year horizon. Plan every year for three years ahead. Let the annual budget targets be developed from the first year of plan.
   - Include all managers in short- and long-term planning processes.
   - Introduce a training and development programme for managers to give them an understanding of long-term and short-term planning.
   - Discourage the idea that meeting the budget is the same as doing the management job.

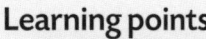

Learning points

- Budget reports should be available three to eight days after the month end.
- Achieve fast reporting, day early cut-off and efficient use of IT.
- Design reports for use by managers, not accountants – they should be simple, graphic and exciting.
- Signal the key factors; do not give the complete detail.
- Design reports for local as well as top management.
- Recognise that manager motivation is not automatically achieved by participation, but is a complex phenomenon resulting from the total system.
- Managers sometimes may not be rationally responsible, but may be convinced that they are, and act accordingly. Behaviour is not completely rational in logical or economic terms; consider emotional needs.
- Modifying the budget system and motivating the managers is a complex problem.
- People may not work as effectively under a new and 'better' system.
- Set surplus centres as close to operations (the 'front line') as practicable, to make managers cost orientated as well as surplus orientated.
- Head office 'advice' may really be orders.
- Region 'agreement' may really be imposed by head office.
- Technical problems with the budget are fairly easy to solve, but the human problems are not.
- The involvement of senior management in the budget process is vital if it is to motivate managers.
- A three-year horizon involving all managers is more useful than mere budgetary control each year. This provides the underlying data for the annual and monthly budget targets.
- Design the budget system with reference to senior management objectives, industry sector key factors and the organisational structure of the union.
- Measure the effectiveness of the budget system by what the managers do, not by what they say.
- Review and redesign budget reports periodically to meet changing needs.
- Recognise that reports for head office may not necessarily meet local management needs; thus leading to two (or more) reporting systems – formal and informal.

Figure 3.10 Giltim Union: Revised regional operating summary, March

| | | This month | | Year to date |
	Actual £000	(Under)/over budget £000	Actual £000	(Under)/over budget £000
Recruitment income	170	(124)	679	(122)
Other income	47	31	84	56
Total income	217	(93)	763	(66)
% gain/(loss)	-	(30.0%)	-	(7.9%)
Variable costs of recruitment and sales	142	(45)	384	(64)
Gross margin	75	(48)	379	(2)
% income	34.6%	(5.1%)	49.6%	3.6%
Fixed costs	41	5	211	10
Operating income	34	(53)	168	(12)
% income	15.7%	(12.4%)	22.0%	
Special costs (surplus)	(13)	(11)	12	11
Regional surplus	47	(64)	156	(1)
% income	21.70%	(13.80%)	20.40%	
Assets employed	1,816	(58)	1,816	(58)
% return	2.6%	(3.3%)	8.6%	8.4%

Source: School of Social Entrepreneurs

The budgeting process

This list of key questions should be reviewed by the chief finance officer or other person responsible for organising the budget and compiling the information. It could also be reviewed by the board finance committee to establish whether all the appropriate steps in the process have been taken.

1. Why is a budget useful?

- It outlines in financial terms the goals and policies approved by the board.
- It is a method of monitoring adherence to, and deviations from, plans throughout the year.
- Its preparation causes the organisation to focus on planning, evaluation of programmes and accomplishment of its mission.

2. Is the budgeting process properly timed?

- Can the proposed staff or project changes realistically be implemented before the financial year-end?
- Is board membership scheduled to change prior to budget approval? (Avoid making a new board responsible for a budget they didn't approve.)
- If the budget is approved by members, when is the annual meeting?
- Must major funding requests be submitted in advance of approval of the overall budget? If so, consider the need for a two- or three-year plan.

3. What type of budget is appropriate for this organisation?

- Is a zero-based budget needed for critical evaluation of priorities to force a serious cutback in the level of expenses?
- Are existing programmes examined as closely as proposed projects?
- Will a functional or line-item budget allow for proper review of programme goals?
- Is the budget based on existing operations, with incremental increases or decreases for economic conditions?

4. Who prepares the budget?

- Is a budget committee needed?
- Would a budget committee made up of accounting department staff, board members and outside advisers be effective?
- If each department does the initial preparation, are standard formats and instructions distributed to ensure consistency?
- Is the final budget comprehensive, including restricted funds, endowments, capital improvements and all financial aspects?

5. What are the stages in budget preparation?

- Develop goals and objectives for a three- to five-year period first (long-range plan, dreams).
- Quantify long-range goals, such as raising an endowment, financing new facilities or increasing staff.
- Evaluate last year's results.
  a) Were objectives achieved?
  b) If not, were they unreasonable?
  c) What caused variances? Were mid-year revisions appropriate?
  d) What changes were indicated by ratio analysis?
- Establish objectives for the coming year.
- Prepare programme justification.
- Prepare estimates of income and expenses of programmes.
- Compile, evaluate and balance the results.
- The budget should be approved first by the staff, then by the board (with intervening stages as the nature of the organisation dictates).
- Amend the budget when the monitoring process shows a need for change.

6. Evaluate programmes and services rendered.

- Who are the stakeholders?
- Is the organisation reaching them?
- Should promotion be budgeted?
- Is the cost per person too high?
- Is a competing organisation providing the same service?

7. Evaluate the pricing of services.

- Should changes be made? Price increases or decreases? (There are, of course, more factors to be considered in altering prices than purely cost considerations.)
- Would audience/membership etc increase with a decrease in prices, resulting in more revenue?
- Are funding sources available to cover free or reduced-cost services?

8. Evaluate fundraising activities.

- Can board members and other volunteers devote sufficient time to help the organisation reach its fundraising goals? If not, should consultants or new staff be hired?
- Is an annual special-giving campaign necessary in addition to the membership campaign? Would it drain the membership?
- Can project sponsors or co-sponsors be found?
- Should a planned-giving programme be established?

9. Evaluate expenses.

- Could alternative approaches improve efficiency and thus reduce costs?
- Is the use of volunteers effective?
- Would 'investing' in a paid development director or volunteer coordinator more than pay for itself?
- Are computers used effectively?
- Are cheaper but time-consuming or inadequate computer programs being used to save money?
- Would networking, email or a website pay for themselves through savings in time and mailings?
- Are fixed and variable costs segregated? If so, are they properly allocated to programmes?
- Are changes in salary level factored in to benefit costs?

10. Consider outside forces.

- Is funding likely to be cut owing to the depressed state of the economy?
- Has there been a shift in population? Have local major employers closed down? Are standards in the profession changing?
- Are accreditation or grant requirements changing?

11. Before final approval, consider these issues.

- Is there any doubt about the reliability of projections?
- Do sufficient cash reserves exist to cover shortfalls?
- Re-evaluate policy goals if cuts have to be made.
- Could projects be carried out in cooperation with, or by, another organisation?
- Would charts or graphs illustrate trends and make decisions clearer?

12. Prepare supplementary budgets to implement the overall budget.

- Cash flow projections
- Investment objectives
- Capital expenditure timing
- Restricted fund budgets

13. Devise a follow-up system for monitoring the budget.

- Use timely financial reports to compare actual expenses and income with those budgeted.
- Revise budget to reflect recurring changes during the year.

(With acknowledgement to Jody Blazek.)

Budgetary control: fixed versus flexible – a worked example

A disabled person's charity has a trading subsidiary, which is a wood workshop. The workshop makes children's rocking horses for local authority children and foster homes at a set price. Figure 3.11 shows budgeted results and actual results for May 2012.

Notes

• In this example, the variances are meaningless for the purposes of control. Costs were higher than budget because there were 50 per cent more rocking horses made. The variable costs would be expected to increase above the budgeted costs. There is no information to show whether control action is required for any aspects of income or expenditure.

• For control purposes, we need to know the following.

1. Whether actual costs were higher than they should have been to produce 150 rocking horses.
2. Whether actual income was satisfactory from the sale of 150 rocking horses.

3. Whether the number of rocking horses made and supplied has varied from the budget in a good or bad way.

The correct approach to budgetary control is to:

1. identify fixed and variable costs
2. produce a flexible budget.

In our example we have the following estimates of cost behaviour.

1. Materials, wages and maintenance costs are variable.
2. Rent, rates and depreciation are fixed costs.
3. Other costs consist of fixed costs of £800 plus a variable cost of £10 per rocking horse made and distributed to the local authorities.

Discussion

1. In producing and distributing 150 rocking horses, the expected surplus should be the flexible budget surplus of £2,700 rather than the fixed budget surplus of £950. Instead the actual surplus was £3,400, £700 more than expected. The reason for this improvement is that costs were lower than expected as the projected income on 150 horses was exactly as expected.

Figure 3.11

	Budget £	Actual results £	Variance £
Rocking horses made	100	150	50
Income (a)	10,000	15,000	5,000
Expenditure:			
Materials	3,000	4,250	(1,250)
Wages	2,000	2,250	(250)
Maintenance	500	700	(200)
Depreciation	1,000	1,100	(100)
Rent and rates	750	800	(50)
Other costs	1,800	2,500	(700)
Total costs (b)	**9,050**	**11,600**	**(2550)**
Surplus (deficit) (a) – (b)	**950**	**3,400**	**2,450**

2. Another reason for the improvement was that the local authorities took all the produced rocking horses. As the cost of producing each unit was less than the price paid by the local authority, a surplus (contribution) was made on each rocking horse. What would have happened if the local authority had not taken and paid for the additional rocking horses?

3. Understanding costs and in particular the difference between fixed, variable and semi-variable is vitally important in understanding finance, and in particular budgetary control reports (costing is discussed in chapter 5). Issues requiring further investigation are as follows.

a) The wages did not rise in exact proportion (controllable variance) and are £750 less.
b) The other variable cost element (controllable variance) is over by £200.

4. The fixed costs are non-controllable and do not require any more attention from the manager's perspective.

Exercise 3.1

ASH Hospice has devolved a number of service functions into business units and treats them like separate organisations. One unit is 'Medical and Surgery Supplies', which supplies products to the hospice wards. The unit uses the 'just in time method' so no stocks are held, as deliveries from the local hospital are made each day. The unit pays £20 for each pack of raw materials supplied, which it then assembles.

The unit has a budgetary control system, which is based upon fixed budgets, ie no adjustment is made for changes in the volume of supplies required. You have recently been appointed as the finance director.

Figure 3.12 shows what the budgetary control (variance) analysis should be

	Fixed budget (a) £	Flexible budget (b) £	Actual (c) £	Variance (b) – (c) £
Rocking horses made	100	150	150	
Income	10,000	15,000	15,000	0
Expenditure:				
Variable				
Materials	3,000	4,500	4,250	250
Wages	2,000	3,000	2,250	750
Maintenance	500	750	700	50
Semi-variable costs:				
Other costs	1,800	2,300	2,500	(200)
Fixed costs				
Depreciation	1000	1000	1100	(100)
Rent and rates	750	750	800	(50)
Total costs	9,050	12,300	11,600	700
Surplus	950	2700	3,400	700

Figure 3.13

Item	Fixed budget £	Actual £	Variances £
Quantity supplied (packs)	1,000	1,150	150
Revenue	100,000	V 120,750	20,750
Costs:			
Supplies	20,000	V 23,000	3,000
Wages and salaries:			
Packing staff	20,000	V 24,150	−4,150
Maintenance	2,000	1,950	50
Supervision	3,000	2,800	200
Management and administration	4,500	4,650	−150
Total	**29,500**	**33,550**	**−4,050**
Packaging function:			
Cleaning equipment	1,000	V 1,035	−35
Sterilising equipment	500	V 460	40
Bagging equipment	250	275	−25
Total	**1,750**	**1,770**	**−20**
Expenses:			
Production	1,250	V 1,495	−245
Maintenance	1,500	1,550	−50
Management and administration	2,300	2,890	−590
Buildings	850	720	130
Total	**5,900**	**6,655**	**−755**
Depreciation:			
Cleaning equipment	400	V 460	−60
Sterilising equipment	1,500	V 1,725	−225
Bagging equipment	2,500	2,500	0
Maintenance equipment	1,300	1,300	0
Office equipment and furniture	950	950	0
Total	**6,650**	**6,935**	**−285**
Total cost	**63,800**	**71,910**	**−8,110**
Surplus (deficit)	**36,200**	**48,840**	**12,640**

You note that actual monthly output is frequently very different from the budgeted output. You are concerned to find that the hospice management team pays little attention to the variances contained in the monthly budgetary report, as they say 'it is now a separate business' and 'we are only concerned with the bottom line'.

The budgetary control report for May 2012 is set out in figure 3.13. You have identified that the items marked with V, are variable and change directly with output.

You should redraft the May 2012 budget report, replacing the original fixed budget with a flexible budget. Compile a report to the management team that sets out the problems with the original budget format and explains how flexible budgeting could improve the monthly budget report.

Answer to Exercise 3.1

Memorandum

To: Management Team
From: Finance Director
Date: 8 June 2012
Reference: Monthly Budgetary Control Reports

Medical and Surgery Supplies budgetary control reports compare the actual revenue and costs with a fixed budget, ie a budget that does not take into account the effect that changes in output volume have on costs.

This causes two problems.

1. The variances for those costs that are variable are misleading. For example, the packing staff wages show an adverse variance of £4,150 for May 2012, but as output was 15 per cent higher than budget there is every likelihood that £3,000 of the variance is simply due to more hours being worked to obtain the higher output.

2. The effect of volume changes on surplus is hidden, as variable costs are not grouped together but are included under their particular expense groupings. This means it is difficult to identify the contribution made, or lost, by increases or decreases in the number of supplies made.

The solution to these two problems is to adopt a marginal costing format and flexible budgeting.

A marginal costing format will group the variable costs together and subtract them from the revenue to obtain the contribution for the month. The fixed costs can then be subtracted from the contribution to obtain the surplus. This approach will clearly identify the costs that can be controlled by the medical supplies manager, ie the variable costs, such as the packing staff wages and those that cannot be changed in the short term, ie the fixed costs, such as management salaries. This should mean that the manager can concentrate upon the costs they can do something about, rather than being distracted by unavoidable fixed costs.

A flexible budget will adjust the budget for revenue, variable costs and the contribution to take into account the volume of output. As a consequence, the variances that are shown on the budget report will be due to price or efficiency deviations and not caused by volume. This will mean that the manager will be able to concentrate on dealing with inefficiencies, as the costs of these will be highlighted, instead of being masked by volume changes. For example, the £3,000 adverse variance for supplies will disappear but there will still be a £1,150 adverse variance on packing staff wages to explain.

Figure 3.14 Medical Supplies Unit – revised budget report for month of May 2012

Item	Flexible budget £	Actual £	Variance £
Quantity supplied (packs)	1,150	1,150	0
Revenue	115,000	120,750	5,750
Variable costs:			
Supplies	23,000	23,000	0
Packing staff	23,000	24,150	−1,150
Cleaning equipment	1,150	1,035	115
Sterilising equipment	575	460	115
Production	1,438	1,495	−57
Depreciation:			
Cleaning equipment	460	460	0
Sterilising equipment	1,725	1,725	0
Total variable costs	51,348	52,325	−977
Contribution	63,652	68,425	4,773
Fixed costs:			
Maintenance salaries	2,000	1,950	50
Supervision salaries	3,000	2,800	200
Management and administration:			
Salaries	4,500	4,650	−150
Bagging equipment	250	275	−25
Maintenance	1,500	1,550	−50
Management and administration	2,300	2,890	−590
Buildings	850	720	130
Depreciation:			
Bagging equipment	2,500	2,500	0
Maintenance equipment	1,300	1,300	
Office equipment and furniture	950	950	0
Total fixed costs	19,150	19,585	−435
Surplus (deficit)	44,502	48,840	4,338

Exercise 3.2 A budgetary control problem

St Wilfred's provides a night shelter and day advice centre for homeless people. The budget has been prepared on providing 4,500 free meals every week. Although meals are free, each is recorded with a ticket, taken so the organisation can show how many people they are helping. The budget calculations and budgetary control report for week 17 is being reviewed by the warden and finance officer. Figure 3.15 shows the budget report.

The report shows that the organisation is better off by £17. Closer scrutiny of the individual variances shows that labour costs were considerably higher than expected but this has been outweighed by a lower than expected cost for provisions.

As the finance officer, you should re-work the budget and report your findings for only 4,000 meals being consumed in a week.

Answer to Exercise 3.2

It now becomes clear that St Wilfred's is actually £358 worse off than it should be at that level of activity. There are no favourable variances and the cost of provisions is actually £200 higher than it should have been for 4,000 meals. You must compare like with like to show the true performance.

Figure 3.15

Expenditure	Per meal	Fixed £	Variable £	Total £	Actual £	Variance £
Provisions	50p	0	2,250	2,250	2,200	50
Labour	20p	240	900	1,140	1,180	−40
Electricity	4p	0	180	180	175	5
Equipment rental		500	0	500	500	0
Maintenance	1p	0	45	45	43	2
Management		300	0	300	300	0
		1,040	3,375	4,415	4,398	17

Figure 3.16

Expenditure	Per meal	Fixed £	Variable £	Total £	Actual £	Variance £
Provisions	50p	0	2,000	2,000	2,200	−200
Labour	20p	240	800	1,040	1,180	−140
Electricity	4p	0	160	160	175	−15
Equipment rental		500	0	500	500	0
Maintenance	1p	0	40	40	43	−3
Management		300	0	300	300	0
		1,040	3,000	4,040	4,398	−358

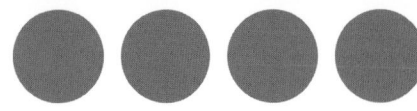

Resource management

4.1
Maximising resources

A voluntary organisation's resources, or assets, are best managed from the perspective of a going concern – that is, without assuming any limit on the organisation's existence. Although the finance officer will strive to get the best return on invested assets, he or she must be sure that the organisation has sufficient liquid assets available to finance current operations. The goal, therefore, is to maintain the optimum balance between available assets and invested, or growing, assets. A going concern operates in a financially solvent fashion. Solvency in this context means the ability to pay the organisation's debts in a timely manner or to meet its financial responsibilities.

This chapter will consider how a voluntary organisation's resources flow and interact, and examine tools for managing that all-important resource: cash. Issues to consider when accepting and protecting restricted and endowed funds are explored, as well as reserves policy and formulation and types of borrowing.

For a voluntary organisation to be financially solvent and operate as a going concern, its managers must, after the budgets are developed, focus on two more objectives.

1. Smoothly financing current operations by making the most efficient use of current, or liquid, funds.

2. Maximising available and obtainable resources to enhance return on the resources or capital.

The task of accomplishing these objectives can be called asset management or resource allocation.

Getting resources

To further examine the resource picture, the organisation's managers must consider the choices available for obtaining those resources. A voluntary organisation's funding comes from one or more of the following sources:

• general public
• government
• business
• internally generated.

There is a wealth of published information and advice about funding and income generation that cannot be summarised here. The intention of this section is to give a taster by exploring, first at a strategic level, ways of maximising the use of resources that might be overlooked and, then at an operational level, policies to maximise the working capital available. For further information see the Further reading and resources section.

4.2
Charity collaborations and mergers

The Charity Commission publication CC34 provides guidance to charity staff and trustees considering collaborative working and mergers.

It has also published toolkits for charity staff and trustees that outline the process of collaboration or merger from start to finish:

- *Choosing to Collaborate: Helping you succeed*
- *Making Mergers Work: Helping you succeed*

The Charities Commission defines collaboration and mergers as:

- **collaboration:** 'Joint working by two or more charities in order to fulfil their purposes while remaining as separate organisations'
- **merger:** 'two or more organisations coming together... Either a new charity is formed to continue the work...or one charity assumes control of the other.

Collaboration and merger activity may be a proactive or a reactive strategic response in three broad areas.

1. **External:** economic environment; funder pressure; changes in public funding; opportunities to scale up; stronger united voice.

2. **Internal:** better use of resources; risk sharing; opportunities for change following retirement of key personnel; other organisational challenges; sustainability; better staff opportunities

3. **Voluntary sector:** greater capacity to influence; better and more diverse services for beneficiaries; enhanced geographical reach; knowledge and information sharing.

The key factor behind these collaborative arrangements should be to ensure that the beneficiaries of the charity are provided with the most effective service now and in the future. It is more likely that a charity will collaborate with another charity. However, charities will sometimes work with public and private sector partners. In all cases, trustees should be able to justify the collaboration as furthering their charity's objects, and ensure that it is an appropriate use of charitable funds and any private benefit is incidental to the furtherance of the charity's purposes. Collaborative working covers a huge range of ways of working together.

The type and structure depends upon the collaboration, but there should be some formalisation of the arrangement. Sometimes a decision to work together can lead to a formal merger of two or more charities and there are different practical and legal issues to consider in these instances. Types of collaboration may include:

- outsourcing
- sharing resources
- sharing knowledge and campaigning
- co-locating
- enhancing diversity in service provision
- joint programmes/projects
- joint ventures
- merger.

It is good practice to have a written agreement even for the most loose and informal collaboration to avoid any misunderstanding. Informal collaboration will usually be more appropriate where the collaboration involves low-risk activities, such as sharing knowledge, experience or best-practice information

While trust plays a vital part in joint working relationships, it is not sufficient to rely on it alone. Written agreements form a common point of reference, may be subject to contract law and may also protect the charities from risks to their assets and reputation. Trustees should consider seeking specialist professional advice as necessary and when entering into a formal collaborative working arrangement.

The Charity Commission has set out 20 questions a charity should ask when considering working collaboratively and most are also appropriate when considering a merger.

Initiating collaboration

1. How can we better meet the needs of our charity and its beneficiaries by working with others?

2. How will potential partners be identified? Do we already have an existing relationship with them?

3. Is the proposed partner charity(s) compatible with us in terms of its charitable objects, culture, governance arrangements, organisational structure and funding base?

4. What are the reasons for collaborating?

5. What will or might our charity gain and lose from collaborating? Have we considered the wider impacts on our charity?

6. Do we plan to approach stakeholders for their views, particularly service users?

7. Does the proposed collaboration further our charitable purposes? Is it an appropriate use of charitable funds? Is any private benefit incidental?

8. Are there significant reputational or financial risks? If yes, are we carrying out a due diligence exercise?

Approaches to collaboration

9. Have we considered what type of agreement will be appropriate for our charity's needs?

10. Do we need to take professional advice about the type and content of the agreement?

11. Does the agreement state the collaboration objectives, benefits for each party, duration and funding arrangement?

12. Does the agreement address the identified risks including any conflict of interest?

13. Are there significant reputational or financial risks? If yes, are we carrying out a due diligence exercise?

Planning and communication

14. Have we established a project board, committee or group to oversee the project? Is there an individual managing the overall process or other arrangements in place?

15. Have we established a project plan with milestones?

16. Have we identified the risks associated with the collaboration and put measures in place to mitigate those risks?

17. Have we estimated the full cost of collaborating and how it will be resourced? This should include costs such as staff time, rebranding, professional fees, relocation and unanticipated costs.

18. Have we conducted a stakeholder analysis and established a communications plan that covers all relevant stakeholders and audiences? How will we manage any joint branding?

19. Have we identified clear measures to monitor the success of the collaboration? How will it be evaluated?

20. Have we developed an exit strategy for ending the collaborative arrangement should circumstances change?

●●●●○○○○○○

'The decision to merge should not be taken lightly.'

NCVO has a collaborative working unit to support charities wishing to work more closely together where merger is not appropriate. For more information visit: www.ncvo-vol.org.uk.

Mergers are common in the commercial sector but have, until recently, been rarer in the voluntary sector. Mergers are complex, and voluntary organisation mergers have more than just financial criteria to consider. While missions may seem the same, there can be complex delivery and cultural problems that can lead to mergers being called off as, for example, the homeless charities Shelter and Crisis and the public health charities RSH and RIPH. Moira Guthrie, author of *Mix, Match, Merge* (City University Business School, 2000) identifies the following six steps to merger.

1. Clarify the key issues, desired benefits and likely costs.

2. Initiate checks on the partner organisation.

3. Each organisation separately assesses the opportunity presented by combining.

4. Each organisation agrees what needs to be done before combining, and a merger steering group works out detailed recommendations on issues that need to be addressed prior to merger.

5. Legal merger takes effect.

6. Post merger integration starts.

David King was Director of Operations of Cancer Research UK, which to date has been the biggest charity merger (merging the Imperial Cancer Research Fund with the Cancer Research Campaign). He identified the following practical issues for a successful merger.

- Planning is the key element in any successful merger, which should include:

  – a proper cost benefit analysis
  – a proper merger plan before you start.

- The vital role of the merger committee:

  – membership should be limited in number
  – the committee should meet regularly.

- All charity's stakeholders (including charity workers and volunteers) should be kept informed.

- The merger should rationalise and justify the trustee board membership.

King also points out that charities can underestimate the management time needed for mergers and the costs involved, particularly:

- consultants' professional fees
- due diligence review
- legal advice and additional audit work
- staff costs and possible redundancy
- property considerations
- promotion of new branding.

The decision to merge should not be taken lightly. It is not the only possible solution – cooperation and joint ventures should also be considered, as they can be less painful and cheaper.

4.3
Cash flow planning

Often the most important resource for a voluntary organisation – apart from its staff and volunteers – is its cash. To maintain solvency, the organisation must have sufficient liquid assets. Certain non-cash assets, such as donations receivable, will eventually become cash and are a part of the liquidity management process.

Such assets are commonly called 'current assets' on a financial statement and are defined as those that will turn into cash within a maximum of 12 months, for example, monthly student tuition fees receivable, bookshop inventory etc.

To maintain solvency, the cash must flow smoothly and be readily available when it is time to pay creditors and salaries.

Accountants' cash flow statements

It is important to realise that the 'cash flow statement', which accompanies sets of company accounts, is not the same as a cash flow forecast. The cash flow forecast is a budget prepared to show anticipated future cash in and cash out, usually on a monthly basis. The cash flow statement is a highly specialised, even arcane, document, which reconciles the accruals method of accounting with the cash position, and is normally prepared by professional accountants with the final accounts. Essentially, it deals with the perennial question: 'Why does the income statement show a surplus, but the overdraft has gone up?' It starts with the surplus or deficit shown by the income statement and reconciles the adjustments made by conventional accrual-based accounting, showing how eventually the figures agree with the year's movement in the bank balance.

Cyclical and seasonal fluctuations

The other side of cash flow planning addresses timing cycles and cash flow management generally. For most voluntary organisations, cash inflows and outflows fluctuate throughout the year for many reasons other than accounting ones, such as the following examples.

- Churches typically receive generous donations during the Christmas season and much scantier ones during the summer vacation.
- Schools often require parents to pay a full year's tuition before the school year begins.
- Some membership organisations, such as unions, collect their members' dues once a year.
- Grants may be received quarterly, or contract money quarterly in arrears.

For the many voluntary organisations that have funding arriving at irregular intervals throughout the year, cash flow planning is essential. The fluctuations in cash probably cannot be entirely controlled.

However, it is important to appreciate that the organisation may be insolvent, at least technically, if there is insufficient cash to pay bills when due.

Cash management is about achieving maximum effectiveness of cash receipts and payments, thereby making sure that the money is working for the charity and returning a satisfactory yield, but is still available when needed.

●●●●○○○○○○○

'Especially close attention is needed if cash flows fluctuate widely, or if months of deficit funding are expected.'

Best practice guidelines suggest that voluntary organisations should do the following things.

- Collect money from debtors as quickly as possible, whilst exercising tact.
- Centralise payments and streamline procedures for different functional areas, such as accounts payable and payroll, by using (for example) BACS payment methods.
- Develop close partnerships with customers and suppliers to negotiate mutually beneficial payment policies.
- Consolidate banking relationships by choosing banks that can offer customised cash management services, for example, handling appeal monies.
- Develop accurate cash flow forecasting techniques and models that are linked to budgets and strategic plans.
- Conduct regular cash management reviews to check controls and ensure appropriate use of current technology, for example, telephone/internet banking.
- Ensure that investing, borrowing, payment and other financial transactions are properly authorised.

Much of the above may be self-evident, but it is surprising how often voluntary organisations ignore the fundamentals of good cash flow management.

Designing cash budgets

Once the annual operating and capital budgets are authorised, they can be converted into a cash budget to verify the availability of resources, in other words, to see if the organisation can finance the plan. The cash budget is prepared on a monthly basis to pinpoint possible cash shortfalls. The task is to summarise the projected sources and uses of cash for the coming year, according to the actual months of receipt and payment.

To do so, first estimate when collections of year-end receivables will occur. Next, calculate the normal time lag, if any, between the invoicing or billing for services or pledges (the point at which income is recognised in the accounts under the accrual system) and the actual arrival of the money in the bank.

Record the expected inflows of cash from revenue-producing activity on a monthly basis.

Correspondingly, chart the expected cash payments according to when the actual payment is to be made. The prediction should be based on past experience and an element of educated guesswork. Expected capital expenditures, sale of assets, borrowing, debt repayment and other financing transactions are then recorded by month.

In the light of any deficits revealed by the cash flow budget, consider whether there is a need to borrow or to redesign the entire budget. Monitoring the cash budget is a continuous process. Especially close attention is needed if cash flows fluctuate widely, or if months of deficit funding are expected. Although it is possible to perform this task monthly by hand, cash flow budgets produced on spreadsheets save countless calculations.

The model cash flow statements for a professional business association providing services to both corporate and individual members is shown in figures 4.1 and 4.2.

The first version of the cash flow produced a substantial deficit in the month of August.

The management of the professional business association has then reworked the cash flow to eliminate the deficit balance in August. This has been achieved by rescheduling the timing of membership fees, receipts from information services and publication sales. On the payments side, payments for marketing have been delayed till later in the year and payments for information services spread more evenly throughout the year. By this process, it has been possible to eliminate the deficit in August while at the same time maintaining both the total receipts and payments for the year as before, and presenting a healthier cash flow position.

Beyond cash flow imbalances

Ideally, a voluntary organisation always has cash in reserve for unforeseen circumstances. A new organisation in particular needs to budget for revenue surpluses in its early years until a sufficient level of cash is accumulated. To a young organisation struggling to meet its payroll, building a cash reserve may seem like a luxury it can ill afford.

Nevertheless, the financially prudent organisation plans from the very start to build working capital reserves equivalent to several months of operating expenses. Whenever cash flow budgets indicate excess cash reserves, plans for temporary investment are needed. As much money as possible should be kept in interest-bearing accounts in order to maximise yield. Once cash reserves exceed the current year's need, the opportunity for longer-term investment arises. This task of resource management requires complex decision making, ideally, by a finance committee with the assistance of professional investment managers. Investment policies must weigh the permissible level of risk to the organisation's resources against the expected return.

More money in the bank

The financially astute voluntary organisation will ensure that its cash balances work in its favour by keeping its money for as long as possible.

Whether the organisation is able to earn interest on the money, or to avoid paying interest on funds it must borrow or on bills it pays late, money in the bank is obviously desirable. A voluntary organisation can also charge interest on late payment and offer discounts for early payments.

The membership renewal system should remind members promptly that it is time to send in their fees or donations.

The submission of quarterly cost reports for grants payable by instalments should never be late. The fundraisers will know the deadlines for submitting grant requests to potential funders well ahead of time. Unfortunately, there are many voluntary organisations with cash flow problems that are slow in sending the renewal notices or grant reports that would provide the funds to pay staff.

On the outgoing side, bills should be paid when the terms for purchase require it and not before. A regular cycle can be established for bill payments, for example, the first and 15th day of the month. These set days should be made known to the staff and creditors, so that they are aware of when they will receive their money. Such a simple policy can save considerable effort and earn interest by keeping the money in the bank longer.

To borrow or not

When the cash flow budget indicates that a deficit in cash will occur during the year, a voluntary organisation faces a tough decision. Does the organisation attempt to borrow the funds, can it find new funding, or does it reduce projected payments?

The answer will, of course, depend on several factors. Is the deficit temporary? Will it reverse itself in a few months? For a new organisation, interim borrowing may not be an option. For a mature one that is, for example, expecting to refurbish old buildings, there may be alternatives. The decision must be based on the facts of the case.

Securing a loan requires good planning. When the need for short-term debt is recognised as a part of the budgeting process, solutions can be found. The budget itself probably shows that the situation will reverse itself with money expected to be received later in the year. For an organisation in this situation, preparing a business plan in order to make a formal application to a bank is a useful exercise. If a bank cannot be persuaded to make a loan, the voluntary organisation should go back to the drawing board and revise its budgets and/or find new funding sources.

A cash deficit created by proposed capital acquisitions may have a simpler solution, as the tangible nature of a capital asset makes it suitable as security for a loan. Therefore, it may be possible, even for a new organisation, to borrow money needed to equip the organisation.

Lenders expect to be able to get their security back if the organisation defaults on payments. However, lenders dislike foreclosing, particularly on a charity, because of the bad publicity they receive; therefore they will not rely solely on the security offered but will look to the longer-term cash flows.

Figure 4.1 Cash flow projection for the year: version 1

	January £	February £	March £	April £	May £
Receipts					
Corporate members' fees	10,000	40,000	20,000	30,000	10,000
Individual members' fees	3,000	10,000	8,000	12,000	6,000
Information services	14,000	14,000	12,000	12,000	12,000
Publication sales	20,000	20,000	20,000	20,000	20,000
Professional training	8,000	8,000	20,000	8,000	8,000
Annual meeting	10,000	5,000	5,000		
Royalty income	0	6,000	0	8,000	
Interest income	200	200	200	200	200
Total receipts	65,200	103,200	85,200	90,200	56,200
Payments					
Salaries and payroll taxes	30,000	30,000	30,000	30,000	30,000
Pension benefits	2,500	2,500	2,500	2,500	2,500
Professional fees	1,000	1,000	12,000	10,000	1,000
Supplies	2,200	2,200	2,200	2,200	2,200
Telephone	1,667	1,667	1,667	1,667	1,667
Postage and shipping	1,667	1,667	1,667	1,667	1,667
Building costs	2,000	2,000	12,000	2,000	2,000
Equipment repair and insurance	1,100	1,100	1,100	1,100	1,200
Printing and publications	12,000	8,000	12,000	9,000	12,000
Travel	1,000	1,000	6,000	1,000	3,000
Meetings and classes	500	500	18,000	500	2,500
Information services	4,000	15,000	15,000	9,000	5,000
Marketing	11,650	11,650			
Purchase of equipment	10,000				
Total payments	81,284	78,284	114,134	70,634	64,734
Excess (deficit) of cash	(16,084)	24,916	(28,934)	19,566	(8,534)
Cash at beginning of month	60,000	43,916	68,832	39,898	59,464
Cash at end of month	43,916	68,832	39,898	59,464	50,930

June £	July £	August £	September £	October £	November £	December £	Total £
5,000	3,000	2,000	30,000	40,000	30,000	50,000	270,000
2,000	1,000	800	1,200	5,000	11,000	30,000	90,000
10,000	10,000	8,000	16,000	14,000	14,000	14,000	150,000
10,000	10,000	10,000	25,000	25,000	25,000	25,000	230,000
2,000	2,000	2,000	22,000	8,000	16,000	6,000	110,000
							20,000
20,000			8,000				42,000
							1,000
49,000	26,000	22,800	102,200	92,000	96,000	125,000	913,000
30,000	30,000	30,000	30,000	30,000	30,000	30,000	360,000
2,500	2,500	2,500	2,500	2,500	2,500	2,500	30,000
1,000	1,000	1,000	1,000	1,000	1,000	1,000	32,000
2,200	2,200	2,200	2,200	2,200	2,200	2,200	26,400
1,666	1,667	1,666	1,667	1,666	1,667	1,666	20,000
1,666	1,667	1,666	1,667	1,666	1,667	1,666	20,000
2,000	2,000	2,000	2,000	3,000	4,000	3,000	38,000
1,200	1,200	1,200	1,200	1,200	1,200	1,200	14,000
9,000	11,000	9,000	20,000	9,000	10,000	16,000	137,000
3,000	1,000	1,000	3,000	3,000	3,000	4,000	30,000
500	0	1,000	2,000	2,000	1,500	3,000	32,000
4,000	4,000	4,000	5,000	5,000	5,000	5,000	80,000
						23,300	46,600
					7,400	10,000	27,400
58,732	58,234	57,232	72,234	62,232	71,134	104,532	893,400
(9,732)	(32,234)	(34,432)	29,966	29,768	24,866	20,468	19,600
50,930	41,198	8,964	(25,468)	4,498	34,266	59,132	60,000
41,198	8,964	(25,468)	4,498	34,266	59,132	79,600	79,600

Figure 4.2 Cash flow projection for the year: version 2

	January £	February £	March £	April £	May £
Receipts					
Corporate members' fees	10,000	40,000	20,000	30,000	10,000
Individual members' fees	3,000	10,000	8,000	12,000	6,000
Information services	14,000	14,000	12,000	12,000	12,000
Publication sales	20,000	20,000	20,000	20,000	20,000
Professional training	8,000	8,000	20,000	8,000	8,000
Annual meeting	10,000	5,000	5,000		
Royalty income	0	6,000	0	8,000	
Interest income	200	200	200	200	200
Total receipts	65,200	103,200	85,200	90,200	56,200
Payments					
Salaries and payroll taxes	30,000	30,000	30,000	30,000	30,000
Pension benefits	2,500	2,500	2,500	2,500	2,500
Professional fees	1,000	1,000	12,000	10,000	1,000
Supplies	2,200	2,200	2,200	2,200	2,200
Telephone	1,667	1,667	1,667	1,667	1,667
Postage and shipping	1,667	1,667	1,667	1,667	1,667
Building costs	2,000	2,000	12,000	2,000	2,000
Equipment repair and insurance	1,100	1,100	1,100	1,100	1,200
Printing and publications	12,000	8,000	12,000	9,000	12,000
Travel	1,000	1,000	6,000	1,000	3,000
Meetings and classes	500	500	18,000	500	2,500
Information services	4,000	8,000	8,000	8,000	8,000
Marketing		10,000			
Purchase of equipment	10,000				
Total payments	69,634	69,634	107,134	69,634	67,734
Excess (deficit) of cash	(4,434)	33,566	(21,934)	20,566	(11,534)
Cash at beginning of month	60,000	55,566	89,132	67,198	87,764
Cash at end of month	55,566	89,132	67,198	87,764	76,230

June £	July £	August £	September £	October £	November £	December £	Total £
5,000	3,000	17,000	15,000	40,000	30,000	50,000	270,000
2,000	1,000	800	1,200	5,000	11,000	30,000	90,000
10,000	10,000	12,000	12,000	14,000	14,000	14,000	150,000
10,000	10,000	20,000	15,000	25,000	25,000	25,000	230,000
2,000	2,000	2,000	22,000	8,000	16,000	6,000	110,000
							20,000
20,000			8,000				42,000
							1,000
49,000	26,000	51,800	73,200	92,000	96,000	125,000	913,000
30,000	30,000	30,000	30,000	30,000	30,000	30,000	360,000
2,500	2,500	2,500	2,500	2,500	2,500	2,500	30,000
1,000	1,000	1,000	1,000	1,000	1,000	1,000	32,000
2,200	2,200	2,200	2,200	2,200	2,200	2,200	26,400
1,666	1,667	1,666	1,667	1,666	1,667	1,666	20,000
1,666	1,667	1,666	1,667	1,666	1,667	1,666	20,000
2,000	2,000	2,000	2,000	3,000	4,000	3,000	38,000
1,200	1,200	1,200	1,200	1,200	1,200	1,200	14,000
9,000	11,000	9,000	20,000	9,000	10,000	16,000	137,000
3,000	1,000	1,000	3,000	3,000	3,000	4,000	30,000
500	0	1,000	2,000	2,000	1,500	3,000	32,000
8,000	8,000	8,000	5,000	5,000	5,000	5,000	80,000
				10,000	13,300	13,300	46,600
					7,400	10,000	27,400
62,732	62,234	61,232	72,234	72,232	84,434	94,532	893,400
(13,732)	(36,234)	(9,432)	966	19,768	11,566	30,468	19,600
76,230	62,498	26,264	16,832	17,798	37,566	49,132	60,000
62,498	26,264	16,832	17,798	37,566	49,132	79,600	79,600

4.4
Prudent investment planning

Once the voluntary organisation accumulates cash assets beyond its operating needs for the coming year, it can begin to develop permanent investment plans. In managing the organisation's investments, the trustees have a duty to maximise the value of the assets and therefore to obtain a good return. However, the trustees should not risk assets by investing in highly speculative ventures; they must balance risk against return.

The trustees must also balance the future needs of the voluntary organisation against current needs, so they should consider whether the maximisation of income for current consumption is in the best interest of future beneficiaries.

Trustees need to balance long-term capital growth against short-term income generation. Capital growth should be, at the very least, sufficient for assets to maintain their value compared to inflation.

Investment management is discussed in more detail in Chapter 7.

4.5
Restricted funding

The funding environment of the voluntary sector has changed dramatically in the recent past. Voluntary organisations are increasingly being funded to deliver specific outputs in return for grant funding or more formal arrangements under contracts.

As a result, there has been a rapid increase in funding for the delivery of specific charitable programmes and a consequent decline in funding of a more general nature.

Over the last decade a 'contract culture' has grown up. Instead of receiving grants, a growing number of charities are entering into legally binding agreements (contracts) with public bodies to provide services to the public on behalf of those bodies. A contract will specify the services to be provided by the charity and what the charity is to be paid for providing them. It will also include provisions, in greater or lesser detail, setting out the legal obligations that each of the parties accepts in order to fulfil the purposes of the contract.

On the positive side, a contract can establish a partnership between the charity and the public body and clarify their relationship by specifying in detail what is expected from each party. A contract can also offer a secure source of funding over the period it covers.

On the other hand, some charities feel that entering into contracts with public bodies would lead to the loss of their independence: their freedom to set their own policies and to decide, within the range of their charitable objects, what services to provide.

Charities must ensure that they take all their costs into account when pricing a service to be provided under contract on behalf of a public body. These costs will comprise direct costs, capital costs and indirect costs (or overheads). Chapter 5 provides details on how projects should be fully costed and priced to prevent the organisation indirectly funding public services from unrestricted funds.

Restricted funding can be defined as funds that have donor-imposed restrictions or where the voluntary organisation raises funds for a specific appeal. There are many reasons for the growth in restricted project funding, but the general scarcity of funding means that charitable trusts, and other funders, are under increasing pressure to obtain maximum value and impact from the projects they fund. As a result, they are reluctant to provide core funds, for which outputs and impacts are much more difficult to quantify.

Perhaps the most important financial requirement relating to such income is the responsibility to isolate the money. Under trust law, the voluntary organisation owes a fiduciary duty to contributors and grantors to use funds for the purposes for which they are given. Accordingly, before accepting restricted funds, an organisation must have in place a mechanism for tracking the receipt of such funding and the expenditure that can be set off against it. The restrictions imposed can vary in their tightness. A wildlife conservation charity raising funds by mailshot may work under the very broad restriction that the funds collected 'are to help preserve wildlife'. At the other end of the spectrum, the funding could be restricted to saving a particular type of tree in a certain part of Africa because its wood is used for musical instruments and the supply is dwindling.

By accepting restricted funding, the trustees of the voluntary organisation have accepted the responsibility of ensuring that the restrictions are met. It is important that in their fundraising – for example, public appeals – voluntary organisations do not unintentionally create restricted funds by the way in which they advertise.

There are, however, some circumstances when a restriction can be removed or made less stringent, for example, where the objective for which the funds were originally raised is no longer relevant, or where the project has been completed or is deemed impossible to complete. In the first case, it will be necessary to contact the original donors or, if that is no longer possible, to obtain the permission from the Charity Commission.

Exit strategies

Since the majority of funding arrangements are uncertain and are limited to a three-year period at most, the voluntary organisation must ensure, well before the funding comes to an end, that it has strategies to cover the next phase.

If the project is to be continued, this next phase will usually involve finding other sources of income, either from another funder or by income generation. If the original objectives have been met, the closure of the project may involve financial liabilities for staff redundancy.

4.6
Endowments

There are two types of endowment fund.

1. Permanent endowment funds are donations that have been given to the voluntary organisation to be held as capital, with no power to convert the funds to income. These may be cash or other assets.

2. Expendable endowment funds are donations that have been given to a voluntary organisation to be held as capital, but where the trustees do have a discretionary power to use the funds as income.

An endowment gift is usually invested to produce income to fund a specific project – such as scholarships – or unspecified operational costs. Although endowment funding is a highly desirable resource, the terms of the endowment must be thoroughly discussed with the donors before the gift is accepted.

When is an organisation ready to seek endowments? Potential endowment funders must perceive it as sufficiently permanent or stable to survive for a long time; this is why universities, hospitals and churches have traditionally attracted such funding.

The other important issue is the terms governing the voluntary organisation's use of the gift. If these are to meet the organisation's needs, the following points must be agreed upon.

- **Life span of endowment:** for how many years must the endowment remain restricted? Can the funds be used for another purpose in times of crisis? If so, what type of crisis? What happens to the endowment funds should the organisation cease to exist or the charitable objective be met?

- **Definition of income:** are realised gains treated as current income? Is the endowment principal – defined as its original sum – certain, or is it the original plus all appreciations less declines in underlying value?
- **Nature of investment:** do the endowment creators wish the assets originally given to be retained? Can they be sold? Must they be sold in a particular fashion, or offered for sale to particular persons first? If sold for cash, is there a restraint on the way in which the cash can be reinvested?

Endowment funding needs to be carefully considered, as it brings many onerous responsibilities.

4.7
Charity reserves

Charity reserves have been a controversial issue for some time. The media has criticised many large national charities for apparently accumulating large reserves while at the same time conducting additional fundraising appeals. Furthermore, many funders automatically look at the fund balances shown in annual accounts when deciding whether to approve applications for funding.

It is generally assumed that voluntary organisations should not hold on to charitable funds for long periods of time, since the organisation was granted those funds to provide services. This may well be the case, but reserves should also be considered from the point of view of resource management. From this perspective, the existence of reserves is a sign of good financial management. This is reinforced by the Charity Commission research study on charity reserves, which also found that the majority of charities were under reserved.

Any organisation requires a minimum level of reserves to fund working capital requirements, and/or contingencies identified at the planning stage as being necessary to safeguard the continuing activities of the organisation.

What are charity reserves?

The Charity Commission publication CC19 defines reserves as: 'income that becomes available to the charity and is to be expended at the trustees' discretion in furtherance of any of the charity's objectives (sometimes referred to as "general purpose" income), but which is not yet spent, committed or designated (ie is "free").' This excludes the following (as defined by CC19):

- permanent endowment
- expendable endowment
- restricted funds
- designated funds
- income funds that could only be realised by disposing of fixed assets held for charity use.

The Charity Commission now takes the view that voluntary organisations should 'explain and justify' the level of reserves they hold. In order to meet this requirement, even the smallest of organisations that aspire to financial security must have a reserves policy.

Reserves policy

The policy should cover:

- the reasons why the charity needs reserves
- the level (or range) of reserves the trustees believe the charity needs
- what steps the charity is going to take to establish or maintain the reserves at the agreed level (or range)
- arrangements for monitoring and reviewing the policy.

The essential steps in developing a reserves policy are as follows.

1. Review existing funds.

2. Analyse income streams.

3. Analyse expenditure and cash flows.

4. Analyse the need for reserves.

5. Calculate the reserves level.

6. Formulate reserves policy.

7. Presentation of reserves policy.

Assessment of reserve needs

The charity's reserves policy should be based on its:

- forecast for levels of income in future years, taking into account the reliability of each source of income and the prospects for opening up new sources
- forecast for expenditure in future years on the basis of planned activity
- analysis of any future needs, opportunities, contingencies or risks, the effects of which are not likely to be able to be met out of income if and when they arise
- assessment, on the best evidence available, of the likelihood of each of those needs arising and the potential consequences for the charity of not being able to meet them.

Checklist

Answer the following questions before checking the answers in the text.

1. Describe the various forms of collaborative working arrangements voluntary organisation can form.

2. How is cash flow planning different from a cash budget?

3. What are the aims of a cash flow statement?

4. With good financial planning what will a voluntary organisation understand?

5. Describe the various reserves a charity can hold.

Action points for your organisation

Review your organisation to see if it:

- has arrangements with other organisations
- prepares forecast cash flow statements
- has a financial plan, which shows how cash balances are created or what it does with excess cash balances
- has recently reviewed its investment manager
- has an accounting system that can track restricted funds
- has fundraisers who are aware of how to word appeals so that they do not create restricted funds
- has a policy on how to apportion overhead costs and obtain full cost recovery
- has a reserves policy.

Case studies and exercises

1 The Women's Centre

This case study looks at the challenges faced by a voluntary organisation that has just lost its funding. It examines how the organisation can exploit its resources to ensure survival; the issues discussed are not exclusively financial ones.

The case study examines the following areas:

- initial reaction
- longer-term response
- the impact on the organisation
- determining factors
- lessons
- conclusions.

The Women's Centre was set up in an outer London borough by a group formed in 1993. Working as a collective, the centre provided a women-only space; ran activities such as health groups, support groups and adult education; provided drop-in and advice sessions; and campaigned on women's issues locally. In a borough that rejected the idea of a women's centre, they turned to a London-wide funding body for capital and revenue funding. This enabled them to open the centre three weeks before the funding body was abolished, funding was lost and the staff made redundant.

Applications for replacement funding to the local borough and the London Boroughs Grant Scheme were unsuccessful. By this time the centre was running on an entirely voluntary basis – the running costs were covered by the residue of the grant funding – but was exploring other sources of funding.

Initial reactions to loss of funding

Inevitably, the reactions of paid staff and the management committee differed from unpaid collective members: the livelihood of paid staff was under threat, whereas unpaid members often had other things to move on to.

For many voluntary organisations – and the Women's Centre is no exception – funding is a form of recognition, which was lost when the funding was taken away.

However, the fact that the centre had opened its building just before the loss of funding, seems to have lightened some of the gloom.

Longer-term responses

Although the loss of funding was in some sense an ending for the Women's Centre, the opening of its new building marked an important beginning. This gave the women considerable energy to face the future.

Although uncertainty about future funding made it difficult to plan, the clear priority was to get the new building used. It was therefore decided to staff the centre with a rota of volunteers, holding self-financing Workers' Education Association classes and renting out space to other organisations (such as the local Legal Resource Centre) for specific sessions.

Before the funding was cut, the Women's Centre had invested in some useful equipment, including a camera, video equipment and a minibus; the minibus brought in some income from hire fees.

It was also agreed to encourage the women using the centre to make a contribution by standing order and pay subscriptions for newsletters.

The collective also changed its method of operation. In the absence of a central decision-making body, and because of the difficulty of finding new women to join the group, the responsibility for specific tasks (such as newsletter production, dealing with correspondence, minibus bookings or garden maintenance) was taken on by volunteers identified from the mailing list.

The impact on the organisation

Loss of funding can have wide-ranging effects: at a personal level on individuals, and at an operational level on the work programme. It was a particularly difficult time for paid staff, who went through long periods of uncertainty and then, in some cases, had to face redundancy and unemployment.

Staff and others felt that the withdrawal of funding showed that their work was not valued. As a result, the centre lost some of its most active members, and the increase in workload and responsibilities this brought for the remaining members led to exhaustion. This temporary crisis was overcome by changes in the organisation's structure and the allocation of work.

It was not long before conflict broke out between management and staff about who held the power in the organisation. This power struggle was not new. In the past it had been papered over or ignored, but now, as the threat to the organisation and fears about its future raised the stress level, it seemed more important.

At the operational level, the loss of funding caused the Women's Centre to restrict the work it did; as is usual in these situations, outreach and development were the main casualties.

In addition to the effects of losing its paid staff, the Women's Centre's ability to carry out its work was seriously hindered by the amount of time that had to be spent fundraising, filling in grant applications and lobbying potential funders.

One positive result was that members felt that the loss of paid staff had strengthened the collective. The disagreements between paid workers and members were now behind them; members had to have a genuine commitment to working for the Women's Centre if they wanted it to survive. They had learned to cut out unnecessary areas of work and concentrate on the essential. The women felt more motivated because they felt that they had something to contribute.

Determining factors

The Women's Centre was seen as the example of an ideology that was represented nowhere else in the area; this further increased its determination to survive.

Lessons

- **Having one main funder:** this made them feel insecure and severely limited their options. However, having more than one funder was considered to be too time consuming, and funders' interests might have conflicted, causing problems for the organisation.
- **Ways of working:** there had been a lack of urgency in what was done before funding was lost: applications should have been made sooner and there should have been more planning.
- **Dependence on paid workers:** this had caused problems when funding ran out. The paid staff who left had a lot of valuable information in their heads, but they had not been properly debriefed; as a result, unpaid members lost the benefit of that information.

Conclusions

The Women's Centre managed to survive, but it was not easy. It achieved this by exploiting a number of assets.

- A clear and adaptable organisational structure.
- A supportive governing body.
- Clear aims and priorities.
- A long existence.
- Strength of members' commitment.
- Contacts and support within the community.
- Economic resources (such as skills, premises, equipment).
- Political resources (the support of powerful people and organisations).
- An understanding of the situation in which it found itself.
- An awareness of the options open to it.

Many of these assets are a source of competitive advantage, arising either from the voluntary organisation's internal strengths or its position within the sector (see Chapter 2). One of the Women's Centre's strengths had been its ability to adapt to its new situation and develop a more appropriate structure. It managed to persuade a large number of women to work at the centre on a voluntary basis, perhaps because it is focused on its aims. It had strong links with the community and important material resources (including the building and the minibus); these tangible assets were used to generate income. On the other hand, as a radical women's organisation it lacked political resources, and its limited knowledge of the situation it found itself in meant that its choices were restricted.

(With acknowledgement to Centre for Voluntary Organisation, LSE.)

2 BCD

This case study examines the familiar situation where a voluntary organisation has obtained funding for a project from a variety of sources, but the total funds are still insufficient. The organisation turned to commercial lenders for the remainder, but without success. Finally, the organisation approached the Local Investment Fund (LIF), a charity in its own right.

LIF provides:

- loans to community enterprises that are unable to obtain all the funds they need from a bank
- help to community groups that are meeting local need by providing goods, services and jobs, and are aiming to be self-sufficient
- funding exclusively to non-profit organisations
- loans from £25,000 to £250,000 at near commercial rates.
- loans that are only part of the total amount needed.

The case study provides a valuable insight into how a project is assessed and some of the concerns of a lender when evaluating a project for funding.

Background

BCD was set up in 1979 to alleviate poverty and advance education by supporting workers' cooperatives and small starter businesses, and by providing training courses for cooperatives and minority ethnic and other disadvantaged groups. It is a company limited by guarantee and controlled by a voluntary management committee elected annually by the membership, which is composed of representatives of the cooperative movement, the local community and tenants. Any surplus goes to the improvement of BCD services and resources.

BCD's flagship project was the short-life rehabilitation of over 10,000 square feet of retail and office space in Acer Street, leased from the London Borough of Conifer.

BCD has a record of success in enabling women, minority ethnic groups and refugees to gain a foothold in the market, and in providing suitable facilities for small voluntary sector and community groups. Its training courses are targeted on existing cooperative businesses, refugees and local people in need of business skills.

Working closely with other local agencies, BCD is now taking advantage of the myriad opportunities brought about through City Challenge, the European Regional Development Fund (ERDF), the Single Regeneration Budget and the local authority.

BCD's plans for rehabilitating Acer Street involved the retention of existing businesses in the area, and the opening of many new units for community business start-ups and youth enterprise activity. These units will be let to community organisations on flexible terms that take account of the fact that many such groups do not have a track record.

These measures are enabling BCD to bring about an integrated range of new openings, and a coherent infrastructure in which Conifer's community-based business and voluntary sector is set to flourish.

The funding proposition

The overall costs of the Acer Street refurbishment and lease purchase are estimated at £837,500.

The project is being supported by ERDF (£212,500) and City Challenge Gap Funding (£350,000).

Commercial finance of £175,000 is required in the development phase, with a further £100,000 needed to purchase a 99-year lease from the London Borough of Conifer at the end of the refurbishment period. A total of £275,000 therefore remains to be financed.

In 1995 BCD approached the LIF for a £275,000 loan as part of the package of finance required for the refurbishment of Acer Street.

Figure 4.3 BCD Acer Street post-development rent budget

Year	1996 2009	1997 2010	1998	1999	2000	2001
% voids	70 20	35	20	20	20	20
Sub rent rise 20% every five years						20%
Head rent review and costs rise 20% every five years						20%
Rent receivable	79,738	79,738	79,738	79,738	79,738	91,698
Less: voids and areas	55,817	27,908	15,948	15,948	15,948	18,340
Total rental income	23,921	51,830	63,790	63,790	63,790	73,358
Head lease rent	6,000	0	0	0	0	0
Repair/maintenance	0	1,000	4,000	4,000	4,000	4,800
Advertising	1,000	1,000	1,000	1,000	1,000	1,200
Legal/technical	2,000	1,000	1,000	1,000	1,000	1,200
Staff costs	12,000	12,000	12,000	12,000	12,000	14,400
Establishment, administration and overheads	2,000	4,500	4,500	4,500	4,500	5,400
Rates liability	0	2,000	3,190	3,190	3,190	3,827
Total expenditure	23,000	21,500	25,690	25,690	25,690	30,827
Net income	921	30,330	38,100	38,100	38,100	42,531
£275,000 repayment	450	33,000	33,000	33,000	33,000	33,000
Balance carried forward	0	471	-2,199	2,902	8,002	13,102
Balance	471	-2,199	2,902	8,002	13,102	22,634

The project met the criteria set by LIF for such projects; what remained to be decided was the amount of finance LIF would provide. Among the documents submitted to LIF was a rent budget, reproduced as Figure 4.3.

Project viability

LIF was particularly concerned about the assumption underlying the level of voids and common areas (that is, the periods between lettings and the common areas which are not lettable), which was that they would reduce from 70 per cent to 35 per cent in the year 1997 and then to 20 per cent for the remainder of the projection.

2002	2003		2004	2005		2006	2007	2008
20	20	20	20		20	20	20	
				20%				
				20%				
91,698	91,698	91,698	91,698	105,453	105,453	105,453	105,453	105,453
18,340	18,340	18,340	18,340	21,091	21,091	21,091	21,091	21,091
73,358	73,358	73,358	73,358	84,362	84,362	84,362	84,362	84,362
0	0	0	0	0	0	0	0	0
4,800	4,800	4,800	4,800	5,760	5,760	5,760	5,760	5,760
1,200	1,200	1,200	1,200	1,440	1,440	1,440	1,440	1,440
1,200	1,200	1,200	1,200	1,440	1,440	1,440	1,440	1,440
14,400	14,400	14,400	14,400	17,280	17,280	17,280	17,280	17,280
5,400	5,400	5,400	5,400	6,480	6,480	6,480	6,480	6,480
3,827	3,827	3,827	3,827	4,593	4,593	4,593	4,593	4,593
30,827	30,827	30,827	30,827	36,993	36,993	36,993	36,993	36,993
42,531	42,531	42,531	42,531	47,369	47,369	47,369	47,369	47,369
33,000	33,000	33,000	33,000	33,000	33,000	33,000	33,000	33,000
22,634	32,165	41,697	51,228	60,759	75,129	89,498	103,868	118,237
32,165	41,697	51,228	60,759	75,129	89,498	103,868	118,237	132,606

●●●●○○○○○○

These targets would have to be met if the loan repayments were not to become a drain on the organisation.

Strengths

- BCD appears to be a well-managed and efficiently run organisation.
- The loan will be fully secured in the event of the failure of BCD.
- The proposal meets LIF criteria in supporting regeneration of impoverished communities through providing economic opportunity.
- The project has the support of local agencies including the Government Office (ERDF/SRB) and City Challenge.
- The project professionals are experienced, with good track records.

Weaknesses

- The project must build occupancy levels quickly to 80 per cent and then maintain them in order to meet projected loan payments.
- This project, taken together with other development projects in the pipeline may exceed staff capacity.

Conclusion

The LIF Council of Management agreed finance of £175,000 for BCD. Although this meant that £100,000 remains to be financed, the organisation was able to secure this from the proceeds of an option to sell on another property within their portfolio.

(With acknowledgement to LIF)

3 Problems with restricted donations

Following the tsunami in Southeast Asia on Boxing Day 2004, many major international aid agencies and NGOs launched appeals, including Médecins Sans Frontières (MSF). MSF launched an appeal for the work they were doing to provide emergency medical aid in the worst affected areas, particularly in the Indonesian region of Aceh.

Widespread media coverage of the impact of the tsunami provoked a massive response from the public, and resulted in MSF receiving many more millions of pounds than it actually needed to deliver emergency services in the region. But because donations had been given to support this specific appeal, the income generated couldn't be redirected to fund its work in other countries. MSF could have chosen to drip feed funds into the affected regions over a longer period instead, but this wouldn't have been in line with the spirit in which the gifts had been given, and would have also been inconsistent with MSF's core mission of delivering emergency aid.

Instead of attempting to return the money, or simply sit on it, a decision was made to contact all donors for permission to use their gift to fund MSF's emergency activities in other regions. This was a huge operation, which involved attempting to contact all donors across the 19 countries it fundraised in. This was a particularly tricky to do in the case of donations made in Germany, since most gifts were made by individuals filling in transfer orders at their local bank, and lacked any accompanying contact details. MSF resolved this issue by crediting each donor's account with a nominal sum and sending an attached message explaining their request. Of all donors contacted, only 1 per cent asked for their money to be refunded rather than redirected, effectively unlocking almost all of this restricted form of funding for MSF.

Overall, MSF was pleased that the response from its donors was so positive, but is actively working to prevent a similar situation happening again. This is to avoid the high administrative costs, as well as possible reputational risks, associated with having attracted more money than is actually needed to deliver the services donors expect to see. In this instance, the trust MSF had built up with its donors was crucial, and helped the organisation make the best use of donations that had initially been given with very specific restrictions. MSF has been very open about the problems it has had with this issue, and is the only NGO we are aware of that has openly published information about its mistakes.

Further information can be found on the Médecins Sans Frontières website: www.msf.org.uk. The Charity Commission guidance *CC40 Disaster Appeals: Attorney General's Guidelines* contains ideas about how to avoid generating a restricted donation surplus.

● ● ● ● ● ○ ○ ○ ○ ○ ○

Exercise 4.1

The new honorary treasurer of Age Concern Winton (ACW) is reviewing the management accounts prior to the management committee meeting with the finance officer.

ACW provides the following services.

- A drop-in day centre, offering various leisure and educational activities.
- A refreshments and lunchtime meal service.
- A new home-visit service, which starts on the first day of the new financial year.

In addition, ACW runs two shops selling donated and new 'fair goods'. It receives income from various financial services (insurance) as well as the occasional legacy.

ACW has a director who is supported by:

- an activities coordinator
- a home visits coordinator
- a catering manager and supervisor
- two shop managers
- a finance officer
- a secretary/administrator.

ACW is based in its own building, which was donated to it five years ago. A local estate agent has estimated the building would be worth £150,000 and derives an annual rent of £10,000 per annum.

The building is divided into 40 per cent of the space being for the education and leisure activities, 40 per cent for meals and 20 per cent for offices. The home visits coordinator is based within these offices and takes up 10 per cent of the space.

An annual budget is prepared each year by the finance officer, with assistance from the honorary treasurer, from the latest estimates based on last year's financial accounts. These also form the financial reports provided to the trustees and staff. The first draft budget and the finance officer notes are shown in figure 4.4.

Notes about the budget

1. A payrise of 3 per cent for the year has been budgeted. On-costs are 10.5 per cent, with 3 per cent contribution to a personal pension scheme paid gross.

2. Home visits – volunteer expenses are priced at £3 per visit. Local authority contract is based on a per-capita charge of £10 per visit, paid 10 days after receipt of a monthly visit report.

3. The legacy has been confirmed and is due to be paid during the fifth month of the year. It has restrictions, and is only to be spent on the education and activities projects.

4. Catering meals are priced at 75p per meal day-ticket, comprising morning coffee, lunch and afternoon tea. The price is based on what the catering manager, supported by the users' catering committee and the local health authority representatives, considers to be an appropriate price and service for elderly people needing a good meal. There are 160 places per day available.

5. Funds within the charity comprise:

   - restricted funds £10,000 for education projects
   - general fund £11,500
   - designated fund for kitchen equipment £5,000
   - cash at bank £21,000
   - 6 per cent capital bond in the local building society, maturing in two years' time, purchase value £10,000. The bond pays no income to avoid paying income tax.

6. Grants are paid mid-quarterly.

7. Shop sales are even throughout the year except in months 5 and 12 when they are respectively half and double normal takings, reflecting one shop being closed in month 5 and Christmas in month 12.

8. Purchases are paid monthly in arrears. Current food stocks are valued at £1,200 and shop stocks at £1,500. New kitchen equipment is to be installed in month 2 and is payable on delivery.

Figure 4.4 ACW budget for the year

1. Salaries (inclusive of on-costs)	£	£
Director	28,000	
Finance officer	20,000	
Co-ordinators	40,000	
Canteen manager	16,000	
Catering supervisor	12,000	
Shop managers	22,000	
Secretary	16,000	154,000
2. Overheads	£	£
Home visit volunteer exps	6,000	
Shop purchases	18,000	
Shops' rent and rates	7,000	
Leisure material	3,000	
Cleaning	4,000	
Audit	3,000	
Food purchases	14,000	
Telephone, post and stationery	7,000	
Shops' telephones	3,000	
Insurances	5,000	
Shop insurances	4,000	
Travel	6,000	
Sundries	8,000	
Shop cleaning	2,000	
Capital kitchen equipment	5,000	95,000
Total expenditure		249,000

Figure 4.4 ACW budget for the year (continued)

Income	£	£
Funds brought forward		16,500
Central grant from local authority		80,000
Activities services grant		30,000
Activities services charitable grant		10,000
Home visits contract		20,000
Shop sales		60,000
Catering sales		30,000
Home visits		6,000
Legacy		10,000
Financial services		6,000
		268,500
Surplus of income over expenditure		19,500

9. Payment for all operational services are made weekly, except for professional and overhead administrative expenses, which are paid quarterly in arrears. There is £5,000 outstanding overhead expenditure at the start of the year.

10. A charitable trust pays a grant of £10,000 for the activity services on the first day after the end of the half-year, in full.

1. Prepare a new budget based on cost centres.
   • The answer is show in figure 4.5.

2. Prepare a cash flow budget
   • The answer is show in figure 4.6.

3. Discuss findings from new management accounts and cash flow.

Discussion

The honorary treasurer is unhappy with the budget, pointing out that activities should be reflected in cost centres and how much each contributes to covering general overheads. Equally, there is no cash flow forecast – can the organisation pay its way for the following year? They are also not happy with the views of the catering manager and believe there should be changes in the planning process in the future for determining the budget for projects/cost centres.

Figure 4.5 New budget

Actual budget					
Cost centres/projects	Catering £	Shops £	Activities £	Home visits £	Total £
Sales	30,000	60,000			90,000
Purchases	−14,000	−18,000			−32,000
Gross profit					58,000
Project income			40,000	26,000	66,000
Total income	16,000	42,000	40,000	26,000	124,000
Direct expenditure					
Salaries	28,000	22,000	20,000	20,000	90,000
Rent .27 rates	4,000	7,000	4,000	200	15,200
Leisure activities			3,000		3,000
Cleaning	1,600		1,600	80	3,280
Shop cleaning		2,000			2,000
Shop telephone		3,000			3,000
Shop insurance		4,000			4,000
Volunteer expenses				6,000	6,000
	33,600	38,000	28,600	26,280	126,480
Contribution to general overheads	−17,600	4,000	11,400	−280	−2,480
Expenses					−64,000
General staff					−720
Cleaning					−3,000
Audit					−7,000
Telephone, post and stationery					−5,000
Insurances					−6,000
Travel					−8,000
Rent e7 rates					−1,800
Sub total					−95,520

Figure 4.5 New budget (continued)

Actual Budget	£
Operating profit (loss)	(–98,000)
Central grant	80,000
Legacy	10,000
Financial service	6,000
Rent in kind income	
	106,000
Surplus on budget	8,000

Answers

Interpretation of data
- During month 4 the charity is currently scheduled to go into deficit.
- The charity either needs to plan how it is to deal with the situation, ie by raising further funds or by entering into negotiations with the bank to arrange a short-term overdraft.
- The information received in respect of the shops does not give meaningful information as to whether one of the shops is making losses or not – further work would need to be done on the shops.

Taking into account the views of the catering manager
- At present, the people receiving catering meals are being charged 75p for the whole day. This includes morning coffee, lunch and afternoon tea. If coffee and tea were charged separately at 25p per day then this would result in an increased receipt per day of 50p, ie:

  – coffee 25p
  – lunch including tea or coffee 75p
  – tea 25p
  – making a total of £1.25.

- Current budget is based on:

  – 250 days (ie 52*5 – 10 days in respect of Christmas and other holidays)
  – total capacity, which is perhaps unlikely
  – more prudent budget is 160 maximum less 25 per cent void = 120
  – £1.25 x 250 days x 120 places = £37,500.

- Calculate a new cash flow. The answer is shown in figure 4.7.

The new cash flow forecast resolves deficit and now moves to surplus, and resolves cash flow problem – £625 extra per month; ie £37,500/12 = £3,125 per month less £2,500 originally received.

Cash position
In respect of the bond of £10,000, the charity pays no income tax. It may be worth considering redeeming the bond and keeping it as a bank deposit in order to smooth the charity through its cash flow problems.

Use of the cash budget
In month 4 ACW was scheduled to go into deficit, and although plans are implemented to avert this, there is only a surplus of £165. This surplus could easily disappear if something unforeseen happens. The budget could be used to take to the bank manager to discuss an approved overdraft. The bond could be used as security, and approved overdrafts carry lower rates of interest than unapproved ones.

Figure 4.6 Cash flow budget

	Cash flow 1 £						
Income	1	2	3	4	5	6	Total
Central grant from local authority		20,000			20,000		40,000
Activities service grant		7,500			7,500		15,000
Activities service fees							0
Home visits contracts		1,666	1,666	1,666	1,666	1,666	8,330
Shops sales	4,800	4,800	4,800	4,800	2,400	4,800	26,400
Catering sales	2,500	2,500	2,500	2,500	2,500	2,500	15,000
Home visits	500	500	500	500	500	500	3,000
Legacy					10,000		10,000
Financial services	500	500	500	500	500	500	3,000
	8,300	37,466	9,966	9,966	45,066	9,966	120,730
Expenditure							
Salaries	12,833	12,833	12,833	12,833	12,833	12,833	76,998
Shops' purchases	1,500	1,500	1,500	1,500	1,500	1,500	9,000
Food purchases	1,200	1,167	1,167	1,167	1,167	1,167	7,035
Operational services	3,000	3,000	3,000	3,000	3,000	3,000	18,000
Professional and administration expenses	5,000			5,500			10,500
Kitchen equipment		5,000					5,000
	23,533	23,500	18,500	24,000	18,500	18,500	126,533
Cash inflow/outflow	–15,233	13,966	–8,534	–14,034	26,566	–8,534	–5,803
Balance brought forward	21,500	6,267	20,233	11,699	–2,335	24,231	21,500
Balance carried forward	6,267	20,233	11,699	–2,335	24,231	15,697	15,697

Figure 4.7 New cash flow taking into account revised charges

	1	2	3	4	5	6	Total
Cash flow 2 £							
Income							
Central grant from local authority		20,000			20,000		40,000
Activities service grant		7,500			7,500		15,000
Activities service fees							0
Home visits contracts		1,666	1,666	1,666	1,666	1,666	8,330
Shops' sales	4,800	4,800	4,800	4,800	2,400	4,800	26,400
Catering sales	3,125	3,125	3,125	3,125	3,125	3,125	18,750
Home visits	500	500	500	500	500	500	3,000
Legacy					10,000		10,000
Financial services	500	500	500	500	500	500	3,000
	8,925	38,091	10,591	10,591	45,691	10,591	124,480
Expenditure							
Salaries	12,833	12,833	12,833	12,833	12,833	12,833	76,998
Shops' purchases	1,500	1,500	1,500	1,500	1,500	1,500	9,000
Food purchases	1,200	1,167	1,167	1,167	1,167	1,167	7,035
Operational services	3,000	3,000	3,000	3,000	3,000	3,000	18,000
Professional and administration expenses	5,000				5,500		10,500
Kitchen equipment		5,000					5,000
	23,533	23,500	18,500	24,000	18,500	18,500	126,533
Cash inflow/outflow	-14,608	14,591	-7,909	-13,409	27,191	-7,909	-2,053
Balance brought forward	21,500	6,892	21,483	13,574	165	27,356	19,447
Balance carried forward	6,892	21,483	13,574	165	27,356	19,447	17,394

Notes: Reworked for the additional fees re teas and coffees

Special financial procedures

●●●●●●○○○○○

5.1
Performance monitoring by financial indicators

This chapter expands on useful procedures for financial planning. Using ratio analysis to assess performance sheds a different light on resource flows and allows the evaluation of revenue sources.

Cost accounting allows the voluntary organisation to control and calculate the costs of services and programmes. Money spent is reclassified according to its functional category – for example, counselling, vaccinations and food services – in addition to generic type, such as supplies, salary and rentals.

Ratio analysis permits financial planners to identify trends, recognise strengths and pinpoint weaknesses that may not be readily apparent. As an addition to the financial statements and budgets, ratios provide an alternative view of a voluntary organisation's financial health.

Traditionally, private sector ratio analysis is carried out by looking at three major areas:

1. profitability

2. liquidity

3. efficiency.

It is important to remember that each of these areas needs to be compared with another set of figures in order to be meaningful. Most commonly, the comparison is with the organisation's previous year's results, but if there are similar organisations, it may be possible to do a comparative analysis.

1 Profitability

Within the voluntary sector, 'profitability' may not be an issue, but if parts of the funds are raised through shops, for example, then for all practical purposes the normal private sector tests would apply. In any case, a wide range of operational indicators can be useful. Comparing the various types of income received over a five-year period can reveal trends that could be meaningful. Knowing how much it costs to serve a user is necessary to evaluate whether the price of services is appropriate. For example, the managers can see which contracts or services have particularly high labour costs per £ of income generated.

2 Liquidity

This relates to the ability to pay debts as they fall due, and is normally assessed by two ratios – the 'current ratio' and the 'acid test'.

The current ratio divides the current assets by the current liabilities. (Bear in mind that the word 'current' in accounting terms means payable or receivable within 12 months.) So if the current assets on the balance sheet totalled £40,000 and the current liabilities £20,000, then the current ratio would be 40/20 or 2:1; in other words, there are twice as many current assets as current liabilities. Traditionally, this has been regarded as a 'safe' ratio, but this is due to the nature of commercial trading. A trader first has to sell his or her stock, which takes time, and then has to collect the money from the debtor, which also takes time. On the other hand, the goods the trader purchased have to be paid for, usually in 30 days. Thus, selling is a two-stage process, whereas buying is a one-stage transaction – hence the idea that it is prudent to have twice as many current assets as current liabilities.

This, however, does not really apply to many voluntary organisations, few of whom hold substantial stocks; so 2:1 is perhaps on the generous side. However, it would normally be regarded as risky to drop below a ratio of 1:1 (when current assets are equal to current liabilities).

The 'acid test' ratio looks at a shorter time-span; it takes into account assets and liabilities due within the next three months at most. Here 1:1 is safe; about 0.8:1 is acceptable.

Figure 5.1 uses ratio analysis to test a voluntary organisation's financial situation; the calculations used are based partly on the financial statements. The implications of the results are discussed.

The current ratio compares the organisation's resources available to pay the bills during the coming year. With its 1:4 ratio, the church obviously has a serious problem. With its 1.9:1 ratio, the Association of Non Profit Managers can comfortably pay the bills and have some cash left over. What if the ratio was above 2:1? Too high a ratio sacrifices income for safety.

The difference between current assets and current liabilities is also called working capital. When working capital is adequate, a voluntary organisation may be in a position to make long-term investments, or begin a new project. This formula can also be calculated and compared for restricted and unrestricted fund current ratios.

The acid test, or quick ratio test, shown in figure 5.2 is used to see if the organisation can pay its bills for this current month or quarter if calculated on a quarterly basis.

Ask the question, 'Is the acid test or quick ratio at least 1:1?' If the ratio is below 1:1, ask, 'Can the organisation survive the month if receipt of funding is delayed?' The church finance committee may wish it had asked these questions sooner as it faces what is now a serious financial situation: debts equalling two times its assets available to pay the debt.

The overall liquidity ratio, shown in figure 5.3, measures how long the organisation could survive if it received no new money. The Association of Non Profit Managers has enough money to pay its normal bills for a little more than three months, but the church has only 1.8 months of money. For an organisation with an endowment or other permanent funds, a similar calculation would be made to compare the permanently restricted, or unexpendable funds, with total annual expenses.

Figure 5.1: Current ratio: overall financial health

Current ratio	Holy Spirit Church ratio		Association of Non Profit Managers ratio	
Expendable current assets*	£20,000	1	£220,000	1.9
Current liabilities**	£80,000	4	£116,000	1

* expendable cash and assets convertible to cash
** amounts payable within the next 12 months

Figure 5.2: Acid test ratio

Current ratio	Holy Spirit Church ratio		Association of Non Profit Managers ratio	
Cash or assets due in 1 month	£20,000	1	£110,000	1.5
Total expenses in same period	£40,000	2	£74,000	1

Figure 5.3 Overall liquidity ratio

	Holy Spirit Church	Association of Non Profit Managers
Expendable fund balances	£20,000	£220,000
Total monthly expenses	£10,833	£67,000
Number of months	1.8	3.3

'Many grant making bodies shy away from funding groups with apparently high administration expenses.'

Holy Spirit Association of NPO Church Managers
Figure 5.4 analyses the percentage of the organisation's support received from members' subscriptions and general donations over a three-year period, to see if this funding has changed significantly. The example shows a 7 per cent decline over three years and could indicate a serious problem unless the organisation has deliberately focused on developing other sources.

Year 1, year 2 and year 3
How does the current year's income portion for a particular income source compare with last year's (see figure 5.5)? Is the change planned or expected? Should the reasons for the change be analysed? Should any action be taken in response to the change?

Prior year, current year and ££
Charity Accounting Standards require total expenditure to be classified under the headings prior year and current year in the annual accounts. It is therefore important to monitor how these figures change. They may serve as some measure of worth for a grant provider, which will be interested to see how much of its money is used directly in charitable service provision. Many grant-making bodies shy away from funding groups with apparently high administration expenses. The example in figure 5.6 shows that expenditure on charitable objectives has fallen by 10 per cent over four years, while administration costs have increased from 2.6 to 10 per cent.

Figure 5.4 Operational indicators: income source comparison version 1

	Year 1	Year 2	Year 3
Membership dues and donations	£105,000	£100,000	£95,000
Total income and support	£300,000	£320,000	£340,000
Ratio	35%	31.2%	27.9%

Figure 5.5 Income source comparison version 2

Association of Non Profit Managers	Prior year £	Current year £
Corporate members' fees	258,000	270,000
Individual members' fees	87,800	90,000
Information services	147,000	150,000
Publications sales	215,000	230,000
Professional training	108,000	110,000
Annual meeting	42,000	20,000
Interest income	3,000	1,000
Total income	**860,800**	**871,000**

Association of Non Profit Managers

Figure 5.7 shows how reliant the voluntary organisation is on particular sources of income to fund its total expenditure. In this example, the organisation is heavily dependent on donations and gifts (which may include income from fundraising events and appeals). This source of income has funded just over half the total expenditure in the first year and is still rising in the second year.

Other ratios are also useful.

• **Staff cost as a percentage of total expenditure.** This indicates the proportion of the total expenditure that is (at least in the short term) fixed. Further analysis can distinguish between the staff costs of those who deliver the organisation's mission and those in management and administration.

Figure 5.6 Cost ratios

	Year 1	Year 2	Year 3	Year 4
Pounds spent on:	£	£	£	£
Direct charitable objectives	280,000	300,000	320,000	304,000
Fundraising and publicity	100,000	110,000	120,000	140,000
Management and administration	10,000	20,000	40,000	50,000
	390,000	430,000	480,000	494,000
Percentage ratio:				
Direct charitable objectives	71.8	69.8	66.7	61.5
Fundraising and publicity	25.6	25.6	25.0	28.3
Management and admin	2.6	4.7	8.3	10.1

Figure 5.7 Cost ratios

	Prior year ratio		Current year ratio	
Donations and gifts	890,677	50%	1,647,832	56%
Legacies	668,278	38%	815,872	27%
Grants received	42,500	2%	134,432	4%
NLCB grants	-	-	159,634	5%
Investment income	48,378	3%	77,605	3%
Other income	116,187	7%	130,486	5%
Profit on disposal of investments	3,929	-	15,532	-
Total income	1,769,949		2,981,393	
Total expenditure	1,676,419		2,366,483	

- **Fundraising costs as a percentage of total expenditure.** This shows the relative efficiency of fundraising appeals and events, at least in financial terms. The recent decline in giving has had the effect of increasing this percentage, as fundraising has become more competitive.

3 Efficiency

This relates balance sheet items to income statement items. The two ratios most likely to be relevant to voluntary organisations are the debtor collection period (credit given) and the creditor payment period (credit taken). Ideally, for maximum efficiency, the debtor collection period should be shorter than the creditor payment period.

Service delivery indicators

Non-financial indicators can also be used when planning services, preparing funding applications or bidding for contracts. Here are some examples.

- Number of beneficiaries, overall and for each service.
- Number of staff per beneficiary by service and overall.
- Cost per beneficiary, overall and for each of the main areas of service.
- Number of information requests on a rolling average.
- Number of press mentions on a rolling average.
- Capital cost of buildings per beneficiary and per unit.

5.2
Cost accounting

This section will demonstrate why costs are important in voluntary organisations and look at some techniques for cost management.

The terms 'cost' and 'cost accounting' have many definitions; here are some useful ones.

- **Cost:** 'a measure of the resources used up in obtaining goods and services'; 'the amount of expenditure (actual or notional) incurred on, or attributable to, a specified thing or activity'; 'to ascertain the cost of a specified thing or activity'.
- **Cost accounting:** 'the establishment of budgets, standard costs and actual costs of operations, processes, activities or products; and the analysis of variances, profitability or social use of funds'.

Figure 5.8 includes some of the most fundamental issues that voluntary organisations have to cope with. It is therefore crucially important, in the interests of both internal cost measurement and management and external reporting, that proper techniques exist to address these issues.

Figure 5.8 Cost accounting

What to charge for services/products.	Establish a pricing structure that covers total costs incurred and so helps ensure future viability of service.
Determine total cost of a project for which funding is sought or contract with local authority.	Help ensure funding for project/grant of contract is based on both a 'competitive price' and covers its costs.
Negotiate charge for internal services/general overheads.	Ensure that core costs of the organisation are allocated to projects on a reasonable basis.
Should the voluntary organisation accept the contract price given by a local authority?	The organisation needs to be certain about what the project's total costs are if it is to accept a contract for services.
Cost control for budget reporting purposes.	Ensure that budget parameters set at planning stage are met, for example, a balanced budget.
Cost management for cost reduction purposes.	Ensure long-term financial viability.
Identify internal strengths and weaknesses.	Exploit cost advantages and/or commit to corrective action.
Maximise resources employed by organisation.	Conduct a strategic review of activities to consider possibility of outsourcing, formulating alliances etc.
Performance evaluation.	Maximise impact on society/outputs for minimum costs.
Implement fund accounting principles.	Trust law requires a separation of funds provided for specific purposes, and the Charity Accounting SORP requires classification of expenditure according to functional categories.

In this section, cost accounting techniques will be described under the following headings.

- **Cost ascertainment:** how much does a service, product or activity cost?
- **Planning:** what level of activity and resource allocation can the voluntary organisation undertake?
- **Resource maximisation:** are we making the best use of available resources?

Cost ascertainment

The question of what a product, service or activity costs is becoming more important for voluntary organisations. As conditions of funding become more stringent, and core funding becomes increasingly difficult to obtain, organisations need to be very clear about costs, not only at the organisational level, but also at project level.

The total cost of a service or product can be broadly divided into the following areas.

1. **Direct costs.** These are costs incurred as a direct result of carrying out a particular activity. Running educational courses, for example, would involve the cost of trainers, room hire, course materials and probably most of the education officer's time, but if the organisation did not run courses, it could probably avoid these costs.

2. **Indirect costs.** These are shared organisational costs that are difficult to apportion to a specific project or activity. Examples include the project manager's time, some administration costs and some premises costs. Organisations are finding it increasingly difficult to obtain funding for indirect costs if these have not been apportioned across other project costs.

In most cases, it is possible to identify accurately the direct costs of a project or service. What is less clear is how to identify indirect costs and the share of these costs that should be allocated to the end product or service.

The process of sharing out the indirect costs among a number of products or services is called 'overhead absorption' or 'overhead recovery'. It can be a very arbitrary process, for example, how much of the account clerk's salary cost should be allocated to each service or product?

It may be easiest to simply divide the total salary cost by the number of projects served, but this may not reflect the true cost of serving a project or product. Later in this chapter we will see how the absorption of overheads can be a more sophisticated operation.

Why absorb overheads?

Overhead absorption is often criticised for its arbitrary nature. So why should the finance officer undertake the task at all? Why not simply concentrate on the direct costs that can be accurately allocated to services and products?

There are two main reasons why it is important to calculate the fully absorbed costs of a product or service.

- **To understand the long-run costs of products and services.** This can be useful in many decisions, including pricing. Some voluntary organisations take the total cost and add a percentage to determine the selling price. This is known as 'cost plus' pricing, but it is not always appropriate in a competitive market: suppliers may have to set prices according to what the customers are prepared to pay, rather than what the supplier would like to charge!
- **Under fund accounting principles specified in the Charities SORP, most organisations are required to identify separate expenditure on restricted funding projects.** This means that they will need to allocate indirect or support costs to services or projects.

The Community Health Project

The following example has been adapted from *The Complete Guide to Business and Strategic Planning for Voluntary Organisations* by Alan Lawrie.

The Community Health Project is a voluntary health education project with five main activities.

1. **Education and training:** courses for teachers and health workers.

2. **Youth project:** specific health work with 12–22 year olds.

3. **Public enquiries:** enquiry point for a wide range of public calls.

4. **Resource centre:** producing and disseminating teaching and resource materials.

5. **Rural project:** community health work with isolated communities.

The current budget
The staff costs are analysed as follows.

The change to a project-based accounting system came about for the following reasons.

- The budget did not show the cost of individual projects.
- Funders and purchasers wanted to become more 'project' based.
- There was an urgent need to cost and price contracts properly.
- It was difficult to raise money for core costs.

The treasurer and manager have reviewed the projects and identified the following cost centres; all future income and expenditure will be allocated to one of them:

- education
- resource centre (including public enquiries)
- youth work
- rural work.

The first task will be to identify and allocate direct costs to each of the above cost centres.

The treasurer and manager have together identified the following basis of apportionment. First, for non-staff costs:

- **building costs:** fixed percentage (based on floor space occupied by each activity)
- **resource materials:** actual usage (based on review of last 12 months' invoices)
- **minibus:** approximate costs of past usage
- **telephone and administration:** a quarter of all telephone costs (£1,500) and one tenth of admin costs (£2,000) were estimated to be the direct costs of the resource centre's public information work.

The results of this review are shown in figure 5.9.

The treasurer and manager have now looked at staff costs and have agreed the allocation of time spent by each staff member to the four cost centres (see figure 5.10).

It was also agreed that 40 per cent of the manager's time and 70 per cent of the administration clerk's time could not be allocated to a particular project and would therefore form part of indirect costs.

At this stage, only the direct costs have been allocated to cost centres, and the position so far is summarised in figure 5.11.

The remaining £39,800 (£23,000 non-staff costs and £16,800 staff costs) represents the indirect costs of the community health project, and is now allocated to the four cost centres according to the floor space occupied shown in figure 5.12.

Having reorganised the information from the income and expenditure budget into a cost centre framework, the treasurer and manager now have a much better idea of the true cost of running the current services. For example, although the trust grant for rural work is £15,000, the total cost of carrying out this work is £16,520, which suggests that it is losing the Community Health Project £1,520 in the current year. The project is now in a much better position to decide whether to continue this work (and subsidise the loss from other income) or to approach the trust for extra funding.

Figure 5.9 Direct non-staff costs per cost centre

	Admin	Materials	Minibus	Telephones	Building costs	Total allocation
Budget	20,000	3,000	5,000	6,000	20,000	54,000
Cost centre						
Education		1,500			6,000	7,500
Resource centre	2,000	800		1,500	8,000	12,300
Youth work		500	1,000		4,000	5,500
Rural work		200	3,500		2,000	5,700
Not allocated	18,000	0	500	4,500	0	23,000

Figure 5.10 Allocation of staff costs to cost centres

Cost centre	Manager	Ed. officer	Info. officer	Res. officer	Clerk	Total allocation
Education	30% ie 8,400	70% ie 16,100	20% ie 4,000		10% ie 800	29,700
Resource centre	20% ie 5,600	15% ie 3,450	60% ie 13,200	75% ie 14,250	20% ie 1,600	38,100
Youth work	5% ie 1,400		20% ie 4,400	25% ie 4,750		10,550
Rural work	5% ie 1,400	15% ie 3,450				4,850
Not allocated indirect cost	40% ie 11,200				70% ie 5,600	16,800
Total	28,000	23,000	22,000	19,000	8,000	100,000

Figure 5.11

Cost centre	Direct non staff costs	Direct staff costs	Total direct costs
Education	7,500	29,700	37,200
Resource centre	12,300	38,100	50,400
Youth work	5,500	10,550	16,050
Rural work	5,700	4,850	10,550
Total	31,000	83,200	114,200
The amounts still to be allocated (indirect costs):			
Non staff costs	£23,000	Staff costs £16,800 (see figure 5.10)	Total £39,800 (see figure 5.9)

Developing a cost-centred approach can raise a number of other issues.

- Many voluntary organisations are very poor at costing their work; the cost involved in operating and providing good management is often underestimated, not properly identified or even ignored. This attempt to do 'quality' work on the cheap can easily lead to a long-term crisis.
- Many organisations that have adopted a cost-centred approach have found that the true cost of providing a service or activity is greater than the funding being offered. This information enables the organisation's managers to be more assertive when negotiating with funders, or taking the strategic decision to subsidise and/or fundraise to cover the loss.
- Problems may arise when people in one cost centre believe they are more 'profitable' than another centre. Cost accounting and absorption costing are management tools that allow decisions to be made about priorities; they are not concerned with assigning value to an activity. Normally, value will be measured in non-financial terms.

The absorption costing model discussed above is not without its weaknesses, however. Among these is the arbitrary way in which indirect overheads are allocated to services or products. With the Community Health Project this was done on a simple percentage basis, and as a result the rural work was seen to be losing the organisation money.

However, the results may well have been different had the percentages used to allocated overheads been different, and a different decision about continuing with the rural work might have been made.

A further weakness of absorption costing is that it fails to explain to management why costs are incurred. This is because, under most accounting systems, costs are accumulated in the general ledger using a natural classification system of salaries, printing, rents, insurances etc and then reported by the department or project manager responsible. As a result, the project manager lacks any real understanding of the activities or processes that are ultimately responsible for these costs. This means that, whenever cost cutting is needed, management will tend to reduce headcount first, since this is by far the largest cost item. But the work remains untouched, to be shared out between fewer people.

Figure 5.12 Allocation of indirect costs

Cost centre	% share	Indirect £	Direct costs £	Total cost centre £
Education	30	11,940	37,200	49,140
Resource centre	35	13,930	50,400	64,330
Youth work	20	7,960	16,050	24,010
Rural work	15	5,970	10,550	16,520
Total		39,800	114,200	154,000

●●●●●○○○○○

5.3
Ensuring full cost recovery

In order for charities to be sustainable in the long term, funding must cover both project costs and a fair proportion of overheads. This is what is known as full cost recovery.

Charities also need to monitor their overhead costs to consider efficiency over time, and ensure the maximum use of their resources.

In 2002 the government acknowledged the need for full cost recovery in the HM Treasury report, *Role of the Voluntary and Community Sector in Service Delivery: A cross cutting review* (2002). However, few voluntary sector organisations report experiencing a consistent commitment to this principle in practice.

In their 2007 report *Know Your Cost Base, Know Your Charity,* Charities Finance Group (CFG) found that many organisations aren't being fully funded for the cost of the public services they deliver.

Full cost recovery makes common sense. How can you make rational decisions and future plans without knowing the true cost of a project or service, and how this impacts overheads and free reserves?

This section introduces the concept of ensuring full cost recovery for funding and describes some of the issues surrounding this.

Core costs

In order for us to establish what is meant by full cost recovery we must first identify the charity's overheads that cannot be directly attributable to a service or project. These are the core costs of the charity. Core costs also relate to the strategic and governance costs for the organisation.

Core costs are wide ranging and can include the following.

Central functions
- Chief executive
- Human resources and personnel costs
- Information technology and computer costs
- Finance management
- Other administration and secretarial functions
- Fundraising (for general purposes)

Operational costs
- Equipment – IT, printing etc.
- Premises – rent, mortgage
- Associated premises costs – heat, light
- Telephone, fax, postage
- Travel and subsistence
- Staff recruitment, training and supervision
- Strategic direction

Governance
- Support of the trustee structure

Other
- Training
- Research and development costs
- Monitoring and evaluation
- Quality assurance
- Accountancy and audit

These costs sit throughout the organisation, and removing any of them would impair the service and work that the charity provides.

The list of core costs cannot be definitive and is typically different for different charities – this highlights the different types of charities in the sector, and the multitude of ways the sector delivers against charitable aims.

Current practice in funding core costs and overheads

Having established what overhead and core costs are, it is important to check whether they are being adequately funded when a funding submission is made.

Unfortunately, in practice, general overheads and core costs are not being funded adequately. The fault for this lies with both the funders and funded organisations.

Funded organisations

Funded organisations often do not know what the full costs of activities are and typically lack the skill base to complete calculations. Funders may be legitimately concerned at the level of overheads and this may be reinforced by the lack of sophistication and transparency around overhead costs in the charity being funded.

Funded organisations may forget to apportion a true level of overhead to a project and therefore will subsidise this from 'general' reserves – this is ultimately not sustainable in the long term.

Calculations have sometimes been completed many years ago and overhead rates that do not apply to the current infrastructure are often used.

Funders

Funders typically have a pot of money to allocate to projects. They may be reluctant to fund overheads, preferring to provide money for project costs, believing that they can fund a wider number of projects, but neglecting the sustainability of these projects.

Alternatively, many funders may add an arbitrary fixed percentage as an overhead charge – such as 10 per cent or 15 per cent – but this figure is often inaccurate and may be well below the actual overhead costs.

Common experience

Experience has shown that being open and transparent in quantifying overheads and core costs allows the funder to develop a real understanding of the true project costs and so develop a more meaningful working relationship with the charity. This has often led to an increase in funding to an appropriate level of overhead costs.

However, if after having completed calculations in a transparent way funders are still not prepared to fund overheads, you may then ask them which part of the costs they wish to ignore. It may focus the funder's attention if a funded organisation says, 'Of course we can run the project, but with reduced funding we will be unable to make any telephone calls, use any computers or ensure the quality control mechanisms around the project.'

Overhead and core cost levels

Having established that a fair proportion of overheads and core costs are, in general, not being funded, is there a standard reasonable rate that could be applied?

All charities are different

All charities have different rates, by the nature of their maturity and what they do.

For example, a mature not-for-profit organisation may have a considerably lower level of overheads than a small, growing, regional charity, due to better economies of scale.

Similarly, a charity based around ophthalmic research may have a greater need for use of Braille texts and 'voice-over' software, which may increase overhead costs compared with similar organisations.

Each charity is individual and will need to engage in active communication with funders to develop an appropriate level of overheads and core cost funding.

There is a perceived wisdom that a low level of overhead costs and core costs is good. If these are too low, the charity may cut back on vital infrastructure or governance costs at the detriment of quality of service delivery. A key example is that charities can spend too much time chasing funding, and not enough time focusing on future strategy and their core objectives.

Growth and development

In *Who Pays for Core Costs?*, Julia Unwin examines the issue of funding overheads in detail. She proposes three distinct funding models.

1. **Full project funding,** in which a reasonable level of overheads and core costs are given to a mature charity in steady state.

2. **Development funding,** through which infrastructure costs are met for a time in order to give a charity time to grow and develop.

3. **Strategic funding,** where a funder recognises the need for a charity to exist as it meets a common strategic need, and funds this over an agreed period.

If a charity is in a growth or development phase, it may be wholly appropriate to provide core cost funding at a higher level than normally expected to help establish the work of the charity and its strategic aims.

Many trust funds and government funders are willing to fund core costs separately from project costs and as a distinct class of funding.

Cost allocation

In order to complete costing calculations, and establish an appropriate level of overheads for a project, we must first understand how to divide a cost used by one or more projects. This is cost allocation.

Costs could be divided amongst different projects in a variety of ways.

1. Headcount

2. Time

3. Floor space

4. Expenditure

The following example will help to make this statement clear.

Example 1: The Hospice

A hospice runs a drop-in counselling centre and safe shelter for young adults sleeping rough. These services occupy different parts of one building. Both services use electricity from the same bill and a social worker is on hand to provide counselling across both projects.

In order to appropriately cost the counselling centre project, we would need to allocate a fair proportion of electricity usage and the social worker's costs.

Electricity may be best allocated by floor area. We therefore include a cost allocation for electricity equal to the floor area the counselling centre occupies.

The social worker's cost may be best allocated by the time spent on each project. We therefore include a cost allocation for the social worker equal to the time spent on the counselling centre.

Imagine that the total project costs for the counselling centre are £50,000 per annum, the electricity bill is an additional £1,000 and the social workers' wage plus NIC and pension contributions, is £25,000.

If the counselling centre takes 25 per cent of the floor area at the hospice and the social worker spends 50 per cent of her time at the centre, then the appropriate full costs for the service (including an appropriate level of overheads) is:

Costs		£
Project costs		50,000
Overhead cost allocation		
Electricity bill	25% x /1,000	250
Social worker	50% x /25,000	12,500
Project cost		62,750

Essentially it does not matter how you choose to allocate costs, as long as your cost 'drivers', such as floor space, time or headcount, are logical and clear. Much of the discussion with funders may centre on the appropriate basis for cost allocation. In fact, some funders will only allow certain bases and not others.

An appropriate model

Having established the basis for cost allocation, how would we calculate an overall project cost for a single project in a not-for-profit organisation?

To complete our full cost model, we need to understand how all costs in an organisation hang together and what the applicable 'layers' of costs are.

Cost structure

Costs within an organisation can be looked at on four levels.

1. Direct costs

2. Direct support costs

3. Indirect support costs

4. Governance and strategic development costs

Direct costs are the costs of those activities that constitute the project itself, such as the costs of hospice staff in the hospice example.

Direct support costs underpin the direct project work and can be directly identifiable as relating to the project, such as the costs of the social worker in the previous example, who splits her time over several projects but who works directly on the counselling centre.

Indirect support costs are central costs, such as the chief executive, computers, payroll, personnel, finance and accounting. These are all activities that support the service delivery, but cannot be directly identifiable as costs against the project. An example here is that the hospice will use computers, as will the chief executive, but how would we fairly allocate these costs?

Governance and strategic development costs are the costs associated with regulatory costs, engaging with trustees and identifying the strategic direction for the charity.

Typically, small charities would not have four levels of costs but would have three, combining direct and indirect support costs into one category as follows.

1. Direct costs

2. Support costs

3. Governance and strategic development costs

This latter model is proposed in the ACEVO template.

Budgets and forecasts

When making funding applications, a charity is typically planning for the future. However, it will almost certainly base its cost estimates on historical financial information and from previous experience.

It may be more appropriate to use budget or forecast information in funding applications, especially where there will be a future change in funding requirements. One example is where a charity may be forced to rent more expensive premises in the next year. It is wholly applicable to pass this cost increase on to the funder, as this becomes the true cost of the project.

The key is to be able to justify your calculations and be transparent in your methodology. Completing proper, well-constructed and well-thought-out funding applications will promote better communication between funder and the funded and hopefully establish a more appropriate and sustainable level of overhead or core cost funding.

Count all costs

Many charities omit or 'cherry pick' costs to ensure that actual funding submissions equal known funding policies. An example is where a local authority is known to only fund up to 10 per cent overheads and, therefore, the charity's submission provides overhead costs to hit this figure. The shortfall will have to be found from somewhere else, typically needing further fundraising cost or reducing free reserves.

It is vitally important that true costs are identified, and the real cost of the project presented in a transparent way. Core costs and overheads exist and should not be hidden.

If the core costs and overheads are not being adequately funded you should bring this to the funders' attention. In an extreme case, this may lead to a charity saying 'no' to the new funding as this would adversely affect reserves, or be too costly in terms of new fundraising.

Using a full cost recovery model

Having established a model, how would we use this to complete full cost recovery and ensure we receive a fair proportion of overheads for a project?

Example 2: The Hospice

The Hospice in Example 1 has a board of trustees, director, bookkeeper and general office administrator. They all occupy the same building as the counselling centre and safe shelter.

The direct costs of the counselling centre have been previously identified as £62,750, including the electricity cost for the centre and the cost for the social worker's time.

The costs for the additional items are:

Cost	£
Board of trustees	2,000
Director (Including NIC and pensions)	40,000
Book-keeper (part-time)	12,000
Office administrator (including NIC)	15,000
All other core costs	75,000

Overall, the counselling centre occupies 15 per cent of the director's time, and governance and strategic development costs for the centre are those represented by 30 per cent of the board of trustees and approximately 10 per cent of 'all other core costs'.

The safe shelter project costs (including electricity and social worker costs) are £188,250.

In order to identify the full costs for the project we will have to allocate a proportion of all overhead and core costs to the counselling centre; how would we do this?

Using our model we have the following structure.

1. Direct costs

2. Support costs

3. Governance and strategic development costs

Direct costs are as previously established in Example 1, £62,750.

Governance and strategic development costs are represented by 30 per cent of the costs for the board of trustees and approximately 10 per cent of 'all other core costs'. This figure is:

(30% x £2,000) + (10% x £75,000) = £8,100

Support costs are 15 per cent of the director's time plus a proportion of all other costs.

We lack a basis to calculate the appropriate cost allocation for the bookkeeper, office administrator and 'all other core costs'. Our best approximation will be project expenditure and it is this that we use as a default.

In this case the counselling centre takes 25 per cent of all costs, ie centre cost as a proportion of all project costs = £62,750 / (£188,250 + £62,750)

Calculating the support costs then becomes:

Cost	£
Board of trustees (already included under governance)	
Director's time is 15% x 40,000	6,000
Bookkeeper 25% x 12,000	3,000
Office administrator 25% x 15,000	3,750
All other central costs 25% x 75,000	18,750
Total support costs	**31,500**

Therefore the total overall project cost for the counselling centre is:

Cost	£
Direct costs	62,750
Support costs	31,500
Governance and strategic development costs	8,100
Total costs	**102,350**

●●●●●○○○○○

'The cost allocation method used must be consistent with prior years and transparent.'

Summary

In order to ensure full cost recovery you need to complete a two-step process.

1. **Account for all costs:** ensure that no costs are omitted, and that you have appropriate information, such as budgets and forecasts, with which to cost the project.

2. **Allocate costs:** ensure that costs are allocated within a framework to appropriately cost direct project costs, support costs and governance and development costs, including a fair proportion of overheads.

The cost allocation method used must be consistent with prior years and transparent, such that open communication between funder and the funded can be completed to ensure an appropriate level of overheads are funded.

Many organisations that have adopted a full cost approach have found that the true cost of providing a service or activity is greater than the funding being offered. This information enables the organisation's managers to be more assertive when negotiating with funders or taking the strategic decision to subsidise and/or fundraise to cover the loss.

Competitive bidding

Many charities are bidding for work in a competitive environment – what is the point in cost allocation and transparency in project funding here? In this case, ensuring full cost recovery is just as important. By understanding costs, a charity will be able to calculate an appropriate cost for the bid, including a fair proportion of overheads.

A decision can then be taken to bid to receive a surplus or deficit throughout the life of the contract.

If the funding available is less than your cost of delivery, you have to make a choice: either don't do the work or fund the difference from another source.

Full cost recovery will help establish appropriate costs for the service and decide a strategic approach to bidding.

By appropriately allocating costs and ensuring full cost recovery for projects a charity is better able to define:

- costs of charitable activities (including support costs)
- governance costs
- costs of generating funds (including support costs).

This will provide a consistent model by which costs can be allocated within the statutory accounts.

The following example highlights the impact of failing to recover overheads when making a bid for a new contract.

Example 3: Swimmers of the World

The charity Swimmers of the World provides grants to help swimming pools around the world. They have a core grant from Sport UK of £400,000 but this is under review. They have expanded rapidly as various countries have used their services to build pools and have now been asked to set up lifesaving training course by the FCO (Foreign and Commonwealth Office). They estimate that the direct costs for the training costs will be roughly £1m per annum.

The overheads of the charity (including strategic development and governance costs) are budgeted as £0.5m. This is 42 per cent of all costs (not unusual for a small, rapidly growing, multi-country organisation).

A contract with the Department for International Development (DFID) provides £1m (71 per cent) of all income; a 30 per cent (£0.3m) overhead charge is taken by Swimmers of the World from this contract for overheads. There is no further income or expenditure other than that shown below. Reserves are £2m of which £1.95m are fixed assets as physical swimming pools round the world.

The charity has been asked to bid for a new contract for lifesaving training courses from the FCO and the chief executive says that Swimmers of the World should put in no more than 10 per cent overheads, as that is all they will pay. As finance director you feel unhappy with this.

The budgeted breakdown of income and costs appears as follows for the next year:

Income	£m	£m
Core grant from Sport UK (unrestricted)	0.40	
Grant – DFID	1.00	
		1.40

Expenditure	
Accountable grant – direct costs of DFID grant	(0.70)
Support costs	(0.40)
Strategic development and governance costs	(0.10)
	(1.20)

Income less than expenditure	**0.20**
Reserves as:	**2.00**
Fixed assets	1.95
General assets	0.05

Questions

1. What would you think about before bidding for the new FCO lifesaving contract (financial and operational)?

Operational issues are key here. Does the charity have the skills to undertake training contracts when it is used to building swimming pools? So many organisations fail to stick to what they are good at, and compromise against their core business, seeing the money not the delivery.

Does the organisation have the administration systems and resources to take on this contract? Is the cash flow sufficient? Many contracts are paid in arrears, and this could eat into reserves. Why do we maintain such large overhead costs – could these be reduced or made more efficient?

On the financial front – how do we equitably allocate costs to each project, specifically as we now have a large step change in funding?

2. If all grant income was restricted and any underspend due to be paid back to donors – how would this change the financial position of the charity before taking on the new contract?

The income and expenditure then becomes:

Income	Restricted £m	Unrestricted £m
Grant – DFID	0.70	0.30
	0.70	0.30

Expenditure		
Accountable grants – direct costs of DIFD grant	(0.70)	
Support costs	-	(0.40)
Strategic development and governance costs	-	(0.10)
		(0.50)

Income less that expenditure	0.00	(0.20)
Reserves B/F		(0.70)
Reserves C/F	-	(0.15)

The loss of core grant from Sport UK means that the organisation can no longer cover its overheads and reserves and is now trading insolvently.

The question then becomes, can the new grant cover the loss in overhead recovery?

3. Would you take the new contract, and if so how much overhead would you apportion to it?

If the core grant comes to an end because of quality issues, there are real problems – basically the organisation may not survive. Concentrating on quality must come before undertaking new work. When is the core grant due to end?

If you don't take the new contract, you may have to cut costs. Equally you may have no charity if the DFID contract finishes, as all your eggs are in one basket. This depends on the DFID contract and the allowable level of overhead recovery.

If you do take the new FCO contract you must be careful to cover overheads, absorb any new resource requirements and find an overhead rate acceptable to your donors.

One thing that is certain is that it is going to take a recovery rate greater than 10 per cent. If you say no to the chief executive and no to the grant, this could seriously impact on the organisation's volume of work.

Increasingly, organisations are just going for 10 per cent recovery. In this scenario they would end up in financial difficulties when either the core grant goes from Sport UK or the DFID contract finishes.

Activity based costing (ABC) and charities

To address these weaknesses, a system of activity based costing (ABC) has been developed and has gained some acceptance within the voluntary sector. At its simplest, ABC attributes the costs incurred by an organisation to processes or activities. It therefore cuts across the departmental boundaries that often appear in organisational charts.

An example of such a process in a commercial company is order fulfilment: from persuading the customer to receiving their order, from fulfilling the order to receiving the cash, each process is performed in different parts of the company.

However, most business activities are organised not on a process basis but on a functional basis, for example, sales, accounts and legal. The same is true for voluntary organisations, which are divided into fundraising, accounts, personnel, etc. In accordance with this functional split, costs tend to be collected by department and, when appropriate, may be allocated out to other departments as a general overhead.

The reporting of costs to the department head is also usually by cost type, for example, salaries, travel, overheads and computer costs. Although this is important to the department head for internal budgetary control purposes, it gives no insight into the business processes that caused the costs to be incurred in the first place. It tells the management the 'what' but not the 'why'.

Take, for example, the finance department, which performs the functions of invoicing, payroll, general accounting, cash receipts and payments – all of them activities that exist as a result of other business processes. They are not an end in themselves, but a consequence of other activities. In most commercial organisations these costs are treated as overheads and may be reallocated to other departments.

However, as we have seen, the allocation is arbitrary. Take the cost of running the payroll – a detailed analysis of how costs were incurred would probably show that it costs very little more to run a payroll for 200 staff than it does for 150. But a common basis for allocating payroll costs is the number of employees. As a result, a department employing 150 staff would receive a disproportionately higher charge than one employing only 50.

The critical difference under ABC accounting is that costs should, if possible, be charged directly to the service or project in such a way that the amount charged reflects as closely as possible the actual cost of the service.

Despite the benefits it can bring, ABC does have a number of problems associated with it. Some of these relate to the voluntary sector.

- When setting up the system it is easy to make it too complicated. Only the most important business processes need to be identified, and the components of those processes should be kept to a minimum. If for some reason more detail is required, this can be obtained by a one-off exercise, rather than by building it into the system.
- A balance needs to be struck between reasonable approximations and excessive detail. This is particularly important when costs have to be allocated.

- Full implementation of ABC requires a sophisticated accounting system to collect and hold data.
- Maintaining time sheets to record how staff spend their time is commonly used as a basis for attributing staff costs and some services to the identified business processes or products. Maintaining such a system, with its associated complications, is an additional overhead that would need to be justified.
- Unlike their commercial counterparts, voluntary organisations often receive donations of time, goods and services that enable them to provide a much better service. How should these donations be valued, and how should they appear in management reports?
- To be effective, ABC needs the involvement and commitment of all staff, not just senior management. It may, however, be seen as a threat by staff, as business processes cut across departmental boundaries and challenge work practices or unproductive activities.

Although direct implementation of ABC across the voluntary sector may not be appropriate, there are some organisations – in particular, the larger charities and those actively engaged in commercial operations – that should seriously consider introducing it. ABC is probably unsuitable for smaller voluntary organisations, however, because it needs sophisticated computer systems to provide information on a regular basis. Such organisations should at least think about conducting a one-off study to identify the business processes and determine the real costs of each one. There may be misconceptions about the true cost of a particular process, product or service that could have serious consequences for the future of the entire organisation.

5.4
Using costs for decision making

This section looks at using costs to help managers in their decision-making activities; cost behaviour patterns; and different classifications of costs for decision making.

Cost behaviour patterns

The term 'cost behaviour patterns' is used to describe how costs behave in relation to the level of activity'. It involves asking the question, 'Does this cost increase in line with activity or does it remain constant?' A variety of factors can cause costs to change – for example, inflation and scarcity in supply – but cost accounting focuses on how they change in response to the level of activity. Activity can be measured in a variety of ways, depending on the organisation, the type of costs being analysed and the reasons for analysing the costs. Common measures of activity might include the level of service provided (local, regional or national), the number of training courses run, the number of beneficiaries using the service, the number of employees and the number of telephone calls to a helpline etc.

Fixed costs

Fixed costs are those that do not vary with the level of activity of a project and remain constant for a reasonable length of time. If, for example, the rent of the premises is £10,000 p.a. then the total cost incurred in the period will be £10,000 for all activity levels, even at zero activity. In the short-term, therefore, an organisation will have to pay these costs even if activity drops to zero. Another term used to describe fixed costs is 'period costs'; this highlights the fact that a fixed cost is incurred according to the time elapsed rather than the level of activity. Drawn as a graph, fixed costs would be represented by a straight horizontal line.

Examples of fixed costs for a community centre operating a kitchen preparing food for homeless people on a contract basis would be:

• rent and rates
• salaries of kitchen staff
• insurance
• depreciation of equipment.

These costs will probably be unaffected by the number of homeless people served over a period. But there may come a point when demand for the service expands and more staff or bigger premises are needed. There will then be corresponding increases in salaries, rent and rates etc.

A fixed cost is therefore unaffected by changes within a relevant range of activity. If activity extends beyond this range, then the fixed costs change. The costs remain fixed for a certain range of activity. Within this range it is possible to serve more homeless people without needing extra staff and therefore the salary cost remains constant. However, if activity is expanded to the critical point where another staff member is needed, the salary cost moves up to a higher level. The cost then remains constant for a further range of increases in activity until another staff member is needed and another step occurs. The critical points are often referred to as 'break points'. This is referred to as 'stepped costs', because when represented graphically it resembles a set of steps or a staircase.

Out of a desire to serve as many beneficiaries as possible, voluntary organisations often increase their levels of activity beyond the relevant break point. This situation cannot be sustained in the long term without affecting the quality of the services provided. Furthermore, it is seldom possible to obtain extra funding to allow for this expansion; a commercial provider, by contrast, is more likely to secure further investment. Identifying the relevant range and break point is, therefore, crucially important for voluntary organisations.

'Variable costs are those that vary according to the amount of activity undertaken.'

Variable costs

Variable costs are those that vary according to the amount of activity undertaken or goods produced. The higher the level of activity, the higher will be the cost incurred. When activity increases, the total variable cost increases in direct proportion, ie if activity goes up by 10 per cent, the total variable cost also increases by 10 per cent, as long as the activity level is still within the relevant range. Using the community kitchen as an example, the two costs likely to be variable are food and fuel.

Semi-variable costs

Also referred to as 'semi fixed' or 'mixed' costs, this is a cost that contains both fixed and variable components, and is therefore partly affected by fluctuations in the level of activity. As levels of activity increase, a variable component is incurred in addition to the basic fixed cost. A typical example of a semi-variable cost is the telephone – there is a fixed standing charge and then a variable usage charge.

5.5
Breakeven analysis

This section looks at a type of analysis that depends on an understanding of cost behaviour. Suppose the community centre was faced with the original decision about whether it should accept the fixed-price contract with the local authority to operate a community kitchen. One key factor in the decision would be: 'How many homeless people does the community centre need to attract in order to break even each month?'

Calculating the breakeven point

Suppose that you have produced the following estimates of your monthly costs.

Fixed costs £ per month
Rent and rates 800; Salaries 1,500; Insurance 100; Other 100; Total 2,500

Variable costs £ per person (average)
Food and drink 3; Laundry 1; Other 15; Total 19

The contract with the local authority would provide a fixed fee of £10 for every homeless person fed. It is now possible to calculate the breakeven point. The first step is to calculate the contribution from each person. Every time the community centre serves a homeless person it receives £10 and has to pay £5 for food etc. The management accounting term for this difference of £5 is the 'contribution'. Therefore, the community centre gets a contribution of £5 per person:

contract income less variable costs = contribution (£10 − £5 = £5).

The contribution is so called because it literally contributes towards the fixed costs, which are incurred no matter how many people are served. Therefore, if the community centre has one homeless person walk in, there is a £5 contribution towards the fixed costs of £2,500. If there are two customers, there is a £10 contribution towards the fixed costs of £2,500, and so on.

To break even, the community centre needs sufficient contributions to pay all the fixed costs. The centre will then have nothing left: no surplus and no deficit – the breakeven point will have been reached.

Limitations of breakeven analysis

The example of the community centre shows that breakeven analysis can be useful for investigating the relationship between an organisation's costs and income.

However, it does have its limitations, most of which stem from its underlying assumptions.

- Costs are assumed to behave in a linear fashion. Unit variable costs are assumed to remain constant, and fixed costs are assumed to be unaffected by changes in activity levels. Breakeven charts can be adjusted to cope with non-linear variable costs or steps in fixed costs, but too many changes in behaviour patterns can make the charts very cluttered and difficult to use.
- Sales revenues are assumed to be constant for each unit sold. This may be true where, as in the community centre, there is a contract for services. However, it may be unrealistic in situations where 'products' are sold, because of the necessity at times to reduce price in order to increase volume.
- It is assumed that activity is the only factor affecting costs and revenues. Other factors such as inflation and technology changes are ignored.
- The analysis can only be applied to a single product or service. Most voluntary organisations have more than one product or service, and the sale or take up of each may be affected by the other.

5.6
Marginal analysis

This sections looks at some common decision-making situations to see how choices are made. If alternative courses of action are being compared, there is little point in including data that is common to all of them. Management's attention should be focused on the costs and revenues that will differ as a result of the decision. In other words, the incremental costs and revenues should be highlighted. In many cases, the fixed costs will not be altered by a decision, since they are not incremental costs; they should therefore be excluded from the analysis. However, in some situations there may be a step in the fixed costs, and this extra, or incremental, fixed cost should be taken into the analysis. The following examples illustrate this.

Hamilton Care case study

Hamilton Care provides residential care for young people in need, under contract from the surrounding local authorities. The contract price paid is on the basis of the number of young people cared for (ie spot purchase). Hamilton Care has the capacity to provide 100 beds in total. These facilities are available for 200 days of the year; at present, 80 beds are occupied for the full term (200 days p.a.). Extracts from their management accounts reveals the following:

Figure 5.13 Residential care facilities

		£
Contract income for services		480,000
Variable costs	320,000	
Fixed costs	100,000	
		420,000
Surplus		60,000

A private sector competitor has recently gone out of business and Hamilton Care has been approached to take the competitor's place.

The regional authority will refer 20 young people a year, but is only prepared to pay 75 per cent of the normal contract price per person.

Variable unit costs will not be altered by the proposal, but fixed costs would increase by £5,000, as extra staff would be needed to help with supervision.

Is it a worthwhile proposal from a financial point of view? Hamilton Care needs to determine the incremental costs and income that will arise from this proposal.

First calculate the number of 'bed nights':

Total days multiplied by current capacity 200 x 80 = 16,000

Then calculate the current 'spot price' per person:

Contract income £480,000 = £30 per person.

Therefore the proposed contract price is: (75% x £30) = £22.50

The variable cost per 'bed night' = £320,000 = £20.00

A financial outline for the proposal has been prepared as shown:

The proposal would generate an extra £5,000 ((20*200)*(22.50-20.00)) and is therefore worthwhile from a financial point of view.

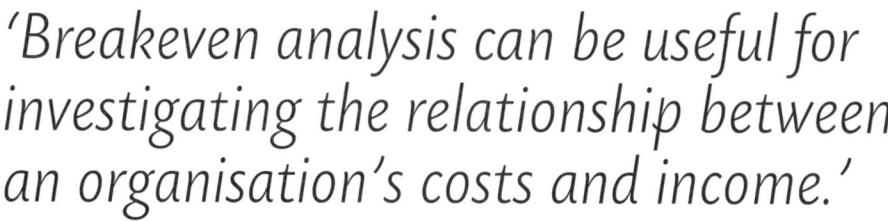

'Breakeven analysis can be useful for investigating the relationship between an organisation's costs and income.'

Closing a project

A national voluntary organization that provides support services and information for elderly people and campaigns on their behalf, has a chain of retail shops through which it sells donated goods. A financial review of the shops is currently under way, and three shops have been identified with a view to perhaps closing at least one of them. The results for the latest period are shown in Figure 5.14

The directors are considering closing down shop C because it makes a loss. However, the fixed costs would still be incurred. The organisation's profit on its retail shops as a whole would fall to £16,000 per year if shop C was closed.

The £5,000 contribution from Shop C would be lost, and so this shop should not be closed, unless a more profitable use can be found for the space it occupies.

The financial effect of closing shop C is shown below.

	Shop A £000	Shop B £000	Total £000
Sales revenue	78	120	198
Variable cost of sales	48	68	116
Contribution	30	52	82
Fixed cost			66
Profit			16

Figure 5.14 Summary of financial results for shops

	Shop A £000	Shop B £000	Shop C £000	Total £000
Sales revenue	78	120	21	219
Variable cost of sales	48	68	16	132
Contribution	30	52	5	87
Fixed cost	23	34	9	66
Profit/(loss)	7	18	(4)	21
	Shop A £	Shop B £		Total £
Sales revenue	78	120		198
Variable cost of sales	48	68		116
Contribution	30	52		82
Fixed cost				66
Profit				16

These examples have been evaluated on purely financial terms; however, it is also important to consider the non-financial consequences of such decisions. If, for example, a nursing home for the elderly is closed, the emotional effects on long-term residents are impossible to calculate, but would certainly need to be considered by the charity.

Relevant costs

Relevant costs are those that will be affected by the decision being taken. In management decision making, all relevant costs should be considered. If a cost will remain unaltered regardless of the decision being taken, it is called a 'non-relevant cost'.

Non-relevant costs

Costs that are not usually relevant in management decisions include the following.

- **Sunk or past cost:** money already spent that cannot now be recovered, for example, expenditure incurred in developing a new fundraising campaign. Even if a decision is taken to abandon further work, the money cannot be recovered. The cost is therefore irrelevant to future decisions concerning the project. However, it should be noted that sunk costs are not irrelevant psychologically; a manager who has expended a lot of time, money and effort in a project will be reluctant to admit that it was effectively wasted. This tends to result in the organisation continuing with projects that should really have been abandoned.
- **Absorbed fixed overheads:** these will not increase or decrease as a result of the decision being taken; see the example above on the closure of retail shops.
- **Expenditure that will be incurred in the future, but because of decisions taken in the past cannot now be changed.** Although this is a future cost, it will be incurred regardless of the decision being taken and is therefore not relevant. An example is expenditure on training material that has been delivered but not paid for – the organisation is obliged to pay for the material even if it subsequently decides not to proceed with the training courses. This is a variant on a sunk cost.

- **Historical cost depreciation:** depreciation calculations do not result in any future cash flows. They are merely bookkeeping entries designed to spread the original cost of an asset over its useful life.

Checklist

Answer the following questions before checking the answers in the text.

1. What is the difference between output and outcomes?
2. Can ABC costing techniques be applied to voluntary organisations?
3. Describe cost behaviour.
4. Why should voluntary organisations undertake full cost recovery

Action points for your organisation

'Audit' your organisation by checking to see:

- whether the trustees receive ratio analysis reports
- whether the organisation understands its costs
- what method of apportioning overheads has been used
- whether ABC could be applied to your organisation
- whether projects are appraised using breakeven analysis
- whether full cost recovery is being applied to all contracts.

Case studies and exercises

Women's Building Project

This case study looks at the use of marginal costing to help a voluntary organisation determine which projects should be accepted in order to ensure maximum contribution to core costs.

The Women's Building Project (WBP) is a recently established charity that seeks to provide women who are disadvantaged (because of low income or for other reasons) with opportunities to gain new skills that can then be usefully employed within the construction industry. This is a unique project that offers training to reskill women, and initial information gathering has identified a number of government and voluntary agencies that have indicated willingness to refer on to WBP.

WBP operates from premises in West London. The site was previously used as a warehouse storage facility and covers about 15,000 square feet. This has been modified by allocating 5,000 square feet to office and administration functions and the remaining 10,000 square feet to be used for training workshops.

WBP has applied to a well-known charitable trust set up by the construction industry for funding for both the running costs of the premises and the provision of free training to women. The trust agreed to provide £50,000 towards the core costs of running the premises, but no funding for the provision of training, which it argued should be self-financing through course fees. Further negotiations resulted in the trust agreeing to provide materials and trainers at heavily subsidised rates, however, WBP would still have to levy a charge to ensure that its costs were covered.

The training courses that WBP planned to offer are listed here.

- **Utility installation:** this will provide the skills and knowledge needed to install electricity, water and gas supplies to new residential premises.
- **Woodwork and joinery:** this will provide women with the hands-on experience and skills they need to use different types of timber in the construction and decoration of residential premises.
- **Metalwork:** this will provide women with the basic skills they need to use metal structures in the construction of industrial premises.
- **Brickwork:** this will provide women with the basic skills necessary to use brick materials in the construction of residential properties.

The training programmes are planned to provide as much hands-on experience as possible within a workshop environment. They will last for three months each, and will be repeated three times a year. The site will be closed for the remaining three months. To ensure maximum learning, the number of women allowed on to the training programmes at any one time will be restricted to 12.

Because of the workshop approach of this training, it has become apparent that only three of the planned programmes can be accommodated in the 10,000 square foot space. Any unused space may be offered to another community organisation wanting office space at £5 per square foot. Each training programme will require its own set of materials, to be used and facilitated by a skilled supervisor.

Detailed costings for each of the four training programmes and the premises as a whole are provided in figure 5.15. A unit of output has been defined as a 'training day' for the maximum of 12 women. For the nine months available in each year, the number of 'training days' will be 180 days per annum or 60 days per term. The costs for each training day will differ according to the type of training programme being run. For example, brickwork training requires more materials (cement, sand, bricks etc) than utility training.

The other fixed premises costs are estimated at £50,000 p.a. and indirect overhead costs are estimated at £30,000 p.a.

At the next trustees meeting, the management team needs to be able to recommend which training programmes to offer. An initial examination of the information has led the project manager to conclude that first priority should be given to utilities, then metalwork, and finally woodwork, as these have the highest course fees and take-up rate.

The treasurer, who is also studying to be an accountant, has decided to take a more rigorous approach. He is particularly concerned that, in view of the restriction imposed by the available floor space, only those training programmes that maximise the contribution per square foot to the annual fixed overheads should be accepted. His calculations are shown in figure 5.16.

Figure 5.16 shows that the conclusions of the project manager and the treasurer are very different. The treasurer is recommending that the metalwork programme be dropped, whereas this was the project manager's second favourite.

The financial effect on WBP as a whole of the two proposals is shown in fig 5.17.

The information on fixed premises costs and indirect overhead costs will be the same for whatever course of action.

Figure 5.15 Training programme costs

Per training day	Utilities	Woodwork	Brickwork	Metalwork
Materials	£30	£35	£40	£60
Supervisors staff costs	£75	£22	£30	£60
Consumables 1	£5	£10.50	£10	£20
Floor space required (square feet)	2,000	2,000	3,000	5,000
Training course fees (per term)	£750	£700	£600	£650
Expected take-up rate (%)	90	80	75	95

Figure 5.16 Training programme costs

	Utilities	Woodwork	Brickwork	Metalwork
Total variable costs per training day (a) (material+ staff+consumables)	£120	£67.50	£80	£140
Total variable costs per term (b) (a) multiply by 60 days	£7,200	£4,050	£4,800	£8,400
Expected variable costs per term (c) (b) multiply by take-up %	£6,480	£3,240	£3,600	£7,980
Expected course fees per term (total course fees (for 12) multiply by take-up %) (d)	£8,100	£6,720	£5,400	£7,410
Expected contribution per term (e) (d) minus (c)	£1,620	£3,480	£1,800	£(570)
Floor space required square feet (f)	2,000	2,000	3,000	5,000
Contribution per square foot (g) (e) divided by (f)	£0.81	£1.74	£0.60	£(0.114)
Treasurer's ranking	2nd	1st	3rd	not run
Project manager's ranking	1st	3rd	not run	2nd

Figure 5.17 Financial results of the recommendations

	Treasurer's proposal	Project manager's proposal
Contribution for year: ((e) multiply by 3 terms)		
1st: Woodwork	£10,440	
Utilities		£4,860
2nd: Utilities	£4,860	
Metalwork		£(1,710)
3rd: Brickwork	£5,400	
Woodwork		£10,440
	£20,700	£13,590
Remaining floor space available to rent	3,000 sq ft	1,000 sq ft
Rental income @ £5 per square foot	£15,000	£5,000
Total contribution to overheads	£35,700	£18,590

Exercise 5.1

The Captain Nelson Foundation has a residential services department, which runs three residential centres for disabled, elderly, former sailors. The details are:

Name of home	Number of beds	Actual beds occupied	Staff establishment
Southways	40	30	8
Northend	40	20	8
Central	50	40	10

Health and local authorities pay the Nelson £3,500 per annum per resident in occupation. Variable overheads are £500 per annum per occupied bed. Fixed costs are staff members whose average salary is £10,000 per annum each and charity head office overheads at £200 per bed.

At a management team meeting reviewing the homes, the finance director states that the homes are currently running at a deficit. The charity can no longer afford these deficits, and so he informs the residential homes director that a revised budget is required which will, at a minimum, break even.

At a subsequent meeting of the heads of home to discuss options, the Central home head suggests that Northend be closed and the residents transferred to the other homes. The residential services director points out that two staff are shortly to leave. By reducing the establishment at Northend to six, it is suggested that this should resolve the problem.

Questions

1. Calculate the current residential homes department deficit by home.

2. What is the required number to break even?

3. Adopting the suggestion to lose two members of staff at Northend, what is the new position for the department? Assume the same occupancy, but a 10 per cent rise in income and costs.

4. Discuss the advantages/disadvantages of the proposed solution. Are there alternatives?

Exercise 5.2

This exercise looks at understanding overhead costs in tendering to run a day centre.

Following reorganisation, Any Council now comprises two main urban areas at either end of its boundary, separated by countryside. One of the urban areas is the County Town, which has an active and large Age Concern organisation – ACCT. In the other, smaller, Urban Town the services are still provided by the Council. The new Council has asked ACCT if it would like to run the same services in the Urban Town. It currently gives a grant of £80,000 to ACCT and it is proposed to offer a further grant of £45,000 to run the Urban Town's services. The Council will transfer its current building rent-free to ACCT. There are no transfers or contractual problems for the existing staff as the council will redeploy existing staff if ACCT takes over.

The current ACCT organisation has a large purpose-built building owned by the organisation, which accommodates 150 people daily in a variety of activities, advice, medical services etc. The building has an average 80 per cent capacity use. The Urban Town centre is half the size of the County town centre with 75 places and exactly half the running costs. The budget of ACCT for the current year is:

Income:	£
Council grant	80,000
Insurance/services	16,000
Donations	17,000
Catering profit	13,500
Total	126,500
Expenditure:	£
Staff	104,000
Costs	22,000
Total	126,000
Surplus	500

The director has made the following notes on the budget, with a plan for the take-over of the new service. They have proposed that both centres will be under their overall management, assisted by the finance officer and catering manager, all of whom would accept a 10 per cent pay rise to reflect additional responsibilities and time for managing both services (all staff costs are inclusive of National Insurance etc).

- A director £25,000 – who has advised that the Urban Town centre will need a Centre manager at £22,000.
- A secretary £15,000 – who has estimated that administration costs at the other Centre will be £7,500.
- A finance officer £20,000 – who has advised that the urban centre will require a finance assistant at £10,000.
- Service coordinators (both part-time at £10,000 each).
- A catering manager £12,000 – who has advised they would need an assistant at the Urban Town centre at £10,000.
- Service session staff £12,000; volunteers' expenses £4,000.
- Building running costs £10,000, the new centre will be half the size.
- Office, administration, audit £8,000, administration costs at the urban centre will be £2,000.
- Lunchtime meals are charged at £1 and two tea/coffee sessions at 25p per session. A profit of 30 per cent is made on catering. The centre and catering services are open for 250 days a year.
- Donations and service income for the new centre will be equal in proportion to current ACCT.

From the perspective of ACCT would you take the council's offer and take over the new service? The proposed new management arrangements would mean moving from being one organisation on one site to being an organisation with a management team managing two sites. Prepare revised budgets for the new organisation.

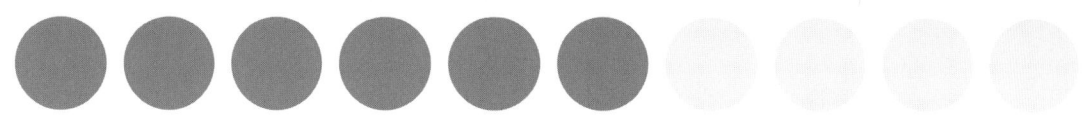

Charity accounts and financial management

6.1
Who uses charities' financial statements?

This chapter looks at the different users of charity financial statements and the types of information that will be particularly relevant to them.

Lots of people might need the information provided by such financial statements. Some of them are directly connected with the organisation, for example, its employees and managers. Others are not directly connected, but may be affected by its management of finance or its financial stability, for example, the general public.

User groups who may require information in a charity's published financial statements include (but are not restricted to):

- the trustees of other voluntary organisations, their governing bodies and any non-trustee members
- managers, employees, prospective employees and volunteers
- donors and sponsors
- grant-making bodies
- the beneficiary stakeholders using the services of the charity
- suppliers
- lenders and potential lenders
- Government departments, including the grant-making regulators such as the DfE's EFA (for academy schools), HEFCE (for universities/colleges), LTA (for social housing), also the Charity Commission and/or OSCR, local authorities, Companies House (as appropriate) and HMRC
- the public, including the media
- academia (for research) and sector information providers (publishers of reference data, charity database websites).

Trustees of charitable voluntary organisations

The trustees are legally responsible for the financial resources entrusted to the charitable organisation, and therefore need to ensure, not only that the financial statements comply with the relevant charity sector accounting code or SORP (Statement of Recommended Practice), but also that they properly describe the charity, its structure, management, external relationships and its aims, activities, achievements, future plans and financial position.

Trustees are often unclear about how the information and figures in the management accounts, which they will be familiar with, become the annual financial statements. There are three key reasons for this.

1. The purpose of management accounts is internal monitoring and control, whereas the annual financial statements are for *stewardship* reporting to an external audience.

2. The format of annual financial statements is prescribed by the charity's SORP (general or specialised) and the regulations or other statutory underpinning of that SORP, while management accounts should be in a format that informs the financial management of the organisation.

3. A number of adjustments may be needed to the management accounts for the full financial year – such as for accruals and prepayments – in order to arrive at a set of figures that complies with accounting principles and best practice for external reporting.

It is important for the charity trustees as a body to take the trouble to understand their annual report and financial statements. Although the chair of the trustee board, sometimes with the honorary treasurer, usually signs the report and the financial statements, any such signing must by law be specifically authorised by the board members, who all share 'joint and several' liability to their charity for any lack of due care resulting in loss.

Managers, employees and prospective employees

The managers of any voluntary organisation need financial information to help them manage the business. They need past information to help them monitor the progress of the organisation (or their part of it), current information to carry out day-to-day operational management and control, and forecast information to plan activities into the future.

Employees and trade unions may consult the financial statements when they are negotiating pay and terms of employment. Current and prospective employees might be wise to examine the financial statements to assess whether the organisation is likely to grow and prosper, or whether it (and the job) may disappear.

Volunteers will be interested in how the organisation is doing, and may particularly want to see whether their work is being reflected. As the debate over valuing volunteers continues, it will be interesting to note how much more interest is taken.

Donors and sponsors

People and organisations who donate money to voluntary organisations, or who otherwise sponsor their activities, might use the financial statements to check that they are happy with the way the organisation is handling its funds.

Grant-making bodies

Many grant-making bodies will use the financial statements to obtain a better appreciation of what the organisation does and how it is managed. In particular, they can sometimes use the financial statements to determine the level of reserves available to the organisation, and on this basis decide whether funding will be granted.

For many voluntary organisations, restricted project funding may form a large part of their reserves as disclosed in the financial statements. However, since these project funds are restricted, they are not available for another purpose.

Grant-making bodies will also use financial statements to determine how well the voluntary organisation is managed. Although useful insights can be obtained by using key ratios, sometimes grant makers have paid too much attention to the figures for management and administration costs in isolation.

The beneficiary stakeholders using the services of the charity

This group of users may be paying for services, or receiving them free of charge, but in either case they will want to use financial statements to assess how effectively and efficiently those services are being delivered. Their particular concern will be whether the voluntary organisation has sufficient resources, in the present and future, to support their continuing needs.

Suppliers

Potential suppliers want to know whether their customer will be able to pay for the goods and services supplied. Many customer–supplier relationships are long term and require a considerable investment of time and money. A supplier will want to be sure of the long-term viability of the other party before making the effort.

Lenders and potential lenders

Banks and others who lend money to voluntary organisations will need information about the organisation's ability to make interest payments in the short term and ultimately to repay the loan on its due date. They will also be concerned about the security for their loan: does the organisation have valuable items, or assets, that could be sold to raise the money to repay the loan if necessary?

The government, including the Charity Commission, Companies House and HMRC

HMRC will need to consult the charity's financial statements to determine whether there is a tax liability arising from any trading activities and, if VAT-registered, that the correct amount of VAT has been paid or refunded. The Charity Commission requires most charities to file annual reports, financial statements and annual returns. For resource reasons this is not as important to its monitoring activities, which have been drastically scaled back in recent years, but it is used as a resource for other stakeholders in the sector. Companies House is the central government repository for all audited and unaudited financial statements of private and public limited companies. Other government departments and agencies may require financial and non-financial statistics to monitor the state of the economy.

The public, including the media

Voluntary organisations and charities rely, to a large extent, upon the goodwill of the public in donating money to their causes, and recognised charities and community amateur sports clubs are also able to take advantage of a range of tax concessions. As taxpayers and council tax payers, the public often use financial statements to decide whether to give to a particular charity or not, on the basis of how efficiently it is managed.

6.2
Introduction to the Charities SORP

Charity accounting changed in the 1990s with the official recognition that charity operations, which became 'big business' in the mid-1980s as the sector took up the challenge of government initiatives such as Care in the Community, were in need of some form of regulation that recognised that even charities bidding for commercial contracts are very different from commercial companies.

Previously charities had, in line with commercial best practice, produced income and expenditure accounts, which in essence were the same as profit and loss accounts. In recognition of these differences – for example, the object of a charity is not to make a profit for distribution to investors but rather to spend all its money, including ultimately any trading surpluses, on its charitable purpose in line with annually reset aims and objectives – the Charity Commission set up a working party to help improve the quality of financial reporting by charities, and to assist those who are responsible for the preparation of the charity's annual report and financial statements. An agreed Statement of Recommended Practice for charity accounts, to be underpinned for enforcement purposes by regulations made under the 1993 Charities Act, and nowadays commonly known as the 'Charities SORP', was published in October 1995. The Accounting Standards Board required it to be frequently updated and it was subject to revision every three years, but in practice it was revised every five years, as reflected in the 2000 and 2005 SORPs. Although the word 'recommended' is used in its title, as with all the industry SORPs, it is generally mandatory, as the SORP forms the basis of the accounting regulations now prescribed in the 2011 Charities Act, so each new version is supported by a new Statutory Instrument. Even for charities formed as companies, and accounting under the Companies Act rather than the Charities Act, its application is best practice, and without it an auditor will be unable give an unqualified opinion that the accounts do 'show a true and fair view' as is required by law.

Developments in SORPs inevitably stem from developments in accounting and financial reporting standards and the identification of issues that arise over time and are inadequately addressed by a current SORP. A new version was due in 2010, however the emergence of the Accounting Standards Board's 'convergence' plans around the migration of UK accounting standards to international financial reporting standards (IFRS) had challenged whether the existing SORPs could have any status under a globally based regime. The 2010 version was abandoned with the next version due after the planned convergence of UK-GAAP with IFRS. Subsequent debate has taken place between those who feel the integrity of the SORP should be maintained and those who are in favour of international harmonisation. After much consultation between the Accounting Standards Board and key stakeholders it was agreed that the charity sector's special and general SORPs would remain valid for the UK and be reissued based on Financial Reporting Standard (FRS) 102. FRS 102 was issued in March 2013 by the Financial Reporting Council (which now subsumes the ASB as one of its internal committees under a new name) and will be effective for financial years commencing on or after 1 January 2015. The exposure draft of the proposed new SORP has been issued for a four-month consultation period from July 2013 and is likely to be finalised by the summer of 2014.

FRS 102 introduces some changes including the following points.

- All entities under FRS 102 will have to publish a cash flow statement, with fewer headings than FRS2 but with a choice of showing the gross or net operating cash flows (under the FRSSE, there is no cash flow requirement).
- The criteria for recognising assets and liabilities have been aligned so they are accounted for when it is 'probable' that the 'economic resource' will be transferred or the money received or paid, instead of when it is 'virtually certain'. Income and expenditure are then recognised as and when net assets increase or decrease.
- Gifted assets and services must, in general, be recognised at their fair value at the date of gift, not when sold off, used or distributed, but where gifts of goods for sale cannot be reliably valued until sold or the cost of valuing them outweighs the benefit of the information to the reader, recognition is to be at the point of sale (for example, charity shops). For volunteers, 'it is expected that the contribution made by [them] cannot be reasonably quantified'. New USA research into this measurement problem, promising auditable figures for the Statement of Financial Activities (SoFA), could soon change that, with the Charities SORP allowing a more representative presentation of volunteer-staffed charitable service provision in the statutory accounts of many of the largest charities.
- Liabilities due for payment more than a year beyond the balance sheet date will have to be discounted to their net present value.
- This includes obligations to provide staff retirement benefits. Under FRS 102 they will have to be accrued as actual liabilities for any unfunded commitments at each year end. The current requirement under FRS 17 is to show a notional liability for a defined benefit scheme in deficit.

The new SORP will have a modular format so that charities only need to refer to those sections that directly affect them. Core modules relevant to all charities cover areas such as the trustees' annual report, fund accounting (restricted and unrestricted funds and any endowment capital) in the SoFA and balance sheet, cash flows under FRS102 as part of the primary financial statements and gift accounting, as well as the general rules for income and expenditure presentation in the SoFA and the classification of assets, liabilities and funds in the balance sheet. There are specialist modules for certain types of charities, such as companies or charities undertaking particular activities, such as joint ventures, grant making or holding heritage assets. Specialist guidance will cover investments, social investments, charity branches, group accounting and charity mergers.

Trustee annual report

In understanding a charity's financial statements, we need to recognise that the trustees are responsible for them. The trustee report enables trustees to discharge their public duty of accountability and stewardship and provide an insight into the charity's activities and achievements.

While figures are the essence of financial statements, the starting point for the public in understanding charity accounts is with words. The Charities SORP places emphasis on the formal narrative in the trustees' report. Charity Commission guidance CC15b provides details about the purpose and content of the annual report. The report has to include information about the charity's structure, governance and management, which involves giving details on the induction and training of trustees, and risk management.

The trustee report includes the charitable objects, aims and objectives for the year, as well as its achievements, (the difference the charity has aimed to make and has made), as well as its strategies (ways and means) for achieving those objectives and details of the year's significant activities. Policy and performance in respect of actual year-end reserves must be given, as well as for the selection of investments if these are significant (including any ethical considerations and distinguishing social (programme-related) investments) and for any significant grant-making activities. A public benefit statement is needed, to confirm whether the charity trustees have complied with their duty to have due regard to the guidance on public benefit issued by the Charity Commission under the Charities Act 2011. A commentary on the financial position of the charity – especially if it is not obvious to the reader that the charity continues to be 'a going concern' – and information on volunteers (if their contribution is significant) should also be included.

The Statement of Financial Activities (SoFA)

The traditional income and expenditure account treatment led to complaints that it did not reflect, or fully explain, all the financial activities of a charity. Therefore, it was considered that the very nature of the raising and using of charity resources required a different approach from that of the business community.

Charities, even those that are companies, do not have investors with equity interests of any kind, so distributable profits (dividends) do not arise. Those who provide the voluntary resources for charities do not expect a financial return on their contributions, least of all on their donations, but more of a 'warm glow' or, in the case of commercial sponsors, an enhancement of their brand or company image by the publicity normally associated with their support. However, the users of a charity's financial statements do need to be able to assess the services that the charity is providing, primarily through its charitable expenditure and its ability to continue to provide those services.

The financial statements should also show how the trustees have carried out their stewardship duties and ensured that their public benefit responsibilities have been met during the year. While it may be that the commercial sector's bottom line – the annual surplus or deficit of distributable profit – provides some of this information, any presentation that focuses only on the bottom line tends to ignore the fundamental differences between accounting for charities and for commercial businesses. What is the bottom line when in effect none exists, because no kind of profit distribution is permitted?

Charities, except where trading (actually or in effect), have no investor-driven compulsion to indulge in the commercial business of matching their income and their expenditure to monitor the annual result. Therefore, they are not working towards a particular year-end result unless, for long-term sustainability, they are building up reserves. In other words, to place undue emphasis on the bottom line at a particular point in time can be misleading, as income and expenditure in any one period are often not directly related; for example, grants received this year may be for projects to be carried out in the following year, or indeed over a number of years. SORP 2005, in line with the evolving financial reporting standards on which it was based, abandoned the old commercial matching concept for income and expenditure in favour of the more fundamental recognition of assets and liabilities as the determining factors for all financial accountability. However, charities do still need to link (though not to match) as far as possible, the different types of incoming resource with any related resources expended.

Revenue and capital

Unfortunately, the traditional income and expenditure account with its focus on revenue, to the exclusion of capital, does not always adequately explain a charity's activities. Businesses primarily invest in fixed assets to generate future distributable profits while a charity may be investing in fixed assets as part of its charitable activity (primary purpose), whether or not it has a duty to consider the needs of future generations of beneficiaries, for example:

- equipping a cancer research laboratory
- building a care home
- acquiring lifeboats.

This difference is extremely important to certain charities, where a significant proportion of their annual expenditure is of a capital nature.

In any particular year, a charity may use part of its income to purchase fixed assets for its charitable activities, but since this expenditure is of a capital nature (even if made out of income rather than endowment capital) it will not be shown in the income and expenditure account. This could, therefore, lead to showing a surplus on the income and expenditure account for that year, which would give a misleading impression, as the asset is to be written off against income over a number of years.

Disclosures

The SORP's great innovation for the charity sector was SoFA. This is a means of showing, in summary form for the year:

- all the charity's funds.
- all its incoming resources (including any disposal gains on capitalised assets held for its own use)
- all its non-capitalised expenditure
- all transfers between funds
- all gains and losses (net) on investment assets and all revaluation gains on capitalised assets held for the charity's own use
- how the fund balances have changed since the last balance sheet date.

This comprehensive primary accounting statement shows what funds the charity has had at its disposal and how they have been used. Of course, it may be necessary to add appropriate additional information in the notes to the financial statements to bring out a special feature, for example, the equipping of a medical research laboratory or the effectiveness of a particular fundraising campaign or significant branch activities.

However, as radical as the SoFA was at the time, it essentially just amalgamates the old-style income and expenditure account with the endowment capital accounting that is unknown in the commercial sector and incorporates the latter's separate statements of other recognised gains and losses, and reconciliation of funds. It can even include an analysis of the movements on each of the charity's major individual funds unless these are too numerous, when that analysis is relegated to an accounts note.

Reasoning

The SoFA recognises that charities do not usually have just one single indicator of performance that is comparable to the bottom line for a commercial business with equity investors. As well as considering the changes in the amounts of the net resources of a charity, it is important to consider the changes in the nature of those resources. As a result, both the SORP and the regulations that underpin it require a primary statement that records all the resources entrusted to a charity and reflects all its financial activities.

The SoFA is divided into two parts:

1. a statement of operational activities

2. a statement of other financial activities.

The SoFA thus moved away from giving undue emphasis to the bottom line based on the long-since superseded accounting concept of income-and-expenditure matching and even dropped the use of the words 'surplus' and 'deficit'. It focuses instead on the annual measurement of the changes in both the nature and amounts of all the net assets of a charity and how these relate to each of its funds.

Format

The SoFA should be prepared using a column format to distinguish endowment capital (where these funds are held) from restricted and unrestricted income. The minimum requirement is:

- one column for unrestricted funds
- one column for restricted funds
- one column for permanent and expendable endowments
- one column for the total for the year.

Therefore, this requires separation of incoming resources and the consumption of resources between these types of funds. There is also a fifth column, showing the comparative total for the previous accounting period, but it is not a legal requirement to show comparatives for each type of fund.

Where there have been no movements in any particular fund or the charity does not have that type of fund, then it is not necessary to include that column. This column approach can be expanded on, for example, unrestricted funds can be split between general-purpose funds and designated unrestricted funds (such as in the case of a school wanting to distinguish its school fees and costs from other general income and expenditure). Whilst any type of fund may be split in this way, if it creates too many columns then the funds analysis details should be shown in the notes to the financial statements.

Standard headings for each row (ie line) can include the following.

Incoming resources from generated funds:

- voluntary income
- activities for generating funds
- investment income
- incoming resources from charitable activities
- other incoming resources.

Resources expended:

- cost of generating funds (broken down between generating voluntary income, costs of goods sold, investment management costs etc)
- charitable activities
- governance costs (this might not appear under the new SORP, however this is still subject to consultation).

This has helped to make charity financial statements more comparable and transparent. Again, this information will always be required, but if there has been no movement on a particular heading in the year or previous year, that heading need not be included.

There is an emphasis, which for auditable charities is a requirement rather than an option, on expenditure analysis in the SoFA by reference to the *purpose* of all activities. A clear link should be established between any related incoming and outgoing resources. This may be difficult where there are a number of different sources of income supporting a charitable activity, but where there is clarity – for example, the provision of care that can be linked with a local authority's contract or grant funding – this should be reflected within the disclosures on the SoFA.

With the increasing 'contract culture' within service-providing charities over the last few years, special attention will need to be given to recognising income to the extent that an asset has been created (or a liability reduced) by the work that has been done. This may require working with other parts of the organisation to establish how much of the work contracted for has been delivered. For example, in the case of digging wells overseas – how the contract has been structured and how many wells have been dug by the year-end date may determine the accounting disclosure, depending on the terms and conditions set out in the contract (or 'preconditions', in a grant-funding agreement.

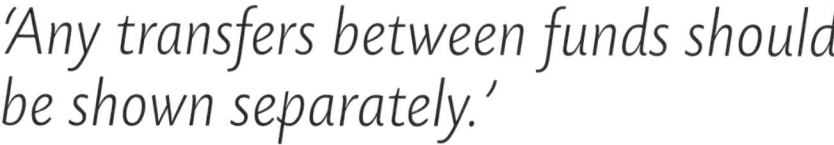

'Any transfers between funds should be shown separately.'

Similarly, therefore, with grants and donations, the charity will need to ensure that all of the donor's preconditions have been fulfilled to enable income to be recognised. If income has been received in advance and not all of these preconditions have been fulfilled, a corresponding amount must be accounted for as 'deferred income', or a liability for repayment may need to be accrued, within the financial statements for that year.

Systems and procedures need to include accounting recognition of material gifts in kind that the charity may receive. While these do not involve financial consideration, if they affect the users' understanding of the financial statements, details should be given.

Support costs should be disclosed within the notes to the financial statements. These are the costs that do not produce a direct output – they do not constitute an activity in themselves but enable an activity to take place. They include management costs, finance, IT and HR (human resources – used to be known as the personnel department), and should be allocated to the relevant cost category on a consistent basis based on usage, per capita, floor space or time spent. Figure 6.1 gives an example.

All costs that directly relate to a specific SoFA cost category should be attributed to that cost. Detailed disclosure on a project-by-project basis can either be shown on the face of the SoFA or in the notes to the financial statements. The costs breakdown shows whether expenditure is in respect of direct charitable activity or grant payments. The notes to the financial statements should also give details of support costs in a structure similar to the one shown in figure 6.2.

Costs of generating funds should be analysed to match the analysis of income. The notes to the financial statements should also show where material costs have been incurred on start-up fundraising projects and other 'fundraising for the future', such as building a donor database, legacy marketing etc, to distinguish them from the recurring costs of current fundraising.

Any transfers between funds should be shown separately, outside of the incoming resources and resources expended sections. Transfers should be shown as gross not netted off, and an explanation should be included within the notes to the financial statements.

Finally, the SoFA encompasses a statement of 'other recognised gains and losses' covering both realised and unrealised gains and losses for investment assets, but only the unrealised gains and losses for any revaluation of tangible fixed assets held for the charity's own use. This is a further area subject to discussion under the SORP consultation.

Figure 6.1

Support cost (examples)	Fundraising	Care home 1	Care home 2	Outreach project	Basis of allocation
Management	£10K	£5K	£5K	£10K	Time spent
Finance	£20K	£15K	£10K	£5K	Transactions processed
Information technology	£15K	£5K	£5K	£ 10K	Number of computers/ software supported
Human resources	£5K	£15K	£20K	£5K	Time spent
Head office space	£30K	£10k	£1OK	£5K	Floor space
Total	£80K	£50K	£50K	£35K	

Balance sheet

Unlike the SoFA, a charity's balance sheet is akin to that of a commercial company, except that the funds section is wholly charitable and not the equity interests of investors (of which there are none for a charity), and the normal commercial accounting rules apply for most other balance sheet items – ie assets and liabilities.

Presentation

A charity's funds should be grouped together in the balance sheet according to their type, distinguishing between endowments, other restricted funds, designated and other unrestricted funds, as the SORP itself explains. Further analysis of major individual funds needs to be given, as appropriate, in the notes to the financial statements.

The assets of the charity should be analysed in the balance sheet between fixed and current assets. The fixed assets section should show separately those for charity use (showing any heritage assets separately) and those for investment, with the latter further separated between commercial and social ('programme related') and for current assets and liabilities these should be analysed between current and long-term elements, with the total (if material) of any provisions for liabilities or charges shown separately. The totals for both short-term and long-term creditors should be sub-analysed in the notes.

In addition, the assets and liabilities should be analysed in a way that enables the reader to gain a proper appreciation of their spread and character. The balance sheet must be approved by all the trustees as a group and signed by one of them.

FRS 17 introduced very detailed accounting rules concerning 'defined benefit' and other staff pension schemes to be shown in the accounts as assets/liabilities, and extensive further disclosures are required where a charity has such a defined benefit scheme.

Guidance on the current and proposed new SORP is available from the Charity Commission: www.charity-commission.gov.uk.

Figure 6.2

Activity or programme	Activities undertaken directly	Grant funding of activities	Support costs	Total
Care home 1	£150K	-	£50K	£200K
Care home 2	£190K	-	£50K	£240K
Outreach project	£50K	£60K	£35K	£145K
Total	£390K	£60K	£135K	£585K

SoFA example: Care Home Trust Limited

Consolidated statement of financial activities (including an income and expenditure account) for the year ended March 2013:

Figure 6.3 Consolidated balance sheets as at 31 March 2013

	Notes	Group 2013 £000	Group 2012 £000
Fixed assets			
Tangible assets	10	830	850
Investments	4	137	129
		967	979
Current assets			
Stocks	11	217	213
Debtors	12	290	287
Cash at bank and in hand		423	319
		930	819
Creditors: amounts falling due within one year	13	242	195
Net current assets		688	624
Total assets less current liabilities		1,655	1,603
Creditors: amounts falling due after more than one year	15	46	56
		1,609	1,547
Funds			
Unrestricted funds			
General	16	1,430	1,363
Designated	16	167	167
Restricted funds	17	12	17
		1,609	1,547

Approved by the board on 13 June 2013 and signed on its behalf by: S.A. Bloggs, Chairman

6.3
Audit and independent examination requirements for charities

Charity Commission guidance CC15b outlines current accounting and reporting requirements updated for charities with financial years ending on or after 1 April 2009. The details are available from the Charity Commission website.

For unincorporated charities, the financial thresholds governing the type of accounts and what type of external scrutiny is required are shown in figure 6.4

The minimum requirement for registration is that a charity must have an income of more than £5,000 a year. Charities with an annual income of not more than £10,000, and nowadays also those not exceeding £25,000, need not submit a copy of their financial statements to the Charity Commission unless they are specifically asked. All registered charities with an annual income in excess of £25,000 have to upload a PDF of their annual report and financial statements to the Charity Commission website, as well as completing the appropriate sections of an online Annual Return for regulatory monitoring purposes.

Independent examination is a simpler and less expensive form of external scrutiny than audit, both in terms of the depth of work to be carried out, and the qualification necessary to undertake such work. The examiner is not required to form an opinion as to whether the financial statements show a true and fair view, but reports, based on the examination carried out, on whether reportable facts have come to his or her attention.

In most cases the examiner will be reviewing receipts and payments accounts and so will not need to be a qualified accountant to carry out a proper independent examination. Where gross income is more than £250,000, charity law requires the examiner to be a full member of a recognised body listed in the Charities Act 2011.

Wherever accruals accounts are prepared, the examiner needs to have an up-to-date understanding of accruals accounting and to be familiar with the SORP.

Many charities will, because of their own constitution/trust deed, still require audit whatever their size. For financial years starting on or after 1 April 2008, company charities that meet the Companies Act definition of a small company may elect for exemption from company audit. A small company is one that meets two of the following three criteria:

1. income not more than £6.5m
2. gross assets not more than £3.26m
3. average number of employees for the year not more than 50.

Figure 6.4

Annual gross income	Type of accounts	Type of external scrutiny
Below £25,000	Receipts and payments option	None required
Above £25,000 but below £250,000	Receipts and payments option	Can choose independent examination or audit
Above £250,000 but below £500,000 and where gross income exceeds £250,000, the charity's gross assets do not exceed £3.26m	Accruals basis mandatory	Can choose independent examination or audit
Above £500,000 or gross income above £250,000 and gross assets exceed £3.26m	Accruals basis mandatory	Audit

All charitable companies have to produce their financial statements on the accrual basis and show a 'true and fair view' to comply with company law. (Charitable Incorporated Organisations are in the same category as other charities in being able to opt out of accrual accounts unless their gross income exceeds £250,000 for the year.) The company's accrual accounts must also include an Income and Expenditure Statement, which is either prepared in addition to, or included within the SoFA. (Where a charity's income is below £250,000 and it has an audit requirement predating the introduction of regulated professional audit and which is considered to be unduly onerous, the charity could consider amending its constitution – with help from the Charity Commission, if needed.)

The charity legislation makes it clear that auditors and independent examiners are required to report certain matters directly to the Charity Commission. The government believes that this obligation is essential to strengthen accountability and maintain public confidence in charities. The Financial Reporting Council's current guidance for charity auditors (PN11) contains a summary of what constitutes a 'whistle-blowing' situation that an auditor should report to the Commission. This is also avoids insignificant matters being reported, which should be handled in a management letter to the trustees. The main types of situation are listed here.

- Significant loss or major risk to the charity from fraud or dishonesty, or else from misappropriation or other cause arising from internal controls failures.
- Suspicions of misuse of the charity for money laundering or as a conduit for criminal activity or as a recipient of the proceeds of serious organised crime or of involvement in or support for terrorism or proscribed organisations in the UK or overseas.

- Evidence coming to light that implies abuse or mistreatment of vulnerable beneficiaries or a significant risk of this.
- Significant or recurring breaches either of a legislative requirement or of the charity's trusts; any deliberate or significant breach of a statutory Order or Direction issued by the charity regulator (for example, suspending a trustee, prohibiting a transaction or activity, or granting a consent in respect of significant assets or liabilities, of the charity).
- Circumstances (if any) reported by the auditor to the charity on ceasing for any reason to hold office as auditor.

(Independent examination is covered in Chapter 9.)

6.4
Converting management accounts to SORP financial statements

Converting internal management accounts, prepared on an income and expenditure basis, to a set of final year-end financial statements is essentially a process of apportionment.

The management accounts contain the income and expenditure results for the different departments of the organisation, reflecting the structure of the organisation.

These may be departments involved in the provision of charitable activities or departments that support the organisation as a whole, for example, the finance or human resources departments.

The expenditure within each of these departments must be identified and apportioned between the main expenditure headings identified in the SORP if the charity is above the statutory audit threshold of £500,000 gross income for the year: charitable activities costs, costs of generating funds and governance costs (relative to ABC and apportionment status – see Chapter 5).

6.5
Interpreting a set of published financial statements

The following questions are a useful checklist to use when looking at a published set of financial statements.

1. Does the trustee report clearly show the charitable aims and (for auditable charities) the year's public benefit objectives of the charity?

2. Is the narrative on the year's charitable activities and achievements, together with the financial review, in the trustees' report supported by the charitable expenditure and financial position disclosures in the financial statements?

3. Does the trustees' report give an indication of planned future activities?

4. Are restricted funds properly identified and explained?

5. Are designated funds and the timescale for expending them explained? Do you consider them definite commitments?

6. Are costs of generating funds properly identified?

7. Are support costs properly identified and apportioned?

8. Are the trading subsidiary (if applicable) activities properly identified?

9. Do charitable expenditure headings properly describe the activity of the charity?

10. Are income sources adequately described and, where relevant, the link with related charitable activities made clear in the SoFA?

11. Do the financial statements clearly show how an income surplus or deficit for the year relates to the funds available as reserves for future activities in the context of the charity's year-end financial position?

12. Is there a reserves policy?

13. Are there any other issues?

Checklist

Answer the following questions before checking the answers in the text.

- What would an external analyst make of your financial statements? Would a potential funder give you money?
- Does your charity comply with the SORP's related regulations?
- Does your management team understand the financial statements? Offer to run a training session for them if they don't.
- How do you present and explain the financial statements to enable the chief executive to meet the trustees' need for comprehensive stewardship reporting properly linked with their in-year internal financial management reports and externally compliant with the regulator's requirements?
- What type of external scrutiny does an incorporated charity with an income of £255,000 require?
- List the material or significant matters an auditor must report to the Charity Commission.
- Where do support costs appear in the accounts?

Case study and exercise

Case study

(This is a fictitious example to illustrate the production of a SOFA.)

The Distressed Equine Animals in Disaster Relief Areas Trust was set up many years ago to rescue horses, donkeys and mules that were suffering from the effects of natural disasters.

For the last 20 years it had operated on a small but consistent scale, but in 2012, due to a highly emotive television programme that highlighted the plight of these animals following an earthquake in Elbonia, the charity has received greatly increased resources. During the 12 months to 31 December 2012 the following transactions occurred:

The charity operates from a building that was bequeathed to it many years ago. It was professionally revalued at £150,000 five years ago and the market value is now approximately £200,000. It is estimated to have a remaining useful life of 20 years. Since the revaluation, £6,000 p.a. depreciation has been charged and the written-down value as at 1 January 2012 was £120,000.

Transaction	£	Notes
Cash donations received	375,000	Elbonia fund £250,000 Unspecified £125,000
Gift Aid	35,000	Received Gift Aid to date £30,000 Awaiting receipt of £5,000 re Elbonia Fund
Investment income from bank deposit account	15,000	Elbonia Fund £10,000 interest Other £5,000
Gift of mobile veterinary clinic (for Elbonia)	30,000	Expected life 3 years; straight line depreciation is used
Horse blankets (for Elbonia)	8,000	£6,000 worth of these had been used by the year-end
Veterinary expenses	115,000	Elbonia £50,000 Other £65,000
Costs of generating funds	50,000	Travel in Elbonia in connection with assisting television production £20,000 £15,000 relates to charity dinner to be held in February 2006
Miscellaneous head office expenses	50,000	Apportioned 60% Elbonia; 40% other

The charity's furniture and fittings are fully written off, but during the year they have acquired six new motor vehicles – three pick-up trucks for use in Elbonia at £20,000 each and three second-hand Range Rovers for general use at £28,000 each. These are all to be depreciated over four years, charging a full year in the year of acquisition.

Accrued audit costs for the year were £5,000. No other costs have been incurred in respect of governance expenditure.

For the purposes of this example, the only items on the balance sheet as at 1 January 2012 were:

Buildings	£120,000
Cash	£80,000
Total	£200,000
Financed by:	
General funds	£200,000

Exercise: Test your knowledge of SORP

Circle the correct answers.

1. Under the Charities Act 2011, within what length of time after year-end must charities file their financial statements with the Charity Commission?

a) 9 months

b) 10 months

c) 6 months

d) None of the above

2. What will an incorporated charity with income of £7,000,000 and assets of £5m require?

a) An audit under the Companies Act

b) An audit under the Charities Act

c) An independent examiners' report

d) No external examination or scrutiny report

3. In respect of investment property owned by an unincorporated charity, which statement is true?

a) It must be revalued professionally every year

b) It must be revalued professionally every five years

c) It must be revalued at least every five years

d) It must be revalued every year

e) None of the above

4. Under the Charities Act 2011, which is the earliest year, an unincorporated charity does not require a full audit?

Year	Income £	Gross assets £
1	490,000	3.5m
2	980,000	4.2m
3	640,000	3.8m
4	690,000	2.9m
5	290,000	2.4m
6	240,000	1.8m
7	190,000	2.3m

a) Year 2

b) Year 4

c) Year 5

d) None of the above

5. Your charity has received a permanent endowment of £100,000. Half the money was invested in shares, which were worth £100,000 at the year-end and the other half was left in the bank. Income received from the shares amounted to £5,000 and gross bank interest received was £5,000. How much was the endowment fund balance at the year-end?

a) £90,000

b) £150,000

c) £155,000

d) £160,000

Figure 6.5 Distressed Equine Animals in Disaster Relief Areas Trust balance sheet

Balance sheet as at 31 December 2012	2012 £000	2012 £000
Tangible fixed assets		
Building		114
Motor vehicles		108
Mobile clinic		20
		242
Current assets		
Debtors (Gift Aid)	5	
Debtors	15	
Cash at bank and in hand	141	
	161	
Current liabilities	5	
Net current assets		156
Total assets less current liabilities		398
Funds		
Restricted funds	170	
General funds	228	
		398

Workings:

Cash Summary	£	Payments	£
Receipts			
Opening balance	80	Vet expense	115
Donations	375	Fundraising	50
Interest	15	HO	50
Gift Aid	30	Motor vehicles	144
		Closing balance	141
	500		500

6. A charity is given a cottage as part of a legacy – probate value £100,000. The legacy was intended by the legatee to provide an income for the charity. The charity decides to use it as a holiday home and receives rent of £30,000. The market value of the cottage was £130,000 at the year-end, based on its rental yield, but its insurance value was £125,000. The cottage has a useful life of 10 years. At what value would it be included in the financial statements at the year-end?

a) £90,000

b) £100,000

c) £125,000

d) £130,000

7. A charity has two funds: a general fund of £10,000, and a restricted fund of £40,000. The charity invested the funds in the same deposit account and earned interest of £5,000. The trustees decided to set up a designated fund with £5,000 of the unrestricted fund. What would be the total of the unrestricted funds held at the end of the period?

a) £5,500

b) £10,000

c) £11,000

d) £15,000

8. If the amount is substantial, how should help received by a charity from volunteers be disclosed in the financial statements?

a) No disclosure necessary

b) Included in the SoFA in the same way as gifts in kind

c) Included in the SoFA if the charity would otherwise have paid staff for the same work

d) Not included in the financial statements but referred to in the notes or trustees report

Answers

1. b

2. a

3. c

4. c

5. b

6. d

7. c

8. d

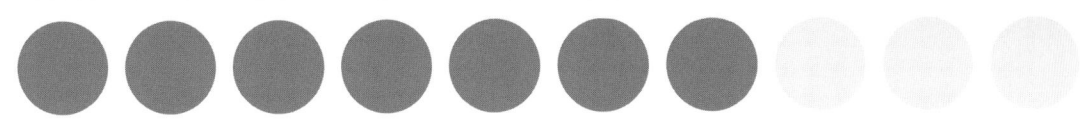

Key issues

7.1
Introduction

This chapter introduces and explores some key financial and management issues in the voluntary sector.

The voluntary sector has seen a number of external influences and pressures that seem far removed from the traditional financial accounting function. For example, registered charities are required to undertake a risk assessment, and there have been greater calls for transparency and reporting on how well the charity has performed in meeting its objectives.

In addition, a voluntary organisation is now expected to manage its finances not just from an accounting good stewardship perspective, but also to be proactive in seeking value for money and best value from its financial activities.

The finance officer now has an integral role in the organisation and is an important member of the management team, as well as a principal adviser on finance matters to the management committee.

Finance and financial objectives, as previously discussed, cannot be viewed in isolation from the objects of the organisation. A commercial organisation normally uses financial objectives to achieve clear financial aims – normally maximisation of shareholder value or annual profits – but a voluntary organisation needs to have effective management to achieve its non-financial aims, whether these are spiritual, as in a religious foundation, or material, as in the relief of poverty.

7.2
Risk management

To comply with the charity Statement of Recommended Practice (SORP) all charities must include in their trustees' annual report a statement on risk. This needs to disclose the major risks to which the charity is exposed as identified by the trustees, the review of those risks and the systems established to mitigate them.

This requirement does not simply refer to insuring against traditional risks such as fire and flood. It goes beyond ensuring that the charity has adequate insurance for financial risk or internal control but concerns the wider concepts of business risk and, particularly relevant to charities, 'reputation risk'. These require more careful consideration; insurance is only part of the solution.

The charity sector does not exist in a vacuum and reflects what is happening in the wider environment. The Charity Commission updated its *Guidance CC26 Charities and Risk Management* in June 2010 following the results of their Economic Survey of Charities, which revealed that 47 per cent of charities thought that the sector would feel the effects of the recession later than the private and public sectors and take longer to recover. The guidance was revised to reflect new developments and the challenging economic climate. In a period of economic uncertainty (as we have witnessed since the global financial crisis of 2007/08) the Commission identified that the major financial risks for a charity are likely to be:

• termination of funding from other bodies
• the future of contracts
• fundraising from the general public
• fluctuations in investments
• an unforeseen rise in demand for their services.

Many charities are responding to the downturn by trying to identify and then focus on their highest priority areas, reviewing the strategic options available to them and weighing up their relative risk versus reward.

This section will explore issues that will help trustees and staff ensure they can effectively identify and manage risk by:

• clarifying what is meant by risk in the context of charities
• understanding the legal requirements
• developing a risk management process.

What is risk?

CC26 defines risk as, 'the uncertainty surrounding events and their outcomes that may have a significant impact, either enhancing or inhibiting any area of a charity's operations...An essential question for charities when considering risk is whether or not they can continue to meet the needs of beneficiaries now and in the future'.

This definition means that risk is not confined to the financial affairs of the organisation, but covers all areas of the charity's operations. It highlights that risk management is not just about risk aversion but can help the charity make the most of opportunities and develop them with the confidence that any risks will be managed.

CC26 provides a comprehensive list of potential risks in Annex 2, analysed under the following categories.

• **Governance risks:** affecting the capability of the board to make effective strategic decisions.
• **Operational risks:** affecting the day-to-day operational capability of the charity. These are usually internal risks and predictable.
• **Financial risks:** most risks will ultimately have a financial impact.
• **Environmental and external risks:** these can often be less easy for the charity to control.
• **Regulatory compliance risks.**

Risk can be seen as having three components.

1. Hazard: risk of bad things happening.

2. Uncertain outcomes: not meeting expectations.

3. Opportunity: exploiting the upside (ie the possibilities of increasing investment returns with the Trustee Act 2000 which gives wider powers of investment but also a statutory duty of care (see information on investments in section 7.5)).

Risks are either 'external' or 'internal' to the organisation. An example of external risk would be changes in economic conditions or public perceptions. An 'internal' risk could be a failure in operational or financial controls, such as fraud. Risk affects all parts of the organisation.

Risk management does not have to be seen as a threatening or negative activity but can be seen as an opportunity, for example, a change of direction that improves service delivery but that involves working with a new partner or a project undertaken in an area of conflict overseas. This example illustrates how the perception of risk can be changed from a defensive isolation activity to proactive risk management. This involves identifying risks and having a strategy to deal with them, which requires a decision to do one or more of the following.

- Minimise the impact of risk, for example, with contingency planning.
- Accept the risk (after controls have been put in place to manage some risk, leaving a residual risk that you are prepared to accept).
- Transfer the risk (insurance or outsourcing).
- Avoid the risk (by avoiding the activity if you judge the risk to be too high).

Underpinning proactive risk management is a sound internal control system, which:

- can respond to significant risks
- is embedded in day-to-day processes
- is capable of responding to external and internal changes
- can immediately report major control weaknesses.

An *organisation-wide risk policy* will provide a trustee board with reports on:

- identification, evaluation and management of key risks
- assessment of effectiveness of related controls
- actions to remedy weaknesses, including considering costs and benefits
- the adequacy of monitoring of internal control system
- the process supporting reporting.

Having such information will not only meet the legal requirements but also will give comfort to the trustees that their charity is well run.

Meeting the legal requirement

Charity trustees are responsible for the management and control of the charity and therefore their involvement in the key aspects on the risk management process is essential, particularly in setting the parameters of the process and reviewing and considering the results. Charities that are required by law to have their accounts audited must make a risk management statement in their trustees' annual report. The statutory audit thresholds effective from 1 April 2009 are:

- an income of £500,000 or more, or
- a gross income exceeding £250,000 with gross assets held exceeding £3.26m.

As a minimum, the statement in the trustees' report could say: 'The trustees have assessed the major risks to which the charity is exposed, and are satisfied that systems are in place to manage those risks.'

If issuing such a statement, the trustees, should have supporting internal documentation that they have undertaken a risk assessment, and would be advised to have this independently confirmed. The form and content of the statement is likely to reflect the size and complexity of an individual charity's activities and structure. A narrative style that addresses the key aspects of the requirements is acceptable. This means:

- an acknowledgment of the trustees' responsibilities
- an overview of the risk identification process
- an indication that major risks identified have been reviewed or assessed
- confirmation that control systems have been established to manage those risks.

Larger charities, or those with more complex activities, are likely to include a more detailed approach to reporting and these are outlined in detail within CC26 as follows:

- a description of the major risks faced
- the links between the identification of major risk and the operational and strategic objectives of the charity
- procedures that extend beyond financial risk to encompass operational, compliance and other categories of identifiable risk
- the link between risk assessment processes and monitoring that are embedded in management and operational processes
- a description of the risk assessment processes and monitoring that are embedded in management and operational processes
- trustees' review of the principal results of risk identification processes and how they are evaluated and monitored.

Developing a risk management model

CC26 sets out a model for risk management and covers the typical stages in the process, which include:

- establishing a risk policy
- identifying risks
- assessing risks
- evaluating what action needs to be taken on risks
- periodic monitoring and assessment

Successful risk management frameworks have been found to be:

- aligned to the organisation's mission
- supported by the trustees, management, staff and volunteers
- communicated effectively throughout the charity
- adaptable to environmental change
- simple but structured.

Charitable organisations need to be clear about their key objectives and the risks associated with achieving them. For example, objectives might be:

- to grow public donations by 10 per cent per annum
- to meet the needs of our client group by 80 per cent within the next two years
- to comply with legislation
- to safeguard stakeholder interests.

Once identified, two questions need to be answered:

1. What risks would prevent us from meeting these objectives?

2. What controls could we adopt to minimise risks to an acceptable level?

Inevitably, this leads to balancing the charity objectives against the control objectives. Risk is inherent in all activity; it cannot be eliminated, but it can be mitigated. For example, the following are key risks for charities.

- Loss of a major funder.
- Regulatory breaches.
- Adverse public relations – reputational risk.
- Industrial action.
- Increased competitive activity for funds.
- Changes in economic conditions.

All of the risks can be managed if appropriate controls are in place. NCVO has been exploring risks for charitable organisations and what they can do to mitigate them. It has formulated a 10-point plan based around the concepts of risk assessment, risk analysis and risk management, which voluntary organisations can follow.

Risk assessment:

1. Develop/review your strategy.

2. Highlight the potential risks.

3. Research the evidence.

Risk analysis:

4. Categorise the risk.

5. Score and prioritise the risks.

Risk management:

6. Devise a risk management strategy.

7. Agree a plan of action.

8. Communicate about risk.

9. Monitor and evaluate.

10. Review policies and procedures.

Risk management for charities is dependent on good internal control systems. The whole organisation must be involved in the process, and that process has to be led from the top of the organisation. The NCVO 10-point plan can be used as the basis for establishing a risk management process. Some accountants can give guidance in this area, for example, Kingston Smith has issued a toolkit for effective risk management providing practical support for charities in improving the way they manage risk. It sets out five key benchmarks and a checklist of questions together with example templates at (available at www.kingstonsmith.co.uk/charities). Whether or not this is done will depend in part on the size and resources of the voluntary organisation. If an organisation has an existing internal audit function, it should take the lead, and in smaller organisations a designated senior member of staff should take the lead. Annex 1 in CC26 guidance provides a risk register template with examples. Figure 7.1 has been created by using this template.

Risk register

Figure 7.1

Area/activity:

Risks identified: (date/source)

Likelihood of occurrence: (score)

Severity of impact: (score)

Overall or 'gross' risk:

Control procedure:

Retained or 'net' risk:

Monitoring process:

Reported to trustees' meeting on [date] by:

Acknowledgement: Kingston Smith

Implementing risk management: a charity case study

The charity Norwood (previously Norwood Ravenswood) established a working party chaired by a trustee, which comprised staff from all levels and aspects of the organisation. An external facilitator supported the working party. Over a period of three months the working party met and first established what they believed were the major risk issues facing the organisation. These were then scored on a matrix scale of 1–5, where 1 meant little risk, and 5 meant very high risk, to the extent that the organisation could close down (the impact). The other side of the scale was based on probability of the event happening, ranging from 1, little likelihood, to 5, very likely to happen.

This could be represented as a grid on which the risks and their likelihood of happening are plotted and highlighted.

The staff on the working party then took back the identified risks to their colleagues and asked them to review them, and either agree or score them differently.

The next meeting of the working party reviewed the staff feedback and plotted these on to a 'risk register' supplied by the charity's external auditors, which identified what safeguards were in place and how effective these were.

The safeguards were taken back again to the staff for evaluation and feedback. The third meeting of the working party fed back these observations. The risk register was completed, which also highlighted the major issues the charity had to address. The trustee who chaired the working party was able to present the register to his fellow trustees and brief them. The trustees were then able to both agree a programme of work and complete a risk statement in their report to the Charity Commission.

●●●●●●●○○○

7.3
Banking and borrowing

This section looks at how to get the best out of financial resources and maximise value in banking and investment, and how to borrow and invest effectively.

All voluntary organisations require the services of banks to hold funds and to pay expenses. Some voluntary organisations occasionally have excess short-term funds that if left in a current account will lose money due to inflation. Some charities are fortunate in having funds that can be invested for the long term, out of which they pay grants to support their work. At the other extreme, some voluntary organisations need to borrow funds to support their work. This section looks at how to maximise your relationship with financial institutions to benefit the organisation, whether you are in surplus or need to borrow. Appendix B lists some of the main types of investments.

Getting the best out of your bank

The banking industry has been under immense scrutiny over the past five years, following the global financial crisis. With that change has come increased regulation and banks that are keen to rebuild the public's trust and confidence to develop their business by ensuring their products and services meet the needs and requirements of its target audience. The Charity Commission actively encourages charities to review their banking service in line with all other suppliers, including auditors etc, every three to five years as best practice, but how many do?

- Have you ever reviewed your banking arrangements?
- When was the last time you did this?
- Have you reviewed the charity banking marketplace?
- Have you considered the competition that exists?

Once you have concluded that you should undertake a review, the next step is to decide which banks to put on the shortlist to tender. Here are five points to consider while making this decision.

1. **Known abilities** – does the bank have a specialist charities team and understand your organisation and the sector

2. **A recommendation** – from colleagues, members, affiliates, trustees, national and local umbrella support agencies can be a strong influence.

3. **Ethics are of increasing importance** – are the banks taking their corporate social responsibility seriously? What are their investment policies? Who do they lend money to? Are they solely profit motivated?

4. **Suitability** – does the choice suit the organisation's need? For example, an overseas aid charity undertaking regular foreign transactions will need to be confident that their bank has sufficient global coverage and expertise to ensure funds reach their destination on a timely basis and at reasonable cost.

5. **Press and satisfaction surveys** – there are a number of charity publications that regularly review the banks and their services (for example, *Charity Finance* magazine, Annual Banking Survey).

6. **Financial strength** – review the bank's credit rating and Core Tier One Capital (ratio of customer assets to customer liabilities – an indicator of how well funded the bank's balance sheet is).

The invitation to tender

A formal tender document should be prepared to provide the tendering banks with the following information:

- an outline brief of your organisation
- the organisation's legal status
- any known borrowing requirements – whether cash flow or capital
- current banking terms
- breakdown of activity – number of transactions by cheque, cash, BACS, internet payment, salaries etc
- the past two years' audited reports and accounts
- the organisation's ethical statement/policy
- forecast monthly cash budgets for at least the next two years
- forecast income statements and balance sheets for the next two years.

The purpose of providing the transaction and balance information is that it tells the banks about the organisation and gives them the opportunity to evaluate whether they can make a reasonable profit on your business. If they can, they will wish to tender; if they cannot, then it is a wasted experience for both of you. Transactions cost banks money; some are more expensive than others. The banks will calculate how much it will cost them to run your account. They will also estimate the organisation's average credit balances, as this gives them an opportunity to earn interest on funds deposited. This will then be taken away from the costs and they will determine the figure (within their own profit recovery margins) that they will charge for running the account. This is the 'hard' financial information for decision making based on cost. However, the organisation should also consider other factors (such as ethical policies) before making a decision.

When tendering, you should create an achievable timetable. You should also make sure that the selection process is to the satisfaction of the board.

The tender process

Here are 10 useful points to remember when bank tendering.

1. When did you last review, if ever?
2. Which banks did you ask?
3. Are they known in the sector?
4. Trustees – whom do they know?

At this point you can decide which banks to invite to tender.

5. Create the timetable.
6. Draw up the tender document.
7. Invite visits from a 'long list' to enable the banks to understand your charity; do not ask them to quote 'cold'.

At this point you will have enough information to create a 'short list'.

8. Undertake the interviews.
9. Plan the transfer over a couple of months.
10. Develop the bank/customer relationship.

Borrowing

Traditional methods of borrowing for charities include term loans (either fixed or variable interest rates in nature), overdrafts and mortgages. There are two less traditional types of borrowing: secured lending against an investment portfolio or taking out long term debt in the form of a social impact bond. Social investment is explained in more detail in Chapter 10.

Charities are becoming more entrepreneurial in identifying and taking opportunities, largely due to external funding pressures. As a consequence, earned income now represents over half of overall total income.

However, new initiatives may require additional funding, which may not be available through the traditional routes of fundraising and philanthropy or may be beyond the current capacity of a charity's reserve funds. With this in mind, borrowing could be seen as an opportunity to help charities fulfil their mission.

With current underlying interest rates at historic lows, it may be an ideal opportunity for charities to consider taking out some form of borrowing. Before considering borrowing, trustees should ask the following questions.

1. Does their constitution and governing document allow them to borrow? If not, they would need to seek permission from the Charity Commission. If the charity is not constituted as a company limited by guarantee, the trustees could be personally liable for ensuring that any loans are repaid. If unsure, the trustees should seek professional advice.

2. What is the financing need? Is the borrowing to:

- undertake charitable purposes
- fund new developments
- fund core costs
- fund working capital
- fund capital expenditure
- do something now rather than later
- preserve investments
- maintain a reserves policy
- bridge the receipt of grant funding?

3. Have the trustees considered other options for raising the money that the charity needs?

4. Does the charity have the ability to repay the loan and interest charges?

5. Do the trustees want to seek professional advice in terms of reviewing the loan documents and checking if the terms of the loan are reasonable?

Before approaching a bank for finance, the organisation should work up a finance proposal. This should set out the aims of the financing and, in particular:

- what is to be achieved
- at what cost
- with what return
- in what timescale.

It should demonstrate the tangible and intangible benefits, and address the following points.

1. Investment – is the amount identified sufficient?

2. Can repayment be made?

3. The proposal should be supported by financial forecasts of:

a) income and expenditure

b) cash flow

c) balance sheet (including effect on reserves).

These should be for a minimum of two years ahead.

Once this information is prepared, a formal proposal can be made to a bank. The proposal should be accompanied by a business plan covering:

1. executive summary

2. background

3. management/governance

4. services

5. the market (competition)

6. method of operation

7. public relations and fundraising

8. implementation/timetable

9. finance requirement and funding

10. future prospects.

There are circumstances where borrowing would be inappropriate, especially where there is a risk that the charity would not be able to repay the debt or if the loan would be used for activities that deviate from the charity's mission statement or objectives. Borrowing to pay bills or fund deficits without means of generating sufficient income or reducing costs to cover the lending should also raise concern for trustees.

NCVO's *UK Civil Society Almanac 2012* estimates that the voluntary sector holds loans worth approximately £3.5bn as at 2009/10 which is just 3 per cent of the sector's net asset value. This appears to indicate that trustees may be unwilling or unaware of the borrowing opportunities available.

Barriers to entry into borrowing for charities are internal and cultural, rather than an overall unwillingness of banks to lend to the sector. Importantly, trustees are concerned about personal liability and are therefore less likely to take on debt. In this case, they should be encouraged to take legal advice regarding the governing structure of the charity, rather than dismissing the possibility of borrowing altogether.

Trustees may have a general aversion to borrowing following the global financial crisis and the amplified losses made due to leverage. However, with increased gearing comes increased risk, as well as increased profitability. Charities need to weigh up the potential for undertaking income and surplus generating projects on borrowed money against the risk of insolvency should the expected cash flows not result.

Although there is still a lack of evidence of an increase in borrowing in the sector, trustees appear to at least be thinking about this as an option. For example, the Charity Finance Banking Survey May 2013 indicated that certain institutions have noticed more of their clients exploring the option of loan finance and social impact bonds. This follows the publicity surrounding last year's Scope bond and the shift from grants to contracts and payment by results, leading to part of the fee being paid in arrears once the contract has been fulfilled. Some charities are exploring loan finance to bridge that gap and seeking finance to put together bids in the first place. Certain sub-sectors within the voluntary sector, such as independent schools, social housing and the care sector, also appear to be increasing their demand for loans.

●●●●●●●○○○

7.4
Cash strategies

Short-term funds – cash management options

'Cash' as an asset class is often neglected. For many charities, cash is a passive asset class and typically consists of simple bank deposits or something similar (such as fixed-term money market rates). In our view, this represents a sub-optimal use of cash. We believe cash should be viewed as an asset class in its own right, which should be actively managed whenever possible.

'Cash' on instant access represents a poor way to manage your cash and you are very unlikely to be making your assets work as hard for you as they could.

Your first step should be to identify, by means of a cash flow budget, the likely 'calls' (regular or one off) on your cash holdings over the next couple of years. Then you will be in a position to identify cash that needs to be kept on 'instant access' and cannot afford to be tied up for any period of time. The cash flow budget will also identify how much can be locked up for certain periods of time, for example, one month, three months, six months, one year, two years etc. By locking cash up in, for example, term deposits, you would be aiming to achieve a higher return over the period of the deposit than by keeping it on instant access.

In determining how to split the charity's cash holdings into the various 'liquidity pots', the main factors to bear in mind are:

- liquidity requirements (as identified above)
- potential returns
- the scale of investment to be made.

What should a charity do with cash that needs to be kept on 'instant access'?

Cash that has to be kept on instant access should be held in an account that will pay as high a level of interest as possible. However, you should be aware that banks or building societies with lower credit ratings sometimes pay higher interest rates. Credit rating is an important factor to consider when choosing an institution to deposit cash with. In the UK, the Financial Services Compensation Scheme only serves to compensate depositors in relation to the loss of £85,000, from 31 December 2010. Any amounts deposited above this amount will be lost if the institution fails.

The other issue to be aware of is the fact that the institutions offering the most attractive rates at one point in time tend not to be among the best performers a few months later. This can be overcome (at least in theory) by continually chasing the best rates and being prepared to open and close accounts on a regular basis. In practice, this requires an on-going level of due diligence by keeping the rates (and credit ratings) available in the market under regular review. In addition, with deposit takers becoming more strict with their account opening procedures (largely due to the tighter regulatory regime that governs them), this can become a fairly labour-intensive process.

One way around this is to deposit cash with institutions that are shown to provide consistently good rates. While these rates might not be the very best available in the marketplace at any one time, they tend not to be far below, and you do not have to go through the hassle of transferring cash from bank to bank on a regular basis.

An alternative option for larger cash deposits above £500,000 could be to utilise specialist treasury management services. An example of an organisation providing this service is Epoch Wealth Management. Epoch can carry out a review of a charity's existing cash position to assess exposure to bank risk and the returns being received. It can then provide recommendations to help improve returns, increase diversification and achieve the charity's liquidity requirements without a high administration burden (information is available at: www.epochwm.co.uk).

What are the risks associated with cash deposits?

In respect of cash deposits, the Financial Services Compensation Scheme provides limited protection in the unlikely event that a bank was to fail (as outlined previously). The key to ensuring the safety of cash deposits is the size and credit rating of the bank. Given the current historically low rates of interest, holding excess cash over the longer term, taking account of inflation, will result in negative real rates of return, so these levels should be monitored closely.

●●●●●●● ○○○

7.5
Investments

Longer term funds – entering the investment maze

The Trustee Act 2000 gave freedom of investment powers to trustees of all trusts, including trustees of charities. After many years of frustration of working within the 40-year-old scheme of the Trustee Investment Act 1961 of 'narrow', 'wider' and 'special' ranges of prescribed investments, or needing to seek special orders from the Charity Commission, trustees may now make any kind of investment that they could make if they were absolutely entitled to the assets of the trust. However, as the Act further states, before exercising any power of investment, a trustee must obtain and consider proper advice about the way in which, having regard to the standard investment criteria, the power should be exercised. Trustees, and those advising them, should read the guidance provided by the Charity Commission – *CC14 Investment of Charitable Funds.*

The investment of charitable trust funds is one of the most important, and also one of the most difficult, duties requested of trustees and the finance officer. This is especially so if an individual has taken on the role of trustee because of the skill they hold relating specifically to their charity, for example, a consultant physician on a medical trust, rather than any financial skills. Equally, most voluntary sector finance officers are unlikely to be appointed with investment training and experience, being more likely to come with an accountancy background. The trustees must be aware of the suitability of the investments currently held, or being considered, and be aware of the need to diversify their investment holdings. Clearly, for anyone unversed in financial matters, the need to seek advice is compelling and, under the Act, a duty.

Pooled versus segregated funds, or product versus service

Charities can choose between pooled funds or an individual portfolio service. One of the distinct advantages that the charity sector has over other investors is the existence of common investment funds, which enjoy the support of the Charity Commission. These special collective investment funds offer a number of clear benefits.

- They are well-diversified investment funds with clear objectives.
- There is a reasonably diverse choice of funds available.
- They are usually cheaper than unit trusts.

Common investment funds have set the marker for the rest of the charity investment sector. A segregated approach must either offer something unusual, or provide a better service at a similar cost. For smaller funds it is difficult to imagine how this can be done.

Segregated funds are usually tailored to individual client needs with individual holdings in cash, fixed interest securities and equities, both UK and overseas. The key factor in the comparison with common investment funds will be the minimum charge. On this basis, most charities that have funds worth less than £1m are probably better off using common investment funds, while most charities with funds over £10m may be better off using a segregated approach, especially if they require a bespoke asset allocation and specific ethical criteria to meet their investment objectives and this doesn't fit with that of any of the common investment funds available. Funds between these two extremes will have to look at their distinct needs and cost. There are over 55 common investment funds to choose from, ranging from equity (UK and overseas) to gilt fixed interest, mixed funds, property and hedge funds.

Choosing an investment manager – key factors

The selection of investment managers needs to be carried out professionally. Charities should go out to tender with the clear aim of matching the objectives of the trust to their investment policy (see Appendix A for suggested criteria). Having appointed a fund manager, it will be necessary to monitor his or her performance in meeting the fund's needs, by holding regular review meetings with the manager and choosing an appropriate performance benchmark to assess their performance.

Review procedure

The normal procedure for a segregated fund would be quarterly reports supplemented by meetings with trustees. Often these meetings are quarterly, although once a fund is established, the frequency may be reduced, however, meetings should be held at least once a year. Trustees are required to have an annual review of investment performance from a longer-term perspective, including consideration of the appropriateness of the benchmark or the agreed investment policy.

Charities investing in pooled funds may well find less frequent reports more appropriate. Most pooled fund managers produce six-monthly reports, which are usually sufficient for trustees to keep in touch with developments. Even so, a formal meeting of the trustees to review the investments annually is still sensible. Where poor performance is an issue, the trustees will probably ask for the manager's comments prior to this annual review.

Performance measurement and targets

Measuring performance of investments is complex, but various measuring methods are available.

- **Measurement techniques, which use quantitative tools and valuations.** However, charities are already a heterogeneous group with wide variation in investment policy and constraint. The use of comparisons to industry averages must, therefore, be treated with caution. It is unlikely that any single yardstick will provide an easy method of judging investment performance.
- **An independent performance measurement service for charities.** The strengths of this lie in the independent verification of returns and its analysis of the relative success in each asset category. Its weaknesses are the cost, which makes it inappropriate for funds of less than £1m and, more importantly, the fact that trustees may be tempted to assume its weighted average return represents a universally appropriate yardstick, which it does not.
- **Bespoke benchmarking set by the charity.** This involves the trustees defining their investment objectives. In particular, they need to set clear income targets, defining precisely the constraints (including ethical issues) that will apply, and providing some indication of the degree of risk that they are willing to incur. Limits can also be set as to how far the fund manager can deviate from the benchmark in response to shorter-term judgements of relative value. Once chosen, the benchmark needs to be regularly monitored.

Costs

The key driver of the recent changes in financial services regulation and specifically the introduction of the Retail Distribution Review in January 2013 has been the lack of transparency in fee charging. Charities should be aware of all the costs upon their funds, and should certainly consider the total costs when appointing new managers. The most common forms of charging are as follows.

- **Management fee:** a direct fee usually charged as a proportion of market value on a sliding scale. This charge is very clear, easily verifiable and usually what trustees think of when talking about costs.
- **Commissions on transactions:** a charge on each transaction based on a percentage of the market value of the deal, again usually on a sliding scale.
- **Pooled fund charges:** these are subject to their own charges, including initial charges, annual fees and sometimes commissions.
- **Bank interest deductions:** many firms derive revenue from the cash balances held by retaining a part of the interest rate charged. This is not always easy to identify, so it is sensible to compare cash rates earned with inter-bank rates at least annually.
- **Administrative charges (including charges for custodian services):** many firms include these services in their standard charges, but those that do not may charge a fixed fee, a value-based fee or a transaction charge.
- **Third-party charges:** most firms pass on third-party charges to clients.
- **Performance fees:** these gear the manager's charges to the success of the fund. The manager may, for example, earn 50 per cent more if the fund outperforms by 2 per cent or more, but 50 per cent less if it under performs by 2 per cent or more. While intuitively attractive, performance fees can be cumbersome to administrate and their use is not conclusively proven.

While not an exhaustive list, this does cover the main charges. The trend is towards fee structures where there is a single sliding scale that covers most (if not all) of the manager's costs. Thus, the lower the sum invested, the higher percentage that fee will represent.

A final word on investments – ethical issues

Ethical investment has been debated within the voluntary sector for many years. Socially responsible investment (SRI) is increasingly offered by fund managers. A number of fund managers have now signed up to the UN Principles for Responsible Investment. Charities, unlike individuals, are constrained by law, which in this area is complex. Trustees are expected to act in the best interest of the beneficiaries. There are, however, some fairly clear areas, for example, cancer charities would not invest in tobacco company shares.

In setting a practical ethical policy on exclusions, three points need to be addressed.

1. What activities should be avoided?

2. What constitutes a material involvement?

3. Where will the information be obtained?

1 Activities for exclusion

Defining the activities for exclusion is the first step, but this is not always straightforward. For example, consider the exclusion of alcohol-related investments. Should the exclusion apply to companies that manufacture alcoholic products, such as brewers, or should it also apply to distributors and retailers? Adopting such a strict definition would exclude, for example, all supermarkets. Trustees must come to an agreement as to precisely what activities to exclude and why these conflict with their charity's objectives. These decisions cannot be based solely on the trustees' own personal views. A number of charities are working collaboratively with corporations and therefore it is important to establish a joined-up approach – one part of the charity might be working with a trading subsidiary of a large conglomerate, however another part of the same conglomerate may, due to some of their activities, be excluded from that charity's investment portfolio.

2 Materiality

In principle, a company with any involvement in an excluded activity should be avoided. This poses a problem both in terms of the degree of exclusion and in obtaining information. In practice, therefore, some definition of materiality is normally applied. Such tests can include proportions of sales, profits or numbers of employees.

3 Obtaining information

The final issue is obtaining information. This is particularly problematic when a strict materiality test is used. For example, a fund manager will know when a company earns 50 per cent of its profits from alcohol, but may not know if the amount is only 0.5 per cent. Annual reports and accounts can be informative but accentuate the positive and bury the negative. The most effective screening service is provided by specialist ethical services, for example, the Ethical Investment Research Service (EIRIS).

Other practical issues that need to be considered are whether to use an ethical pooled fund or a segregated approach. Pooled funds tend to be expensive. Using a segregated approach requires the organisation to be very clear on the issues raised previously in this chapter. The other practical issue is long-term consequences, and these fall into two main areas:

1. monitoring performance

2. cost.

Monitoring performance

There is no conclusive evidence for or against ethical investment on long-term performance grounds. There is clear historical evidence that ethical restrictions can have short-term implications, with such constraints meaning that some opportunities have been lost. It is also possible for fund managers to shelter behind the ethical constraints when defending poor performance.

Cost

An ethical portfolio may cost more to manage than a conventional one, as an additional workload is involved in vetting ethical restrictions, either by the fund manager or through purchasing an independent screening service. However, for large funds, such costs will be a small additional amount.

Socially responsible investment (SRI)

A number of fund managers manage funds with SRI constraints. These can be in segregated or pooled funds with charities able, in some cases, to decide which additional exclusions they wish to see. Fund managers offer investments in organisations that they have screened against their own internal SRI criteria. Charities need to ensure that they are happy with the fund manager's method of assessing companies – some fund managers' methods may be more in line with the aims of the charity than others.

●●●●●●●○○○

7.6
Performance

Meeting the need of SORP 2005 and the Standard Information Return

The charity sector reflects what is happening in the wider environment. The addition of the term 'reporting' in SORP's title requires charities not only to demonstrate a greater transparency in their affairs, but also to ensure that the their trustees are managing their charity effectively.

Voluntary organisations have a variety of different stakeholders – some internal to the organisation, for example, management committee members, and others external, for example, funders. For charities having to comply with the Charities SORP, information about the achievements of the organisation is required, as well as factual data. The often under-resourced finance office may find servicing and providing information to these different stakeholders a problem. There are a number of possible reasons for this.

- The training and experience of the finance staff is usually in financial accounting not management accounting.
- The finance department is often a single- or two-person function, which focuses on 'getting the books right' and does not have the time in reality, or in priority, to produce information for various groups.
- The finance officer fails to see that different groups require different information and produces just one set of information, however more information is needed than this one-size-fits-all approach.

These problems can be resolved if the finance officer works on communicating effectively and adopting a customer focus function by:

- identifying who the stakeholders are, both internal and external
- establishing what the particular needs of those stakeholders are, for example, timing of reports – it is pointless producing a budget report two months after the end of the budget

- recognising that there is a 'hierarchy' and segmentation of information demand – departmental managers require budgetary control information only about their department, hence the importance of establishing a financial accounting system that reports on cost codes and budget centres, whilst more senior managers, notably the chief executive officer, are going to require an overview of the entire organisation.

As well as providing timely and relevant financial management information within the organisation, the finance department is also required to produce information for a variety of external stakeholders. The production of end of year accounts is not the final stage in the process; in some respects it is the beginning.

Voluntary organisations are now required to provide information about their performance, not just for public relations, but also for those registered as charities as a statutory requirement, both through the Charities SORP and the Standard Information Return. Action for Deaf People was in the vanguard of these developments when it produced an annual report that identified targeted activities and measurable performance targets to prove whether it had achieved them.

The role of the finance department in producing this information will be crucial, both in assisting the organisation to produce quantifiable data and being able to convert such data into meaningful, value-for-money analysis.

This will mean using benchmarking techniques, where actual performance can be compared against predetermined targets or budgets. Such processes will be measured over time and involve both internal and external (comparison with similar organisations) analysis.

Developing benchmarking means that the organisation has to understand what it is doing, and can lead to challenging questions of why a service is delivered in a certain way, as well as opportunities to improve.

SORP requirements

SORP 2005 and the Standard Information Return for registered charities are at the forefront of making charities explain not just their aims and objectives, but also the strategies and activities they are following to achieve them. If a charity does not have a strategy with measurable targets how can it know if it is achieving its objectives?

SORP brackets the information required in the trustee annual report as follows.

- **Administrative details:** which includes the name of trustees, the chief executive and other relevant persons and principal advisers, banks etc.
- **Structure, governance and management:** SORP 2000 introduced a requirement for a statement on risk, which we covered earlier in this chapter. This section has now been expanded to enable the reader to understand how the charity is constituted and its organisational structure. An important new addition is to explain how charity trustees are recruited and new ones inducted.
- **Objectives and activities:** this requires the charity to explain both what the aims and objectives are and what strategies it has in place to achieve the stated objectives. Significant activities during the year should also be reported, relating to the type of charity activities, for example, a grant-making charity detailing its grant-making policies.

- **Achievements and performance:** this links to objectives and achievements. What the charity has achieved during the year should be reported, as well as how it compared against the objectives that had been set. This section also asks for disclosure on fundraising or investment performance and for comment on factors within and outside its control that are relevant to the achievement of those objectives; this could include employees and users.
- **Financial review:** as well as describing the charity's principal financial management policies, this section should also include the reserves policy, principal funding sources and, if investments are held, whether any social, environmental or ethical considerations have been taken into account.
- **Plans for the future:** this section links back to the aims and achievements section, but is about the future and should set out key objectives and what plans exist to achieve them. Note that the future plans become the following year's report on what was achieved.

The Standard Information Return

Larger charities (£1m plus) currently have to complete an expanded Standard Information Return for the Charity Commission. Charities that have adopted the SORP reporting requirements should have no problems completing the information sought by the return which asks questions such as:

- What does your charity aim to do?
- Who are your beneficiaries?

It reflects SORP's focus on objectives, activities, outcomes and impact.

Appendix A:
Tendering for an investment manager –
a suggested questionnaire

1. Introduction.

2. The fund's investment objectives.

3. Details of the investment firm, which should include:

- the firm's ownership, financial strength and structure
- the size and number of funds under management, including an analysis by client type and growth in funds under management during the last three years
- charities for whom they act
- the number of staff involved in investment management, research and administration
- details of the investment managers who would manage funds, how many other funds they currently manage, their experience in investment management, length of service and other responsibilities
- details of who would be making investment decisions and dealing with the charity and whether these people would be available to report directly to the trustees
- indication of turnover of fund managers and administrators over the last three years.

4. Services available: this should indicate the range of fund management services the firm provides for charities, showing which services are offered to clients of different sizes and stating any minimum segregated portfolio size.

5. Investment process: this should provide a brief overview of the firm's investment philosophy and process for charitable funds including:

- investment philosophy and how investment strategy is drawn up
- internal decision-making process for stock selection
- definition of risk and what techniques are used to quantify it
- constraints placed on total investments at stock and stock levels, and checks made on adherence to client and house guidelines
- policy towards the use of pooled funds
- research capacity and methodology.

6. Performance: tables comparing the firm's charities returns for the last five years against a suitable index, for example:

- unconstrained discretionary portfolio against WM unconstrained Charity Index or the relevant ARC Charity Indices, which look at actual peer group performance on a risk basis
- charity fixed interest, UK equity and overseas equity total returns, comparing results with the FT All Gilts Index, FTSE All Share Index and the FTSE World Index (ex-UK) respectively.

7. Fees: this should ask for:

- a description of the charging structure identifying all fees, commissions, initial charges and other charges derived by the firm and on what basis fees are calculated
- a full pro-forma example of the fees they would expect to charge in a full year
- estimates of costs of transferring the present account.

8. Administration and reporting: this should seek to discover the custody arrangements, administration and reporting service provided and an outline of the administrative arrangements that they would supply:

- how regularly reports and valuations will be provided and what information they would contain (ask for an example)
- whether the service includes custodial facilities where appropriate, and if so on what basis of charging
- how, and with whom, is un-invested cash deposited, and on what basis this facility is charged for.

9. General: this should invite the firm to highlight any additional information they think adds value, for example, their knowledge of the charity sector.

10. Who will be coming to the presentation?

Appendix B:
Common types of investment

Deposit account with bank or building society

These may give immediate access or be on seven-day or longer notice periods.

- The rate of interest will usually increase as the amount invested and the period of notice increases.
- Be wary of depositing large sums with less well-known financial institutions.

Common deposit fund

This is a special deposit fund available only to charities in England and Wales. It uses a system of pooling cash deposits, so that the amount available for investment is increased and the return improved. The fund manager will invest these funds with several different banks or deposit-takers so that the risk is spread.

- Immediate access.
- Interest is paid gross.

Equities

These are shares in quoted companies.

- Dividends are usually paid twice yearly, with no guarantee of how much.
- Market value can go up as well as down.
- Risk can be diversified by investing in companies in different market sectors.

Bonds

These are fixed interest securities, such as government stocks (gilts), corporate bonds, debentures and preference shares issued by central and local government.

- The risk of losing the principal capital is negligible, hence the rate of return is low.
- Investment portfolios may well include gilts because they are a way of balancing the overall risk profile.

Unit trust

A pooled investment fund that invests in quoted shares.

- Allows the charity to enjoy the benefits of more diversification than it would otherwise be capable of, as the portfolio will comprise fixed interest and equities.
- Entry and exit charges, as well as annual management charges, are usually levied.

Common investment funds (CIFs)

Pooled funds are similar to unit trusts but have benefits for charities. CIFs have the same advantage of diversifying investments across different stocks and shares. They are approved by the Charity Commission and are themselves registered as charities.

Property

An investment suitable only for voluntary organisations with large investment portfolios and governing documents that give them the power to do so. They are long-term investments and cannot readily be sold should the organisation require quick access to resources.

- There are costs associated with managing and maintaining the property.
- Trustees are likely to need professional advice on the long-term growth and income prospects of property.

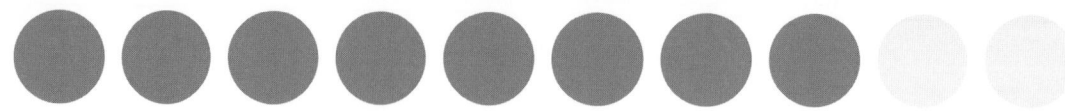

Taxation

8.1
Introduction

Tax law does not recognise voluntary organisations; it only recognises charities, which are defined by legislation introduced in the Finance Act 2010 for Gift Aid that took effect for all tax purposes from 6 April 2012, as follows.

- It must be established for charitable purposes only.
- Charitable purposes are the purposes given by Section 2 Charities Act 2011.
- The charity's governing document must restrict the charity to using all its income and assets for charitable purposes.
- It must be within the court jurisdiction of a country in the EU, Norway or Iceland.
- It must meet the registration requirements of that country, which for England and Wales are in Section 30 Charities Act 2011.
- It must be under general control and management by fit and proper persons and HMRC has the discretion as to whether it matters and to whom it applies the condition.

This chapter will only discuss charities. Responsibility for determining whether an organisation is charitable or not sits with the Charity Commission in England and Wales (in Scotland HMRC makes this decision). However, HMRC decides whether a charity meets the definition for tax purposes.

Each tax has its own concepts and philosophy, which should not be used in relation to a different tax. An example is the income tax concept of trading – this does not apply to VAT, which has its own concept of 'business activities'.

This chapter gives an overview of some of the complexities of tax for charities. It should not be used as a replacement for professional advice. All areas of taxation are extremely complex, and the financial cost of a bad decision could far outweigh any savings on professional fees. Many decisions and contracts cannot be restructured for tax purposes once set up, so it is essential to get competent advice to ensure that you get it right first time. Most problems occur for a charity when its circumstances change. Most large firms of accountants have specialist charity tax departments; you should consult them whenever you think there may be a problem. This guide can only indicate where the tax 'landmines' might lie.

The examples given throughout the chapter illustrate dilemmas that charities can face. They are there to assist with learning and decision making – they are not a technical guide for DIY tax.

8.2
Charities and direct taxes

Charities benefit from a very favourable regime in relation to income/ corporation tax, as long as they are careful about how they arrange their affairs. The rules for income tax and those for corporation tax are more or less identical; charitable trusts are subject to the income tax rules, *companies limited by guarantee* and *unincorporated associations* are subject to the corporation tax rules.

The supreme rule is that as long as the charity income in question is applicable for charitable purposes only as defined in Section 2 of the Charities Act 2011, and actually applied for charitable purposes, then much of it is exempt from income and corporation tax.

The following is a list of types that are exempt.

Rent or other receipts from rights over land

This applies whether the charity is located in the UK or elsewhere. There is another condition that states that the income must, 'arise in respect of rents or receipts from an estate, interest or right vested in any person for charitable purposes', so the property must be vested in the charity.

The legal definition of land in the Interpretation Act 1978 states, 'Land includes buildings and other structures, land covered with water, and any estate, interest, easement, servitude or right in or over land'. The type of income taxed will be principally rent, but will include feu duties, lease premiums and income from the letting of sporting rights.

Profits from the development of land are not covered by the exemption. On first sight, such profits may appear to be capital items and as such outside the scope of income tax. Prior to the introduction of capital gains tax, such profits would have escaped tax altogether if it were not for two strategies of the tax authorities. First, such profits could be regarded as 'an adventure in the nature of trade' and therefore taxable as trading profits; or second, they could be caught by a specific piece of anti-avoidance legislation and treated as taxable. The basic message is to take care when developing land, and where possible place any such profits in a trading subsidiary (see opposite).

Interest received by charities

This includes bank interest and loan stock interest, governmental and commercial, arising both in the UK and abroad. Where UK income tax has been deducted at source this is reclaimable from HMRC by the charity, though most types of interest received by charities will be paid gross.

Tax-effective donations

This applies to donations made under the Gift Aid scheme since 6 April 2000. A donation that is not made under the Gift Aid scheme is ignored by income tax. This might appear to be positive, but it is not. A donation that is ignored by income tax cannot be subject to a reclaim from HMRC, and cannot reduce higher rate tax for the donor. So, if the donation fulfils the requirements of the Gift Aid scheme (see Section 8.3), the charity can reclaim 25p in every pound (20/80 of the net amount received) from HMRC. The reason is that the tax system treats the donation as already having had basic rate tax, currently 20 per cent, deducted from it. Because this income is exempt from income tax for a charity, the charity can reclaim this tax deducted. The scheme is curious, but it means that tax relief is shared between the charity, which gets the basic rate tax, and the donor, who can deduct the donation from their higher rate tax bill. This is dealt with further in Section 8.3.

Company donations

Donations to charities by companies are treated in a different way, in that the charity does not make a tax reclaim on them. They therefore need to be kept separate in the charity's records. Donations received under the payroll giving scheme are also not eligible for a tax reclaim.

'The rules for income tax and those for corporation tax are more or less identical.'

Dividends

Formerly, charities could obtain a refund of the tax credit from HMRC, but this is no longer possible. The dividend income itself is still tax free for charities, whereas it would be taxable if received by an individual.

Profits from trading

The final major category of charity income that is eligible for income tax relief is profits from trading. There are pitfalls here, however, because not all trading is exempt. This is a summary of types of trading that are eligible for relief, which will be explained in more detail later.

- Primary purpose trading.
- Trading ancillary to primary purpose.
- Trading carried out by the beneficiaries of the charity.
- 'Small' trading as defined by statutory guidelines.
- Trading falling under extra-statutory concession C4.

Taxable trading

Trading carried out by a charity, which does not fall under one of these categories, will be taxable, and, if profits are made, the charity could end up paying hard-earned charity funds to HMRC. An example would be trading purely for fundraising purposes and which is on a material scale. Any trading like this should not be carried out in the charity itself but should be placed in a non-charitable trading subsidiary. The subsidiary then donates the profits under the Gift Aid scheme back to the charity, meaning that what were taxable profits are now exempt as a tax-effective donation. This rather arcane system ensures that no trading profits suffer corporation or income tax, but does need to be followed properly. The Charity Commission offers assistance in ensuring that the paperwork is correct, and the HMRC website offers guidance on tax-exempt trading.

Primary purpose trading

Primary purpose trading occurs when a charity has to trade to fulfil its reason for existence, as it is within its objects. Some examples are:

- fee-paying schools
- sale of tickets giving admission to shows staged by a charitable theatre group
- the provision of health care services or residential accommodation by a hospital or residential care charity in return for payment
- the sale of certain educational goods by an art gallery or museum.

Ancillary trading

Profits from trading that is ancillary to the primary purpose are also exempt from income tax. Examples are:

- sales of goods or services for the benefit of students or the provision of a crèche for the children of students by a school or college
- a college renting accommodation to students
- sales of food or drink restricted to visitors by an art gallery or museum or to a member of the audience by a theatre
- the sale of confectionery and flowers to patients and visitors by a hospital.

Care needs to be taken where some of this trading ceases to be ancillary and becomes trading in its own right. This could occur, for example, if the café in the art gallery becomes dominated by customers who do not visit the art gallery. In that case there would be a mixed trade and the legislation requires this to be treated as two separate trades – one exempt and one taxable. The profits of the taxable trade must be calculated using proper accounting principles (GAAP), which will usually mean making apportionments of expenses on a reasonable basis as well as identifying the taxable turnover.

Beneficiary trading

Beneficiary trading is also eligible for relief. Example of trades where the trading is carried out by beneficiaries of the charity are sales of goods manufactured by disabled people who are the beneficiaries of the charity, or a restaurant run by students as part of a catering course at a college.

'Small' trading

There is one other statutory exemption for charity trading and that is 'small' trading. The definitions are a little complex, but in effect state that profits are exempt if the total turnover from what would be taxable activities is less than £50,000, or 25 per cent of the charity's total gross income, whichever is lower. This is aimed at non-primary purpose, non-ancillary, activities that would otherwise have to be put in a trading subsidiary. They can remain in the charity as long as they continue to fulfil the requirements.

Fundraising events

There is an exemption for fundraising events carried out by charities that qualify for the VAT exemption for such activities. The tax authority's main concerns are that those attending are aware they are at a charity event and that the events do not compete with commercial activities. In theory, the exempt events are supposed to be 'one off', but in fact up to 15 such events at the same venue within one year can be exempt. Examples are barbecues, auctions, festivals, concerts, balls and discos. All income from such an event is covered, including sponsorship and sales of goods before, during and after the event.

Business sponsorship

There are some types of activity where particular care needs to be taken, such as business sponsorship. The key here is the nature of the relationship between the charity and the sponsor, and who is getting what out of the arrangement. On the one hand, a simple acknowledgment of assistance in a theatrical programme is treated as a simple donation, on the other hand, the selling of a list of donors to a commercial body is considered to be straight trading and should be put through a trading subsidiary to protect the profit from tax.

The sale of donated goods in charity shops is regarded as an indirect donation rather than trading and as such is not taxable.

Capital taxes and charities

When a charity disposes of an asset it owns, such as a parcel of shares, it will not be subject to capital gains tax (CGT), as long as the gain is applied for charitable purposes only. Inheritance tax is not payable by charitable bodies, but is payable only by individuals and certain non-charitable trusts.

Conclusion

Charities should not pay direct tax, as long as they arrange their affairs properly. The exemptions are always subject to the requirement that income and gains should not be spent on non-charitable objectives, otherwise they will be withdrawn and tax becomes payable. An example of a non-charitable objective would be a loan to a person who is not a beneficiary or employee that was not a proper investment acceptable to HMRC, carrying a commercial rate of interest and commercial repayment terms.

8.3
Donor relief

This section looks at the following donor reliefs in terms of the detailed requirements for each to be successful:

- Gift Aid
- corporate giving
- gifts in kind and loan of employees
- share gift relief
- payroll giving
- personal charitable trusts
- inheritance tax (IHT) relief.

Gift Aid

In the case of payments by individuals, Gift Aid measures apply to all gifts, which are qualifying donations made on or after 6 April 2000. Gift Aid was originally introduced by the Finance Act 1990. Changes came into place in 2010, so that gifts to charities in Norway, Iceland and EU states outside the UK may also qualify for relief and to prevent abuse.

The following donations will qualify.

- Donations by individuals who are resident in the UK.
- Donations by individuals who are Crown servants or members of the UK armed forces serving overseas.
- Donations by other non-resident individuals, provided they have income or capital gains charged to UK tax at least equal to the gross amount of the donation (ie the donation before deduction of basic rate income tax).

A donation must be a payment of a sum of money. A donation cannot be made in kind, by loan waiver or by debt/loan conversion. If a donor wishes to donate goods, the charity must be asked to sell the goods on the donor's behalf and then obtain confirmation from the donor that the proceeds are being donated to the charity. From April 2013, donors can sign a one-off Gift Aid declaration that covers donations for the relevant tax year up to a fixed level of sale proceeds.

The amount is £1,000 for charities that run their shops as trading subsidiaries, which accounts for the majority of charities that run shops, and £100 for charities that operate their shops directly.

The key document from the charity's point of view is the Gift Aid declaration. Before a charity can reclaim tax on donations by individuals, it must have received a Gift Aid declaration from the donor containing seven pieces of information.

1. A declaration that the donations are to be treated as Gift Aid donations.
2. The donor's name.
3. The donor's home address.
4. The charity's name.
5. A description of the donations to which the declaration relates.
6. A note explaining the requirement that the donor must pay an amount of income tax or capital gains tax equal to the tax deducted from his or her donations. (Declarations can be given orally, of which more overleaf, and these do not need to contain this item.)
7. The date of the declaration.

There is no requirement for a declaration to contain the donor's signature.

Oral declarations need to cover the same items as above. The donor has an entitlement to cancel the notice, and it is not effective unless/until the donor is sent notice.

Confirmation by the donor that the donations are to be Gift Aided can be in various forms. HMRC gives the following suggestions.

• I want my donations to be Gift Aid donations.
• Please reclaim tax on my donations.
• Tick here if you want us to reclaim tax on your donations.

Donors are able to give the charity a declaration in advance of their donation, at the time of their donation, or at any time after their donation (subject to the normal time limit within which tax can be reclaimed – normally around six years) to cover a single donation or any number of donations.

Charities need to ensure that they have a record-keeping system that is able to store indefinite records of the declarations. Once a declaration is in place the charity will need to ensure that the donor remains a taxpayer.

HMRC will periodically inspect charity Gift Aid claims.

An error rate is determined from the sample and extrapolated potentially to all claims made in the previous four years. From 12 March 2008 HMRC will allow charities to repair errors in a sample before extrapolation. HMRC has also introduced a 'de-minimis'/yellow card error regime as shown in Figure 8.1.

Benefits

In theory there should be no benefit provided in return for a donation. However, in practice this often happens, for example, reduced admission charges for donors who donate via Gift Aid. There are, therefore, rules about the maximum level of such benefits. If these limits are breached then the donation is no longer a tax-effective donation and becomes trading income. The limits are shown in figure 8.2.

These limits apply separately to each donation. The value of benefits is also accumulated for each donor to the same charity during the tax year and if the value exceeds £2,500 (£500 where the donations were made between 6 April 2007 and 5 April 2011) then cancellation of Gift Aid ensues for the total donations for that donor for that tax year.

Figure 8.1

Repaired error level	Amount at stake	Action at audit 1
Less than 4%	Less than £100	No recovery in year of audit or earlier years – no 'card'
Less than 4%	Less than £500	Recovery in year but not earlier years – no 'card'
Less than 4%	More than £500	Recovery in year but not earlier years – 'yellow card'
More than 4%	Less than £500	Recovery in year but not earlier years – 'yellow card'
More than 4%	More than £500	Recovery in year and earlier years

Figure 8.2

Amount of donation	Maximum value of benefits
£0–£100	25% of donation
£101–£1,000	£25

£1,001+ made before 6 April 2011: 5% of donation (up to a maximum of £500)
£1,001+ made on or after 6 April 2011: 5% of the donation (up to a maximum of £2,500)

'Corporate donations are not subject to tax deducted at source.'

This rule means that charities will need to keep a cumulative record of donations per donor. Benefits are valued on a market-value basis. From the charity's point of view, the mechanism for reclaiming tax, after receipt of the payment, is to complete the new reclaim form and send off to HMRC. Careful calculations are needed where large donations are made by the same person.

Higher-rate taxpayers can claim the difference between the basic and higher rate for themselves (currently 20 per cent to 25 per cent, the latter applies to those earning over £150,000 from 6 April 2013). Donors can now get higher-rate tax relief in a previous year, and tax repayments can be passed on directly by HMRC under Gift Aid.

Corporate giving

Since the Finance Act 2000, corporate donations are not subject to tax deducted at source, so the charity cannot reclaim any tax on them. The company treats the amount paid as a charge on income, deductible from profits chargeable to corporation tax. There are also special rules for companies owned by charities, allowing them to set off the donation in an earlier accounting period than the one in which the donation was made.

Under normal corporation tax rules, companies can only claim a deduction for a charge (such as a Gift Aid donation) in their tax computations in the accounting period in which the charge was paid. If a company wished to pay the charity an amount equal to its corporation tax profit, it would be obliged to determine that profit by the end of the accounting period. This would be difficult to do because the accounts of the company would not have been drawn up at that stage. Unlike other types of companies, charity-owned companies have nine months from the end of the accounting period in which to determine the amount they wish to give or are obliged to give under a profit shedding deed. They can then claim the deduction against the corporation tax profits of the accounting period to which the payment relates.

Gifts to charity of company equipment, trading stock or staff help

Businesses can get tax relief if it makes a gift of equipment to a charity or community amateur sports club (CASC). The business must have used the equipment in their normal business activities for it to qualify, and it must be considered plant and machinery for capital allowance purposes – this could include things like office furniture, computers and printers, vans and cars, tools and machinery.

If a business donates goods that they make or sells 'trading stock' to a charity or CASC, the business can claim a deduction against its taxable profits for the cost of the donated goods but does not have to deem any income to have been received in respect of the gift. Outright gifts of trading stock of medical supplies or medical equipment for humanitarian purposes are also treated as sales at nil value. In this instance there is no requirement that the recipient is a charity.

A business can second an employee to a charity (but not a CASC) and deduct any expenses of the secondment (including the employee's salary costs) in its tax computations. The same applies to any employees volunteering in work time.

Share gift relief

Individuals and companies can obtain tax relief on the value of certain qualifying shares and securities and land and buildings given to charity. Qualifying investments include those listed on a recognised stock exchange including AIM and overseas stock exchanges, units in an authorised unit trust and shares in an open-ended investment company. Charities must give written acceptance of gifts of property, in the form of a certificate, that they have acquired a qualifying interest (in case they do not want them). Individuals can claim a deduction of the gift against their income for income tax purposes and companies can claim a deduction from corporation tax.

It is good practice for the charity to keep records of the date of transfer of the shares to help the donor if necessary. If the charity offers any consideration to the donor for the gift of shares, the value of the consideration must be deducted from the amount of the relief. It is advisable for donors to establish the market value of the investment at the time it is given to the charity – finding it out later may involve time-consuming research.

Payroll giving

Another extension in flexibility of giving was introduced by the Finance Act 1986, whereby employees can have their donation deducted from their gross salary by their employer, who then passes the money to an agency charity, which acts as a clearing house. The funds are passed by the clearing house agency to the charities previously chosen by the employee. There is no need for reclaim of tax by the agency or the final destination charity, because the donation will be made gross out of the employee's income before tax. This saves the charity administration. The effective cost of the donation to the employee is 80 per cent of the committed amount for a basic rate taxpayer and 55 or 60 per cent for a higher-rate taxpayer (earnings for National Insurance purposes are not reduced by payroll giving).

No long-term commitment is necessary by the employee; only the signature of a simple deduction agreement is required. As the scheme is bolted on to PAYE, only employees whose employers have agreed to offer a scheme will be able to take advantage of payroll giving. Donors cannot receive benefits under the scheme.

The main agency charity acting as a clearing house is the Charities Aid Foundation. The HMRC lists a number of organisations that are approved and monitored by them for the purposes of payroll giving in the workplace.

Personal charitable trusts

For a personal charitable trust, a donor sets up his or her own grant-making charitable trust. The trust deed can be worded so that grants can be made for the full range of charitable purposes. This would enable the trust to make grants to recognised charities and to non-charitable bodies where the fund will be used for a charitable purpose.

The trust will need to be registered with the Charity Commission, and can be funded by gifts of capital, such as legacies, or payments under Gift Aid. The trust will reclaim tax on such payments and hold them for gross distributions for charitable purposes.

Control of the trust can be secured by the donor being a trustee and retaining the power to appoint new trustees, or it can be written into the trust deed that the trustees shall distribute the money in accordance with the wishes of the settlor. Care needs to be taken with the wording. It should be made clear that the property in the trust is no longer the settlor's; it is now held for charitable purposes, and money can only be distributed for charitable purposes, not private purposes.

The main advantages of such a trust for the donor include the following.

• The donor can support a range of charities without having to enter into a long-term commitment to them.
• The donor can respond to emergency or disaster appeals promptly and with funds that have already received tax relief.
• Payments can be made to individuals and bodies not registered as charities, thus increasing flexibility of charitable giving, as long as the money is spent solely on a charitable object.

'VAT is not a tax on profits; it is essentially a tax on transactions.'

The downside of the trust is the cost of establishing it in terms of legal fees, and then on-going administrative overheads, though both of these need not be excessive.

The attraction of such trusts to wealthy individuals, and to companies, is obvious. It should be noted that these trusts may accumulate funds, as long as it is in their trust deed, to build up a capital fund, the income from which will be used for charitable purposes, or for a specific future capital charitable legacy, such as the purchase of a building to be used by a charity.

Inheritance tax relief

If an individual's estate is worth over £325,000 (the nil rate band) when they die, inheritance tax may be due. From 6 April 2012, if an individual leaves 10 per cent of their estate to charity then the tax due may be paid at a reduced rate of 36 per cent instead of 40 per cent. The 10 per cent is calculated on the taxable estate after deducting the nil rate band, but after adding back the gift to charity.

Conclusion

The UK now has a very generous tax regime in relation to charitable donations. It is up to the sector to take advantage of this, by producing attractive tax-effective donation products in the way that the USA non-profit sector has.

8.4
Charities and VAT

Value-added tax (VAT)

VAT is not a tax on profits; it is essentially a tax on transactions, which is ultimately borne by the final consumer, at least in theory. The actual distribution of the tax burden differs from this where there are anomalies in the types of supply organisations make, as we shall see with charities, and this can mean that the effective incidence of the tax stops short of the final consumer.

VAT is a tax which is levied on turnover (as defined in the VAT legislation), and calculated on the value, actual or deemed, of the supply of goods and services known as 'taxable supplies', which are supplied by the registered taxpayer. Taxable supplies are supplies of all types of goods and services other than those that fall within the exemption list. These supplies have to be made 'in the course or furtherance of business'. This is not really defined in VAT legislation, but the intention is to distinguish between the activities of businesses, which are subject to VAT, and the private activities of individuals, which are not subject to VAT. Case law suggests that 'business' implies a certain (but possibly limited) degree of commercial intent and that the following factors *may* indicate that an activity is non-business.

- The nature of the activity is clearly charitable or social.
- Fees are set to be as low as possible to maximise affordability for charitable or social reasons.
- The activity possesses important features that would be very unusual in a 'commercial' environment.

It is not just a matter of knowing whether an activity is regarded as business, but also whether its outputs should be standard rated (20 per cent at the time of writing), reduced rated (5 per cent at the time of writing), zero rated or exempt. There may well be an advantage for a charity if it has an activity which is taxable because some, at least, of the charity's input VAT will be recovered.

The variety of types of income received is growing with the development of increasingly ingenious fundraising schemes, and with more charities embracing trading opportunities. Another important development contributing to this variety is the advance of so-called 'contract culture'. The extension of competitive tendering of services previously run by local authorities (for instance) has created a market within which charities can, and do, compete for contracts, for example, in the provision of care. The consideration for the provision of such services may be business and exempt or taxable. By contrast, a grant that is made to a charity without the requirement of service provision is outside the scope of VAT as it is not a consideration for a supply to a customer.

VAT is blind to whether an activity is for charitable purposes – unlike direct taxation as discussed above. Estimates vary on the cost to the sector as being between £400m and £1bn. VAT is charged on taxable supplies of goods and services made by a taxable person. The term 'person' includes individuals, partnerships, trusts, companies and charities. If a person is making taxable supplies, then the value of these supplies is called the taxable turnover. If a person's taxable turnover exceeds certain limits, known as the registration threshold (for the current threshold check on HMRC's website), then they are a taxable person and should be registered for VAT.

'If in any doubt take professional advice.'

For charities, a good rule to follow in defining whether activities fall within VAT or not, is to assume business activities as falling within the scope of VAT and non-business activities as falling outside its scope. However, if in any doubt take professional advice. A taxable supply is a supply of goods and services other than an exempt supply. A taxable supply is either standard rated (currently 20 per cent), zero rated (0 per cent) or reduced rated (currently 5 per cent). In addition, exempt supplies (which are not taxable) do not allow for any recovery of VAT on related costs. The difference between zero rated and exempt supplies is that VAT on costs incurred in making zero rated supplies can be reclaimed.

Figure 8.3 illustrates the differences between standard rated, zero rated and exempt supplies.

Charitable organisations may make supplies that are zero rated – these include hard copy books, periodicals and other publications, certain aids designed for use by people who have disabilities, the sales of donated goods and distribution of goods overseas.

Figure 8.4 will help you determine which activities are classified as 'business', and whether they are standard-rated (SR), zero-rated (ZR), exempt (EX) or outside the scope of VAT (OS). Some of its content is from *VAT Leaflet 701 Charities* and aims to provide a summary. It starts with general activities and then delves into more specific aspects of charities, where the VAT treatment of income may be less obvious.

This list is not exhaustive but includes the most important aspects. Many charities will have a mixture of outputs in all three categories (SR, ZR and EX). VAT recognises taxable persons (ie the legal entity), not taxable activities, which means that all the activities of that person are taken together for the purposes of registration.

Reliefs

The following reliefs apply for charities in relation to their supplies:

- zero rating for the sale of goods donated to a charity
- zero rating for the donation of any goods for export by a charity
- the possibility of exemption of all income that would otherwise be standard rated from a fundraising event.

There are other exemptions that charities may need to apply in relation to their income, such as the exemption of education, health and welfare.

Figure 8.3

Charity:	Standard rated £	Zero rated £	Exempt £
Inputs	80,000	80,000	80,000
VAT	16,000	16,000	16,000
Outputs	120,000	120,000	120,000
VAT	24,000		
Pay (reclaim)	8,000	(16,000)	0

Figure 8.4 Generic VAT treatment of activities

	Business	Non-business	Treatment
General fundraising		Donations, including covenants, Gift Aid, legacies, flag days	OS
		Selling bequeathed property	OS
	Concerts, galas, performances Admission charges to premises – unless 'one-off' events		EX
	Sales of donated goods		ZR
	Sales of bought-in goods excl. books		SR
	Sales of bought-in books		ZR
	Sponsorship where benefits provided		SR
		Sponsorship where acknowledgement only	OS
	Affinity card sponsorship		SR
		Affinity card donation	OS
	Selling advertising space: equal to or more than 50% commercial		SR
		Selling advertising space: less than 50% commercial	OS
	Lotteries		EX
Central/local government funding	Grants with services rendered as condition		Dependent on type of service
		Grant with no service	OS
Financial income	Interest		EX, but effectively ignored
		Dividends	OS
		Profits from share dealings	OS
Letting charity property	To another charity		EX
	Community building to local groups etc		EX/SR (option to tax)
	To businesses		EX/SR (option to tax)
	Sale of farm produce		ZR

Figure 8.4 Generic VAT treatment of activities (continued)

	Business	Non-business	Treatment
Voluntary services		If provided free as part of charitable purpose	OS
Relief aid	Export of goods by gift overseas as part of charitable purposes		ZR
Churches		Fees for rites, eg weddings, funerals	OS
		Offerings from congregation	OS
Clubs, associations	Subscriptions giving benefits		SR
		Subscriptions giving voting rights only	OS
Sports clubs	Subscriptions to play at a club or use sports facilities only		EX
Welfare charities applying services not for profit	Provision of care for the sick, elderly etc		EX
	Protection of children		EX
	Spiritual welfare		EX
		Relief of the distressed below cost, ie recipient pays less than 85% of cost	OS
Approved hospital	Provision of care or medical treatment and goods in connection therewith		EX
School		Education provided free, or for a fee less than cost by a local authority	OS
	Education for a fee at or above cost by DE approved school		EX
	Education for a fee at or above cost by other institution, eg playschool		SR
	Sale of educational materials in class		EX
	Sale of educational materials in school shop		SR
University		HEFC grant	OS
	Educational courses		EX
	Research activities		EX
	Sporting, recreational courses		SR
	Business consultancy		SR
	Secondment of staff		SR

Goods donated to a charity

How does the first relief benefit a charity? First, that in the absence of the relief, part of the proceeds of sale would go to HMRC rather than the charity. Second, that all VAT incurred on the costs of selling donated goods is fully recoverable. Any goods that are purchased and then sold must be standard rated, unless they are otherwise zero rated goods, such as books. There is no corresponding relief for goods bought below market value, so the sale of these is standard rated. Goods that are purchased for resale and that would be zero rated in a normal commercial situation remain zero rated, for example, books and pamphlets.

Goods donated by a charity

The second relief has its beneficial effect in relation to purchases, whereby charities are allowed to reclaim the VAT on goods that are given away by being sent from the UK to outside the EU. This is achieved by allowing charities to treat this activity as a zero rated business activity. If the relief did not exist charities would not be able to reclaim VAT paid on the purchase of such goods.

Fundraising events

The third relief (which is compulsory where it applies) benefits charities in that part of the takings that would otherwise go to HMRC remains with the charity, but has the disadvantage that any VAT incurred is irrecoverable and becomes a cost to the charity. The following conditions apply to the event.

- It must be planned to raise funds.
- It must be advertised or held as a fundraiser.
- Up to 15 events of the same kind in the same location can be held per year (however, small-scale events, where gross takings do not exceed £1,000 per week do not count towards the 15).
- It must not be in competition with a commercial operator.

Overseas challenge events are not usually covered by the exemption for fundraising events, and most challenge events should be dealt with under the special 'Tour Operators' Margin Scheme (see VAT notice 709/5).

If this exemption applies, all types of income directly connected with the event that would otherwise have been standard rated become exempt, including admission charges, catering, sales of merchandise, sponsorship and the sale of advertising space. This only applies where sponsorship and advertising are directly connected with the event. The downside of this exemption is that any VAT incurred on the costs of mounting the one-off event will be irrecoverable.

Sponsorship

Sponsorship can sometimes cause VAT problems for charities. Sponsorship can be a genuine donation, a trading transaction or a mixture of the two. If anything is supplied, or deemed to have been supplied, in return for financial support, then a supply has been made for VAT purposes. HMRC accepts that a payment where only an acknowledgement has been given will be treated as a donation and therefore outside the scope of VAT. If a contribution is made to the charity on the condition that a company's name or trading style is advertised or promoted, this constitutes advertising and is a standard rated supply by the charity. In particular, any exposure given to a commercial logo is interpreted by HMRC as 'advertising'. Furthermore, if the company receives some other benefit in return, for example, tickets to a concert that is not an exempt supply, this is a standard rated supply by the charity. Where there is an element of donation in the payment it may be possible to split the amount, putting the VATable supply through the charity's trading subsidiary and the non-VATable element through the charity. Professional advice ought to be sought on any such split.

'It is sensible to consult professional advisers.'

Affinity credit cards

If a charity receives income in return for endorsing a credit card, this would normally count as a business activity and therefore be standard rated. The enrolment fee from affinity credit cards has, via a non-statutory concession, become capable of being split into two parts. One part relates to payment for services provided by the charity, such as the use of logo and mailing list, a second part, which is a donation for which the charity provides nothing in return. The normal split would be 20 per cent for services and 80 per cent for donation, but this is simply a guide to what is normally acceptable, and each case should be considered on its own merits. HMRC usually accepts that all commission arising from usage of the card subsequent to the initial commission is treated as donation payable to the charity.

Income from branches or fundraisers

An important point to determine is how far the income of branches or fundraisers apparently independent of the charity should be included within the charity's own activities. It is a matter of legal interpretation as to whether a 'branch' is legally part of the charity or a separate legal entity. It is up to the charity to work out where, between those two points, each branch lies. If a branch is judged to be independent, it may have to register in its own right (but only if it makes taxable supplies). If HMRC suspects that an organisation is being broken down artificially into separate units to keep below the VAT registration limits, it may apply the disaggregation provisions, which gives it power to treat the wider organisation as a single taxable unit. The main issue here is that small-scale taxable activities may be carried out by branches that ought to be included in the charity's VAT registration and may be overlooked.

Irrecoverable VAT

The major problem in relation to charities and VAT is irrecoverable VAT. Much of the sector's activities are either exempt from VAT or outside the scope. This means there is no taxable activity to set input VAT on purchases against. The input VAT cannot be claimed and 'sticks' in the charity as an additional cost. Some charities have a mixture of income, which renders them partially exempt if they are registered for VAT because of their different activities. An organisation is partly exempt when it has a mixture of taxable and exempt activities. The main objective will be to ensure that the quantum of the irrecoverable VAT is as low as it fairly can be. There are various ways in which this can be done, and it is sensible to consult professional advisers in order to maximise recovery.

The general inability of charities to reclaim VAT means that taking the most advantage of the charity reliefs for purchases is even more important. Zero rate reliefs include:

• charity advertising
• goods connected with collecting donations
• purchase of radios and talking books for use by visually impaired people
• supply of buildings for charitable use
• lifeboats
• various types of equipment for disabled people
• medical equipment.

VAT planning and maximising recovery

Tax planning is important for voluntary organisations, particularly registered charities. Organisations that are not compulsorily required to register for VAT may still consider doing so under voluntary registration. This is because it may allow a partial recovery of VAT incurred. Such a decision requires being able to answer the following questions.

• Will the VAT the organisation is able to recover exceed that which it will have to declare to customs on standard rated activities? If not, then...
• will the organisation's customers be able to bear the cost of VAT that will now be charged?
• Will the costs of setting up the financial system to record and claim VAT be covered by the VAT efficiencies?

Voluntary organisations should always be seeking to recover as much VAT as possible. Because voluntary organisations have a mixture of activities that are taxable, exempt and outside the scope, there are issues as to how much of their costs is recoverable and how much is irrecoverable. Issues, particularly around the expenses attributable to head offices, where some of these costs can be recovered, require careful planning and negotiation with HMRC.

Case study

A charity, which had objectives including the funding of research and provision of welfare to children who had a particular disease, had remained unregistered for VAT since its formation. The taxable income it generated had historically been low, as its main sources of income were research grants (outside the scope), donations and legacies (outside the scope) and fundraising activities (mainly exempt). The opportunity to register for VAT arose when it decided to open a charity shop selling goods donated by the public (specifically zero rated). The shop was very successful and soon the charity had five shops with a turnover of £250,000.

On speaking with professional charity VAT advisers, VAT registration was sought retrospectively from the date the first shop was opened. This ensured all VAT incurred during this period attributable to the shops could be fully recovered, alongside a healthy proportion of overhead VAT. In addition, all VAT incurred on the annual ball and other fundraising events was fully recoverable as it fell below the partial exemption de-minimis limits.

The charity enjoyed a one-off windfall of £75,000 and an enduring annual VAT recovery of circa £12,000. As the majority of taxable income is zero rated, there is little VAT to pay on income. The professional advisers charged a one-off fee of 10 per cent of the windfall received plus VAT (which was fully recoverable).

A charity registering will need to be mindful of the administrative requirements that accompany registration. Once registered, a charity will need to complete regular returns, keep adequate books and records to support such returns and be prepared for potential VAT inspections.

A charity registered for VAT will need to take advice, as it may be able to claim back an element of its overhead VAT on expenditure that is not specifically allocated to either a business or non-business activity (or between taxable or exempt). This is sometimes referred to as 'the pot' and can be apportioned using a variety of methods that will need to be agreed with HMRC.

Exercise appraising a charity's tax position

In this exercise we review a charity's operations from the perspective of reducing the burden of tax. Direct taxation implications are discussed first. The answer then appraises the indirect tax position.

Wretched of the Earth is a charitable trust that was registered in 1962. Its purpose is to relieve poverty, distress and suffering in any part of the world.

The charity operated from a building just off Soho Square, which was donated to it 15 years ago. On the ground floor, there is a 'restaurant', which offers frugal meals supposed to replicate the inadequate nourishment suffered by much of the world's poor. The restaurant is surprisingly popular, many of its clientele being overweight workers in the media industry located nearby.

The charity was formerly a quiet operation, which had concentrated on convincing the Department for International Development (DFID) to give it a grant. Now, however, Harry Flashpoint, who was brought in by the trustees to give the charity a higher profile, runs it. Harry feels that his conspicuous lifestyle should be partly funded by the charity because the charity is benefiting.

On Friday nights, there is a 'rave for the poor' at the charity's premises. This has become massively popular due to the presence of trendy disc jockeys and various glitterati. The very high entrance fee means that only those with a large disposal income can get in, which increases the exclusiveness of the event.

Part of the premises is used by the charity as a shop, from which goods made by artisans in Africa are sold, together with donated goods and a small range of bought-in jewellery.

The charity's income and expenditure for 201X/1X is as follows:

Income	£
Collecting tin donations	1,500
DFID grant	227,000
Other donations	7,000
Legacies	12,000
Net profit on restaurant	75,700
Net profit on raves	125,000
Proceeds of sale of donated goods	12,000
Net proceeds of artisan goods	500
Net proceeds of bought-in goods	7,500
Total income	468,200

Expenditure	£
Setting up irrigation project	200,000
Costs of shop	8,000
Central charity administration	40,000
Clothes, meals, for Harry	50,000
Roll Royce hire for Harry	16,000
Harry's salary	50,000
Total expenditure	364,000
Surplus	104,200

Answer to exercise

Wretched of the Earth

A) Direct tax

1. Charity has trading activities:

- restaurant
- shop
- bought-in goods
- raves.

These activities will probably be taxable. A possible answer to rectify the situation would be to set up a trading company/ies, which Gift Aids its profits. Are the trading activities profitable? From the information supplied the relevant income is:

Restaurant profit	75,700
Raves	125,000
Bought-in goods	7,500
Artisan	500
	208,700

Issues of direct expenditure and the allocation of overheads as previously discussed in this guide would then have to be considered and a business plan drawn up.

B) Indirect tax

VAT treatment of income and expenditure:

Income	
Collecting tin donations	OS
DFID grant	OS
Other donations	OS
Legacies	OS
Restaurant turnover	SR
Entrance fee to raves	SR
Proceeds of donated goods at shop	ZR
Sales of artisan goods	SR
Sales of bought-in goods	SR
Expenditure	
Setting-up of irrigation project	OS
Costs of shop	SR
Central charity administration	SR
Clothes, meals, for Harry	SR
Rolls Royce hire for Harry	SR
Harry's salary	OS
Other points	

If this standard rated trading activity's turnover exceeds the allowance in the Finance Act it would have to be put in a VAT-registered trading subsidiary to avoid income tax. If possible as much of the input tax on administration should be put through the subsidiary for recovery of VAT.

Code

EX = Exempt
OS = Outside the scope of VAT
SR = Standard rated
ZR = Zero rated

Checklist

Answer the following questions before checking the answers in the text.

1. What is required to be in place to ensure that Gift Aid can be claimed on a donation?

2. What are the major tax concessions that a charity should be aware of?

3. What is a taxable person?

4. Define standard rate, zero rate and exempt.

5. List which voluntary sector income sources are outside the scope of VAT.

6. What factors need to be considered in deciding whether VAT voluntary registration is appropriate?

Action points for your organisation

Audit your organisation to see if:

- it is maximising VAT recovery – for example, when was the last time the organisation had professional advisers assessing the tax position of the organisation?
- the trading subsidiary is profitable and keeping to its business plan
- the fundraisers are fully briefed on tax effective giving
- the fundraising department has plans for maximising tax effective giving among the charity supporters
- the charity's fundraising material is creating a tax liability or restricting funds in an appeal.

Exercise

St Mungo's Monastery is located just outside Eastry in Kent and was established in the late 19th century with a number of endowments from a wealthy individual. It is a registered charitable trust. The monks are subject to the disciplines of the Order of the Sacred Veil and are not generally allowed out of the monastery.

The monks are a very active group, engaged in a number of activities. The monastery owns a vineyard that produces 'tonic' wine, which is usually strong and is very popular. The monastery owns a large acreage, some of which has been turned over to market gardening, again carried out by monks. They also run a residential home for elderly men (who are not monks) attached to the monastery.

There is also a public house, The Laughing Abbot, owned by the monastery but staffed by outsiders.

All the activities of the monastery are carried out by the charitable trust.

Income and expenses are as follows:

	£
Local authority contract for residential home	500,000
Set-aside funds from the European Commission	75,000
Grant from the local authority	120,000
Sale of bar meals in the pub	65,000
Sale of drinks in the pub	250,000
Hire of rooms for functions	15,000
Collections at services in the monastery church	175,000
National Lottery grant for repair of church	200,000
Monks' salaries donated	350,000
DSS Income Support and State Pensions of elderly gentlemen	91,000
Sale of wine to wholesalers	1,200,000
Sales of produce from market garden to supermarkets	750,000
Monks' salaries paid	330,000
Salaries to full-time outsiders	510,000
Wages of part-time staff	60,000
Payments to freelancers and consultants	145,000
Redundancy payment to outsider	40,000
Repairs to church	300,000
Business rates	34,000

	£
Council tax	6,250
Various materials used in manufacture of wine	350,000
Living expenses of monks	55,000
Donation to archdiocese	150,000
Advertising of tonic wine	30,000
Fundraising from bazaars, jumble sales, etc	133,000

The part-time staff members are paid out of petty cash with no deductions for income tax or National Insurance (NICs). At least one of the so-called freelance staff has duties that hardly differ from an employee.

Answer the following questions.

1. HMRC is planning to visit the charity to ensure that PAYE has been properly deducted. What precautions should be taken by the charity?

2. State how the VAT system would treat each of the monastery's activities.

3. What recommendations would you make in relation to the monastery's activities in order to reduce the liability to pay direct taxes?

Answers

1. **Part-time staff:** depending on the level of pay, part-time staff should have income tax and NICs deducted in just the same way as full-time staff. A calculation should be made of the liability going back as far as necessary if tax and NICs have not been properly deducted. This is a liability of the charity, not employees. Penalties amounting to a maximum of the tax/NIC may also be payable, which cannot properly be borne by the charity and so must fall on its trustees personally. These will reduce, depending on the level of cooperation with HMRC, so the charity should be cooperative. Proper pay deduction records should be maintained from now on, and the correct form issued at the end of the tax year. Form P46 (or P38S for students) should be signed by each part-time employee and retained for HMRC to inspect.

Freelancers and consultants: HMRC will endeavour to treat as many of these as employees as they can, so evidence of the proper self-employed status of each should be sought. If in doubt, they should be treated as an employee and subjected to the PAYE scheme. This will upset the consultant, but this is less damaging than using charity funds to pay their tax/NICs. HMRC will use the following tests.

- **Control and work performance:** employees will not be able to decide in general where, when and how the work is performed. Self-employed people have the power of delegation and do not have to work certain hours.
- **Financial risk:** employees do not risk their own personal capital if the work is not up to standard.
- **Equipment:** employees do not usually use their own equipment to carry out the work.
- **Holidays and sickness:** self-employed people do not get these.
- **Exclusivity:** in general, employees will work for one employer, but this is not so with the self-employed. If HMRC has granted the particular consultant self-employed status and issued a 'Schedule D number' this should be obtained, but it is not conclusive evidence.
- **Redundancy payment:** this should be non contractual. Care needs to be taken in this area for the payment to qualify for the £30,000 exemption. The remainder of it is taxable and tax should be deducted under PAYE. Any ex-gratia payment will be a breach of trust, unless consent is obtained from the Charity Commission.

2.

Local authority contract for the residential home	EX
Set-aside funds from the European Commission	OS
Grant from the local authority	OS
Sale of bar meals in the pub	SR
Sale of drinks in the pub	SR
Hire of rooms for functions	SR
Collections at services in the monastery church	OS
National Lottery grant for repair of church	OS
Monks' salaries donated	OS
DSS Income Support and State Pensions of elderly gentlemen	OS
Sale of wine to wholesalers	SR
Sale of produce from market garden to supermarkets	SR
Monks' salaries	OS
Salaries to full-time outsiders	OS
Wages of part-time staff	OS
Payments to freelancers and consultants	See note 1
Redundancy payment to outsider	OS
Repairs of church	SR
Business rates	OS
Council tax	OS
Various materials used in manufacture of wine	SR
Living expenses of monks	SR
Donations to archdiocese	OS
Advertising of tonic wine	SR
Fundraising from bazaars, jumble sales, etc	EX

Note 1: Depends on whether the consultants are registered for VAT.

Code

EX = exempt
OS = outside the scope of VAT
SR = Standard rated
ZR = Zero rated

3. A trading subsidiary should be established. The trust deed should be checked to see whether investing in such a subsidiary would be ultra vires. The deed may need adjusting and this should be cleared with the Charity Commission.

If the subsidiary is to be financed partly by loan capital, the loan should be properly documented and treated as if it was on an arm's-length basis, with security, interest and repayment terms made explicit.

If the following activities remain in the charity they will become taxable, (unless they can be classed as 'ancillary') as Schedule D Case I, profits unless they fall within HMRC's exemptions for small traders because they are not for the primary purpose of the charity, ie the advancement of religion:

- running of the pub and hire of rooms
- production and sale of wine
- sale of farm produce
- running of residential home.

Other points

- The VAT regulations should be complied with. The trading subsidiary will be making the taxable supplies and VAT should be accounted for on the normal basis. Record-keeping rules should be complied with.
- The residential home has exempt income and any input VAT relating to this activity is not reclaimable.

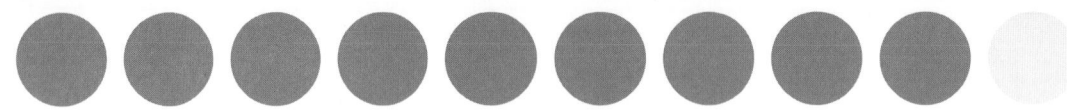

Accounting for smaller voluntary organisations

9.1
Introduction

This chapter introduces the regulation and accounting requirements for smaller voluntary organisations, which we define as having an income of less than £250,000. Many smaller voluntary organisations will be unincorporated charities with income above the threshold of £10,000 a year, and these are now subject to greater scrutiny and accountability than in the past. Please note that Chapter 6 considers the regulatory framework that unincorporated charities work under. Charities that are constituted as a charitable company will operate under a different regime. The chapter also discusses the requirements of an independent examination, an alternative to having a full professional audit.

9.2
Accruals accounting for the smaller charity

The Charity Commission updated its guidance *CC15b Charity Reporting and Accounting: The Essentials* in January 2013.

Charity accounts must be prepared either on the receipts and payments basis or the accruals basis. Which of these is needed will depend on the income of the charity and whether or not the charity is incorporated as a company.

Accruals

All charitable companies must prepare their accounts on the accruals basis in accordance with SORP. They contain a balance sheet, a Statement of Financial Activities and explanatory notes.

For small non-company charities, the Commission provides templates for receipts and payments or accruals accounting to help them produce accounts in the required form and to meet the requirements of the law and the SORP's recommendations. The templates are available through the Charity Commission's website.

The smaller unincorporated charity, unless preparing its accounts under the receipts and payments method, can also follow the Financial Reporting Standard for Smaller Entities (FRSSE), except where it conflicts with SORP 2005, in which case SORP 2005 should be followed. The incorporated charity must follow SORP 2005.

The accounts should include a Statement of Financial Activities (SoFA) in place of a profit and loss account; the principles of fund accounting should be adopted and investments should be shown at market value.

Accounts structure

The accounts structure follows the normal structure of accounts under the accruals accounting method and would include a statement of financial activities, a balance sheet and notes to the accounts.

The statement of financial activities will, in most cases, be the same as a traditional income and expenditure account, with the addition of the balance brought forward from the previous year.

Charities can choose between analysing their resources expended by either the functional classification recommended by SORP 2005 and outlined in CC17 or by natural classification as outlined in CC39.

The balance sheet should explain in general terms how the funds may or, because of restrictions imposed by donors, must, be utilised.

Charities do not need to state whether the accounts have been prepared in accordance with any applicable accounting standards and statements of recommended practice, or give particulars of any material departure from those standards and statements of practice and the reasons for doing so.

Emoluments of employees earning more than £60,000 need to be disclosed. In bands of £10,000, transactions with trustees and other connected persons also need to be disclosed.

The accruals method for SORP accounting for charities with income under £250,000 does not differ materially from the treatment of larger charities preparing their accounts under the SORP accounting method.

Trustees' report

The accruals pack also provides a minimum framework for the completion of the trustees' annual report. Trustees may choose to provide additional information, but will include reference and administrative information, structure, governance and management, objectives and activities, achievements and performance, financial review and funds held as custodian trustee.

9.3
Receipts and payments accounting

Receipts and payments

This is the simpler of the two methods of preparation and may be adopted where a non-company charity has a gross income of £250,000 or less during the year. It consists of an account that summarises all money received and paid out by the charity in the financial year, and a statement giving details of its assets and liabilities at the end of the year. Charitable companies irrespective of their level of income are not allowed by company law to adopt this method.

The Charity Commission booklet *CC16 Receipts and Payments Accounts Pack* has more information.

The practices described in this pack will meet the requirements for accounting periods ending on or after 1 April 2009 and have been subsequently amended for charitable incorporated organisations. Charities are advised to follow the recommendations, since they represent best practice, but are not obliged by law to do so. The accounts will not claim to show a true and fair view of the charity's financial activities and state of affairs. Accounting standards do not generally apply to such accounts. However, the accounts should be prepared on a consistent basis from year to year, and if asset valuations other than cost are provided, they should be reasonable, relevant and reliable.

What are the legal requirements?

Charities registered in England and Wales that are not companies are allowed, under section 133 of the Charities Act 2011, to prepare receipts and payments accounts, provided the charity's gross income is not over £250,000.

Trustees should also check that their governing document does not require their charity's annual accounts to be prepared as accruals accounts. A requirement that asks for 'true and fair' accounts or for the preparation of a balance sheet will imply that accruals accounts are needed.

In Scotland, the Charities Accounts (Scotland) Regulations 2006 apply. This allows charities that are not companies to prepare a 'receipts and payments account' for a particular financial year and a 'statement of balances' as at the year-end, if in that financial year the charity's gross receipts amount to £250,000 or less (or £100,000 for accounting periods starting before 1 April 2011). In Northern Ireland and the Republic of Ireland, there are no regulations governing either the form or the contents of charity accounts. The Charity Commission for Northern Ireland's website notes that it 'has yet to consult and decide on what the Charity Accounting and reporting requirements for Northern Ireland will be.'

Annual report

The trustees of all registered charities in England and Wales are expected to prepare an annual report that summarises their activities over the past year. Charities that receive more than £25,000 a year are required by law to send their reports to the Charity Commission. In Scotland, each recognised body must produce a report containing the information specified in the Charities and Trustee Investment (Scotland) Act 2005. In Northern Ireland and the Republic of Ireland, there are no legal requirements to prepare annual reports.

Trustees' responsibility for annual report and accounts

The trustees of a charity are responsible for preparing the accounts and annual report. Whether or not trustees delegate the preparation of accounts to others (perhaps to their accountant, treasurer or employees), the trustees remain responsible for ensuring that the accounts and report comply with the law. The legal requirements for producing and laying accounts before the annual general meeting, and for allowing other trustees access to the accounts with a reasonable amount of time before the accounts are approved, hold for both smaller and larger charities. The accounts have to be approved in the same way as for a larger charity and accounts must be delivered to the Charity Commission. The accounts of an unincorporated charity not exceeding £10,000 gross income and total expenditure for the year will not normally be required to be audited or independently examined, nor will they need to be submitted to the Charity Commission. Members of the public are entitled to request copies of the accounts.

Charity Commission CC16 receipts and payments accounts

For England and Wales, the Charity Commission has prepared a standard pack (CC16) for use in preparing a charity's receipts and payments accounts and statement of assets and liabilities. No charity is obliged to use the pack, but its use or adaptation for use is recommended by the Charity Commission. The pack contains notes and instructions for trustees on how to complete the accounts in accordance with the law and is designed to meet minimum levels of accountability. Copies are available without charge from the Charity Commission. The format is readily adaptable by umbrella bodies to suit their particular needs.

9.4
Independent examination

This section expands on an area already covered in Chapter 6.

Whether a charity needs an audit or independent examination depends on its size. To meet the requirements of the Charities Act 2011, all charities with an income in excess of £500,000 or gross assets of more than £3.26m where gross income is more than £250,000 in the financial year will require audit. Whether independent examination is required or not depends on the legal status of the charity, ie whether it is incorporated or unincorporated. Those unincorporated charities with an income between £10,000 and £250,000 will require, as a basic minimum, an independent examination. Incorporated charities fall under the auspices of the Companies Act 2006 in respect of the requirement to audit and the preparation of an accountant's report.

Some charities may still require an audit due to governing documentation, a requirement under another statutory or regulatory regime or funder's requirements.

What is independent examination?

This is a less onerous form of scrutiny than an audit, although the level of assurance given by independent examination is higher than that given under the exemption report regulations for companies. It is primarily based on a review of the accounts and consideration of any unusual items or disclosures identified. It indicates whether certain matters have been brought to the reviewer's attention. The examination must be carried out in accordance with the directions issued by the Charity Commission. The examiner is not required to form an opinion as to whether the accounts give a true and fair view.

The level of assurance provided by independent examination may be lower than that provided by audit, but it can be a very attractive option. This is particularly true where a charity's accounts have traditionally been 'audited' to satisfy members or the terms of a charity's trust by an individual without formal auditing qualifications.

If the accounts are prepared on an accruals basis, the independent examiner must check them for compliance with the regulations in terms of format, content and review accounting policies, and enquire about post-balance sheet events. The examiner must also compare the accounts with the trustees' report to make sure they are consistent.

Who can do an independent examination?

An independent examiner is defined as, 'an independent person who is reasonably believed by the trustees to have the requisite ability and practical experience to carry out competent examination of the accounts'. The Charities Act has defined independent as having, 'no connection with a charity's trustees which might inhibit the impartial conduct of the examination'.

The independent examiner will need to have good analytical and communication skills in order to be able to raise questions and to interpret and challenge responses. They should have practical experience, which should be indicated by involvement with the financial administration or independent examination of similar charities.

Once a charity's gross income exceeds £250,000, the examiner must be a person who is a member of one of the bodies listed in CC32 of the Charities Act 2011.

Independent examiner's report

The content of this report is determined by the regulations, should be signed by the independent examiner personally, not on behalf of his/her firm, and must state any relevant professional qualifications or professional body of which he/she is a member. Examiners should avoid making positive statements of opinion or belief that could only be substantiated by carrying out an audit. The examiner should report clearly and unambiguously where the charity's accounts appear to be in order.

Carrying out an independent examination – directions and guidance notes

The current guidance issued by the Charity Commission is *CC32 Independent Examination of Charity Accounts: Trustees' Guide.*

Whistleblowing

This additional role, given to the auditor or independent examiner of an unincorporated charity, of reporting certain facts directly to the Charity Commission is designed to increase public confidence. However, a similar obligation does not exist where the charity is incorporated. This duty occurs where the auditor or independent examiner has reasonable cause to believe that the matter is, or is likely to be, of material significance in relation to the charity, requiring the Commission to implement its functions under Sections 46, 47 and 50 (general power to institute enquiries) or 76 and 79–82 (power to act for protection of charities) of the 2011 Act, Section 156.

Auditors and independent examiners should not have to change the scope of their work to discover whether or not reportable issues exist.

A duty arises if something is discovered whilst carrying out the audit/independent examination that, in their opinion, is of 'material significance' and assists the Commission in its supervisory functions relating to the investigating and checking of abuses within charities. If evidence of misuse is discovered, the auditors are asked to extend their work.

The Financial Reporting Council (previously the Accounting Practice Board) practice note sets out the three types of issues likely to be reportable.

1. A significant inadequacy in the arrangements made by trustees for the discretion and management of a charity's affairs.

2. A significant breach of the legislative requirement in respect of the charity's trusts.

3. Circumstances indicating a probable deliberate misuse of charity property.

The Council requires that the auditors discuss concerns with trustees as part of the process of forming a judgement (unless the matter casts doubt on the integrity of the trustees) as to whether a particular issue needs to be reported directly to the Charity Commission. It is not intended that the auditor/examiner should report on insignificant issues, particularly where such issues have been satisfactorily resolved.

The regulations provide rights of access to all documents relating to the charity and which the auditor/independent examiner properly considers necessary to inspect. This includes the right to require information from past or present trustees, officers or employees.

A report to the Commission must be made in writing. Failure to report a matter could result in disciplinary procedures by the relevant professional body. The revised Practice Note 11 has extended its guidance on *ISA 250: The Auditor's Right and Duty to Report to the Regulators in the Financial Sector.*

9.5
The future of charity accounting for small entities

In March 2013, the Financial Reporting Council (FRC) published a new form of the *UK Generally Accepted Accounting Practice* (UK GAAP) and the new reporting standard FRS 102. A new revised SORP has been issued to the charity sector for a four-month consultation starting in July 2013, which the FRC board will need to approve. This is unlikely to happen before summer 2014.

Smaller charities will have a choice of applying either the FRSSE or moving to the new GAAP. All other charities will be required to apply the forthcoming FRS 102. However, if the FRSSE is unable to address an issue, the charity would need to use existing accounting policies and if no policies are in place, then would need to refer to FRS 102.

There is still uncertainty regarding how the new SORP will apply to small companies, and the framework at the smaller end appears fragmented; a new consultation regarding the FRSSE is likely to take place in the near future.

Exercise

1. The main obligation in preparing a charity's accounts is to show a true and fair view of its incoming resources, their application and its state of affairs, except in the case of:

   a) small charities that elect to prepare a receipts and payments account

   b) charitable companies

   c) charities with branches

   d) charities financed from permanent endowments.

2. An incorporated charity is promised a grant of £300,000 in the year to 31 March 20013 (the charity's year-end) for the salary costs. The grant was not received until May 2013. Actual income received in the year was £200,000. On what basis would the charity be required to prepare its accounts for the year to 31 March 2013?

   a) A receipt and payments basis and would require a reporting accountant's report.

   b) A receipt and payments basis and would require an audit.

   c) A full accruals accounting basis and would require a reporting accountant's report.

   d) A full accruals accounting basis and would require an audit.

3. When should the value of resources accruing to a charity be recorded in the SoFA?

   a) When the financial year ends.

   b) Only when the cash has been received.

   c) As soon as it is prudent and practical to do so.

   d) Even if the conditions for receipts have not been met.

4. The Charities Act 2011 states that the accounting records must:

   a) show the solvency of the charity at any time

   b) show the financial position at any point in time

   c) disclose the financial position at the end of the financial year

   d) be written up on a daily basis to show the current financial position.

5. A non-incorporated charity expects income of £60,000 for the year ended 31 March 2013 and has had this level of income for the last five years. In the past it had an audit because its trust deed required an audit and the trustees thought it was necessary. When can this charity take advantage of the charity regulations to avoid the cost of an audit?

   a) Only after changing the trust deed.

   b) As soon as the trustees inform the existing auditors.

   c) Immediately.

   d) As soon as the existing auditors have resigned.

6. In response to an appeal, your charity has received a gift of shares worth £20,000 and cash of £50,000 to be used for relief in Cuba. During the year the shares have produced income of £15,000, and the sale of 50 per cent of the shares generated proceeds of £25,000. At the end of the year, the charity spent £60,000 on Cuba. How much is the fund balance at the year-end?

   • £30,000
   • £35,000
   • £40,000
   • £45,000

7. A non-incorporated charity prepares its accounts on a receipts and payments basis to 31 March 2013. It received £245,000 in the year. In addition it has claimed back Gift Aid of £30,000 on its donations. This money was received after the year-end. The trustees do not wish to change the basis of accounting unless this is required. In this case, the accounts should disclose:

- income of £245,000 and be prepared on a receipts and payment basis
- income of £275,000 and be prepared on a receipts and payment basis
- income of £275,000 and be prepared on an accruals basis
- either income of £245,000 or £275,000 depending on whether the tax refund is received before the accounts are approved.

8. A small charity producing receipts and payments accounts:

- need not distinguish restricted funds from general funds
- may produce a statement of assets and liabilities instead of a balance sheet
- must file their accounts within nine months of the financial year-end
- must have the accounts independently examined.

9. A charity sells donated goods through its subsidiary, which raised income of £100,000; shop expenses were £40,000 giving a profit of £60,000. The charity's consolidated SoFA should show:

- income of £100,000 under trading income
- income of £100,000 under donations
- net profit of £60,000 as a single line
- none of the above.

Answers

1. a

2. d

3. c

4. b

5. a

6. c

7. a

8. b

9. b

Overseas charity

Receipts and payments account for the year ended 31 March 2012

	Unrestricted £	Restricted £	Total 2012 £	Total 2011 £
Incoming receipts				
Donations – child sponsorship (CSP) and gifts	22,848	-	22,848	24,052
Donations – monitoring visits	5,000	-	5,000	5,000
Grants and corporate donors	6,340	8,125	14,465	-
Fundraising events	13,943	-	13,943	-
Interest received	311	-	311	103
Other receipts	820	-	820	-
Tax reclaim	2,628	-	2,628	4,208
Total receipts	51,890	8,125	60,015	33,363
Payments				
Direct charitable expenditure				
Child sponsorship programme (CSP)	25,584	-	25,584	16,104
Monitoring visits and associated costs	3,728	-	3,728	3,776
Other expenditure				
Fundraising costs	3,106	1,616	4,722	-
Printing, postage and stationery	869	515	1,384	1,004
Travel and subsistence	234	-	234	5
Telephone, internet and website cost	1,237	-	1,237	1,487
Marketing, entertainment and related expenses	66	153	219	309
Office rent	1,728	-	1,728	1,728
Insurance	183	-	183	182
Purchase of computer and printer	-	576	576	1,084
Repairs and maintenance	-	-	-	267
Conference cost	326	380	706	-
Sundry	223	-	223	-
Bank charges and interest	168	-	168	90

Receipts and payments account for the year ended 31 March 2012 (continued)

	Unrestricted £	Restricted £	Total 2012 £	Total 2011 £
Total payments	37,452	3,240	40,692	26,036
Net receipts for the year	14,438	4,885	19,323	7,327
Cash fund balances at 31 March 2011	22,428	-	22,428	15,101
Cash fund balances at 31 March 2011	£36,866	£4,885	£41,751	£22,428
Total receipts	51,890	8,125	60,015	33,363

Statement of assets and liabilities as at 31 March 2012

Monetary assets	General purpose Funds £	Restricted Funds £	2012 TOTAL £	2011 TOTAL £
Bank and cash balances				
Bank current account	9,858	4,885	14,743	3,757
Bank deposit account	26,960	-	26,960	18,671
Petty cash	48	-	48	-
Total	£36,866	£4,885	£41,751	£22,428

Restricted funds		
Building project	4,675	
CAF	210	
	£4,885	(see Note 4)

Other monetary assets		2012 £	2011 £
Debtors:	Tax credits	3,563	791
	Deposit – rent and keys	270	270
	Overseas currencies held	240	155
	Petty cash	-	28
		£4,073	£1,244

Approved by the trustees on 31 August 2012 and signed on their behalf by: J Smith.

Overseas charity

Notes to the financial statements for the year ended 31 March 2012.

1. **Accounting policies:** the financial statements have been prepared under the historical cost convention and are in accordance with applicable accounting standards, and the Charities Accounting Statement of Recommended Practice (SORP).

   - Income is accounted for on a receipts basis. This includes donation, interest and tax reclaim.
   - Direct charitable expenditure includes the direct costs of the charity's activities.

2. **Trustee remuneration:** the trustees received no remuneration in the year.

3. **Staff remuneration:** no salary or allowance was paid to the two volunteer staff.

4. **Restricted fund:** restricted funds are for the following purposes.

   - **Building project:** the grant has been awarded for the building project that is due to take place later on in the year.
   - **CAF:** Charities Aid Foundation (CAF) grant was for trustees and staff to attend selected fundraising courses forming part of The Fundraising Programme run by the Directory of Social Change. Since the year-end the unexpended amount of £210 has been repaid.

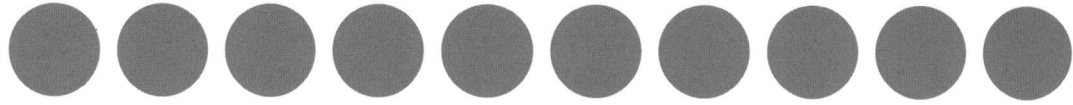

Social investment and social enterprise

10

●●●●●●●●●●

10.1
Introduction

Social investment has received much attention over the last few years. The government is currently championing it as a new form of financing the non-profit sector. Advisers and fund managers are assisting in putting together such investments, and charitable foundations are being encouraged to seriously consider using part of their endowments to invest. David Cameron, speaking in June 2013 at the Social Impact Investment Forum, said that 'social investment can be a great force for social change'. At the time of writing, the government is committed to finding a way of giving tax breaks to investments that qualify as having a 'social impact'. It also hopes to remove the, 'inconsistencies and omissions in the existing regulatory framework' that may be providing barriers to investment.

In the year to March 2012, the social finance sector was worth £202m, according to the *Growing the Social Investment Market* report published in July 2013. In that period, 29 social investment finance intermediaries (SIFIs) actively invested. The Institute for Voluntary Action Research's (IVAR) report looking at social investment charities comments that, 'it is thought by some that social investment could play a significant role in capitalising charities, which could in turn, help charities to achieve their objectives by making them more sustainable.'

Social investment is starting to gain traction and is now attracting financing from retail as well as institutional investors. However, is it something new or an existing form of investment that is now being repackaged or considered differently by the non-profit sector?

In this chapter we will look at the following areas.

- We will attempt to define social investment, taking into account the Charity Commission's views.
- We will consider the different forms that social investment can take.
- We will consider, in turn, what this type of investment might mean for an investor organisation and an organisation considering taking social investment.
- We will consider some examples of social investment.

In Chapter 7 we noted that the sector has traditionally shied away from borrowing. This may become a hurdle that prevents social investment becoming more widely adopted. Indeed, social investment may well not be the answer to financing some organisations, due to the scale of investment or the means by which the investment will need to be repaid.

Different investments are being offered in different ways and it is important for both an organisation seeking investment and for the charity looking to invest that they achieve the best type of financing.

Social investment is unlikely to be the best fit for most small non-profit organisations, whereas it could work well for larger non-profit organisations. When does it work for organisations that are neither one nor the other? The steps that need to be taken by an organisation considering setting up their own social investment can be complicated and for all but a small number of charities could be prohibitive.

10.2
Definition

Social investment is an emerging investment class that involves a generation of blended social and financial return on capital for the investor. Social investment can include equity, bonds (charity bonds or social impact bonds) or other forms of debt that are typically issued by charities and social enterprises. The social return is achieved as a result of the deployment of capital raised by the issuer in sustainable and social beneficial activities.

An organisation wishing to explore social investment

Such investment is not limited to a charitable or community organisation or excluded from an organisation that is not charitable. However, the investment needs to be undertaken for exclusively charitable or community charitable purposes. Some incidental private benefit is accepted; without this, much social investment would be impossible.

A charity wanting to engage in social investment must ensure that the investment is made within the powers of the charity and that the investment is prudent. Social investment is a means of achieving the objectives of the charity, which also obtains a return in financial terms on the investment. The return may be at or near a market return or significantly below.

Charity Commission guidance for charities investing in social investment

The Charity Commission has issued guidance to charities making investments – *Charities and Investment Matters: A guide for trustees* (formally referred to as CC14). The Commission identifies two separate types of investment that might be defined as social investments. These are performance related investments (PRI) and mixed motive investments (MMI).

It should be noted that the Charity Commission is continuing to research PRI and MMI. The Commission accepts that the guidance is currently lacking in some areas and it hopes to improve on this.

To move this forward, it has worked with IVAR and in March 2013 they jointly produced a report – *Charities and Social Investment.*

Performance related investment (PRI)

The aim of a PRI is to use a charity's assets directly to further its aims in a way that may also produce some financial return for the charity. PRI is different from financial investment as the justification for making the PRI is to further the charity's aims; this means that charities are not bound by the principles or law for investment.

In order to fulfil their duties and act within the law, trustees:

- must be able to show that the PRI is wholly in furtherance of the charity's aims
- should make sure that any benefit to private individuals is necessary, reasonable and in the interests of the charity
- should consider reasonable and practical ways to exit from a PRI if it is no longer furthering the charity's aims.

PRI often takes the form of loans, equity investments or pooled funds.

If the PRI is a loan, the loan agreement should set out:

- how it will be used to further the charity's aims
- a rate of interest – considering the impact on their charitable aims and the rate that the borrower might be able and willing to pay
- the timescale and terms of repayment. Trustees can be flexible in considering these arrangements.

A charity can also guarantee a loan.

The Charity Commission expects most social investment to be in the form of loans, and it views equity investment as the exception (see Charity Commission guidance CC14). Ownership gives a right to a dividend if paid and a right to vote at the AGM. Trustees need to ensure that there are processes in place so that the funding will continue to be used to further the aims of the charity.

Trustees must act in the best interest of their charity when making a PRI and ensure that:

- their charity's funds are only used to further its stated aims
- they have regard to private benefit mentioned above.

Before making the PRI trustees should be clear that:

- it contributes to the charity's strategic aims
- they compare PRIs with other ways of advancing the charity's aims in terms of effectiveness and risk
- they consider whether they need to take advice, given the level of risk to the charity, and any knowledge or expertise that they have in the charity.

Trustees may wish to consider setting up a separate committee to consider PRI. They can also delegate decisions on PRI to a third party or staff but need to ensure that they provide a clear direction in writing about the nature and type of PRIs they consider will further the charity's aims and ensure that they have procedures in place for monitoring and reviewing PRI performance.

The terms of the PRI agreement should cover instances where the PRI-funded activity ceases to further the charitable aims. It should be practical to end the PRI and return funding. It is acknowledged that this may be more difficult if equity has been taken.

Some private benefit is acceptable if it is necessary in the circumstances, reasonable in amount and in the interests of the charity. If it becomes unacceptable the investment should be exited.

Mixed motive investment (MMI)

Where an investment cannot be wholly justified as either a financial investment or PRI, it may be possible to justify it as a mixed motive investment. Investments still need to be justified as being in the best interest of the charity. Trustees should consider:

- the justification for making the mixed motive investment; this will need to be established before making the investment
- the suitability of a mixed motive investment for the charity – does it provide part financial return and part contribution to the charity's aims?
- whether there is a need to take professional advice before making the investment – this might be about the fit with the overall business plan of the charity, whether the investment contributes to the charity's aims, the legal issues attached to the proposed investment as a whole and any tax implications for the charity
- whether any private benefit arising from the investment will be acceptable and appropriate
- how the MMI will be monitored
- the size of the MMI in the context of the charity's overall investment portfolio and the charity's attitude to risk
- the risk that the charity's resources are used for purposes that are inconsistent with charitable status and the law on investing charitable funds.

The Commission uses the example of a permanently endowed charity needing to demonstrate that the extent to which the charity's aims are furthered is roughly equivalent to the reduction in income.

When is an MMI not justified?

An MMI *is not* justified when it is made for purposes other than furthering the charity's aims and securing a financial return. If one or more of the trustees (or connected persons) would derive an unauthorised private benefit, the level of private benefit to other individuals is not appropriate and the risks involved do not justify the level of resources to be invested.

10.3
What is the social investment needed for?

An organisation first needs to consider why it needs social investment over other types of available funding. As already mentioned, social investment is not always the best option because the funds will need to be repaid through loan repayment, equity dividends or delivering performance.

CAF Venturesome suggests in its leaflet *Multiply your Social Impact* that social investment can work when organisations are looking for funding to:

- help them make the transition to a more sustainable business model
- bridge to confirmed grants (which are increasingly paid in arrears)
- enable contracts delivering public services
- develop assets for use in delivering their activities
- manage cash flow effectively through the year.

Once an organisation has decided it wishes to pursue social investment it needs to consider whether it wishes to receive direct investment or whether it wishes to work with an intermediary. Either way, the organisation will need to put together a robust business plan for the proposed investment and prepare to go through a due diligence process. The business plan will need to include a realistic financial plan for repaying the finances borrowed or for servicing the equity requirements of the investors.

The organisation may decide it is easier to work with an intermediary as it can support the organisation through the process. The downside might be that the organisation loses some control over its project and incurs additional costs as it pays for the intermediary's services.

It usually takes around 18 months for organisations wanting to access investment to become ready for investment. The amount of work involved can often be a shock to the organisation, and the outcome of achieving social investment may lead to a change in an organisation's culture, business model and staffing. Internal reporting mechanisms will need to change, as well as the ability to gear up to take on a new project.

In working directly to raise finance, the organisation will need to be prepared to manage a number of different relationships and stakeholder requirements. Successful social investment relies on an engaged board, confident and skilled management, effective business planning, a reliable revenue stream and a strong asset base. Strong relationships between investors and investees, based on mutual trust and a shared vision and strategy for what the investment would achieve are crucial. (IVAR)

It is likely that the organisation will need to work with solicitors, and possibly accountancy firms, as the business plan is dissected to ensure that the promised returns can be achieved.

A number of factors may prevent organisations considering social investment. These include risk aversion, limited track record of successful social investments, organisational culture and the legal and regulatory framework in which the investment takes place. (IVAR)

●●●●●●●●●●

10.4
Charities seeking to invest

Charities can be unclear about what is available in this field and what social investment means for them, particularly charities considering making a social investment. Trustees should consider setting up a social investment policy. This will assist the organisation as it considers an investment opportunity. Investments need to be in the best interests of the charity and the Charity Commission wants to ensure that charities remain focused on their charitable objectives.

Trustees must also be able to make informed and independent decisions about investments they are involved in.

A charity wishing to invest needs to ensure that their investment is prudent. In essence, the investing organisation needs to ensure that it has assessed the risk of any such investment, is in a position to be able to monitor its performance, has regard to diversifying its assets (which may not be easy when starting to invest in this area for the first time) and avoids investing in an organisation that would undermine the objectives of the charity.

Most investments would require a due diligence process to be carried out. In situations where a number of investors are interested in investing together, the due diligence can be carried out together, thereby reducing cost. A number of solicitors now have experience in providing this type of support to investing charities, such as Bates Wells Braithwaite, Russell-Cooke and Berwin Leighton Paisner.

Trustees should consider whether they can achieve a financial return from their investment. They need to consider whether the income foregone on conventional investment by making a social investment is offset by the social impact gained. Some may decide that grants provide a better return. They also need to be very clear on whether such an investment will create *private benefit* to third parties. This could include benefit to the directors of companies in which they choose to invest.

An investor needs to be able to balance the likely financial return with the risk that arises. Most social investment creates higher risks than conventional investment.

This is often because such investment is undertaken to remedy market failures to deliver in that field. Indeed, it is this failure of the market to invest, or to invest in sufficient quantity in a field, that often draws charities into social investment.

A further point worth noting is the time and commitment that will be needed by the investing organisations. Social investment is currently a complex area and investors have to weigh up the time commitment against the size of the investment requested.

According to IVAR, on the positive side, the benefits of social investment are viewed as achieving social impact, providing capital to financially excluded organisations and communities and offering alternative forms of finance to their beneficiary organisations.

Monitoring

Monitoring social investment performance remains a difficult area. Work is continuing in this area, with a number of organisations looking into ways of monitoring this type of investment. One of the barriers is the number of different types of investment available, each with different structures and outcomes.

The Charity Commission suggests that monitoring is in two parts: financial and furthering the charity's aims. It agrees that the balance between these two elements may change.

The Commission suggests using impact reporting or social return on investment (SROI) to 'measure, manage and communicate' how the investment furthers the charity's aims. (It accepts that these methods are emerging.)

It also suggests monitoring the financial return on the investment and whether it remains suitable for the charity. (This, the authors suggest, is where the guidance is weakest and needs to be strengthened.)

Exit strategy

Exit strategies can be a difficult area. Most investors will be looking to exit from the investment within a period of time. This can be because the loan has been repaid or the equity realised. A charitable investor should be considering the exit strategy from the outset, whereas a commercial investor will be more interested in the return. It is too early in the era of social investment to offer many examples of successful exit strategies, but it will be interesting to follow the development of the market to see how exit strategies work in practice.

If an investment is unsuccessful, there will obviously be financial loss. Charitable investors are particularly encouraged to take and record their decisions properly. If this has been done, they should be able to address questions or challenges that may arise around their actions.

Accounting treatment

The accounting treatment for social investment has been considerably revised in the draft Charities SORP consultation launched in July 2013. The accounting treatment of social investment has been given a separate module (21).

The Commission suggests treating PRI and MMI in different ways. Both classes of assets should be treated as a, 'separate line on the balance sheet of a charity or identified as a separate class of investment in the notes to the accounts, depending on the materiality of the holding'.

Guidance is given on how to measure social investments. Should an impairment arise, a loss on a PRI should be treated as a cost within expenditure on charitable activities whereas a loss on an MMI should be treated as an investment impairment within the gains/loss on investments line in the SoFA. Any reversal of an impairment charge, 'should not result in an asset's carrying amount exceeding its carrying amount prior to its initial impairment'.

Gains on disposals of PRI should be treated as 'other income' in the SoFA after offsetting any prior impairment loss. Any gain on the disposal of an MMI is to be recognised in the gains/losses on investment line, again after offsetting any prior impairment loss.

10.5
Who are the investors?

Traditionally it has been the trusts and foundations sector that has led the way on funding social investment opportunities. It has done this in a number of different ways: through direct investment, investing in funds such as Venturesome and joint investment with others.

In recent years, four large social banks have become involved in social finance. They appear to be concentrating on investing in a small number of investments at a greater financial level than most social investment opportunities require. Currently social investment is often at a relatively low financial level. The scale of social investment and the ability for the banks to make a return appears to be a large factor.

It is interesting to note that according to the *Growing the Social Investment Market* report, 90 per cent of lending in 2011/12 was secured against borrowers' assets, up from 84 per cent in the previous year. Unsecured lending in the same period was £20m over the year compared with £26m the year before. This assumes that the organisation receiving the loan has an asset base to secure the social investment against. The report goes on to say that, 'this showed there was still not "sufficient identified high-risk unsecured social investment" for third sector organisations'.

10.6
Examples of support available in the sector

Advisers

A number of advisers are able to work with organisations, including ClearlySo – a financial intermediary in the social investment sector, advising social businesses and enterprises on raising capital.

Triodos Bank is a long-standing leader in the social investment market. It plans to offer more charity bonds as more charities and social enterprises look to this form of financing to develop their commercial activities and support their charitable objectives.

Support for organisations

In June 2013 the Big Lottery Fund (BIG) announced that it had committed £3m since March 2012 to support the development of 14 diverse social investment proposals via their Next Steps fund. This support leveraged in over £21m of social investment, ranging from Bristol Together preventing recidivism by ex-offenders through work placement opportunities, to Golden Lane Housing providing new specialist accommodation to help people with learning difficulties live independently. BIG has also delivered the government's Social Incubator Fund on behalf of the cabinet office.

Available funds

A number of funds have been set up to fund social investment. Some examples are included below (this is not an exhaustive list).

- The Big Lottery Fund (BIG) has set up two new social investment funds – Big Potential and its Co-commissioning Fund – with a combined value of £50m. These funds will be open for three years. The Big Potential fund will be for voluntary, community and social enterprise organisations to move towards investment readiness. The Co-commissioning Fund will aim to grow the market in social impact bonds and other outcomes-based investment instruments so that more people can lead fulfilling lives, in enriching places, as part of successful communities.

- CAF's social investment arm, CAF Venturesome, identified in 2002 a new way of supporting charities and making them more resilient, while at the same time providing social impact. Venturesome offers a revolving loan fund to investors; when funds are repaid, the same money is used again to invest in other organisations. To the charity receiving investment, it offers an opportunity not just to survive, but also to thrive and become stronger, which in turn allows it to focus on delivering its mission. Venturesome is concerned that there is a lack of *appropriate* financing available to the sector. Over the last 10 years, alongside other social investors, it has proved that it is possible to support these organisations. Venturesome currently has four live funds.

1. **The Development Fund,** providing high-risk capital to generate social impact by building the capacity of charitable organisations through unsecured loans for growth and transition.

2. **CAF Social Impact Fund,** which is low-risk working capital for charities and social enterprises through underwriting facilities and short-term unsecured loans.

3. **The Community Land Trust Fund,** for community-owned affordable housing projects. It provides high-risk pre-development and development finance through unsecured loans and secured development loans.

4. **SE-Assist,** to enable companies to provide social enterprises with mentoring, consultancy and social investment to build local social economies' capacity of charitable organisations through unsecured loans.

Over the last 11 years CAF Venturesome has offered £30m in loan financing and supported more than 360 organisations. Venturesome's write-off rate has been below 6 per cent with 80 per cent meeting or exceeding the capacity-building targets put in place at the time of investment.

- Big Society Capital has been set up with the proceeds from dormant bank accounts. It will receive up to £400m with a further £200m investment from UK high street banks over the next five years. It has a social mission to develop and shape a sustainable investment market. It can only invest in social investment finance intermediaries (SIFIs) – organisations that provide affordable finance and support to social ventures.

10.7
Examples of social investments

There are a huge number of social investments. The three below give an idea of the different options available.

Golden Lane Housing

On 1 July 2013 Golden Lane Housing announced that it had raised £10m in an oversubscribed charity bond offering. It closed early due to unprecedented demand. The bond offer raised interest from both retail and institutional investors. Triodos Bank supported Golden Lane in bringing the investment opportunity to the market.

Golden Lane Housing is a wholly owned subsidiary of Mencap. The funds raised will be used to acquire freehold properties, which will be specially adapted to house people with a learning disability. The bond offers a yield of 4 per cent per annum for the first five-fixed-year term, providing both a financial and a social return.

Peterborough Social Impact Bond

This was the world's first social impact bond. Launched in 2010, it aims to reduce reconvictions among male offenders sentenced to fewer than 12 months in prison and released from HMP Peterborough.

Social Finance set up the bond and a number of investors, mostly charitable trusts and foundations, came together to offer £5m to fund experienced social sector organisations that were providing intensive support to 3,000 short-term prisoners over a six-year period. The project works with offenders both inside prison and after release to support their resettlement into the community.

The project is called The One Service. If it successfully reduces reoffending by 10 per cent in any of the three cohorts, or by a minimum overall, investors will receive an outcome payment from the government.

Combination of methods

Nottingham Building Society and Framework, a homelessness charity, have combined a charity bond offering with a commercial loan. The investment vehicle ensures that the commercial loan is offset through a retail charity bond. In doing this, Framework is seeking to eventually raise £10m to provide 150 units of move-on accommodation for homeless people across the East Midlands over the next three to five years.

Nottingham Building Society has lent an initial £800,000 on a 5.5 per cent interest rate to help provide an initial 14 of these units. The interest rates will be partly offset through four retail savings bonds developed by the Building Society. Savers will be able to choose from four accounts on various rates and terms. The lower the interest rate paid on their savings bond, the cheaper the loan to Framework will be. This could see Framework's interest payments reduce to 2.48 per cent, resulting in savings to Framework of £360,000 over a 20-year period.

10.8
Forms of social investment

Most forms of social investment are traditional: loans, share or partnership capital, combinations of loans and equity funding and unsecured loan notes. There are three other forms of investment, which are outlined below.

Charity bond

A charity bond is a simple, fixed-income, investment product. It is similar in structure to any standard corporate or government bond where the borrower enters into a formal contract with investors to repay a loan at maturity, with interest paid at fixed intervals over the life of the bond. The bond itself can be issued as either secured or unsecured debt. The payment of interest and repayment of capital is not tied to specific social outcomes as it would be for a social impact bond. (Source: Triodos Bank)

Social impact bond

Social Finance defines social impact bonds as 'based on a commitment from government to use a proportion of the savings that result from improved social outcomes to reward non-government investors that fund the early intervention activities'. The form of the special purpose vehicle set up to deliver this can vary and can involve a combination of loans and equity.

Revolving loan

A revolving loan fund relies on organisations repaying loans that they have taken out. The loan repayments are then used to loan on to other organisations. Organisations investing in these loan funds will participate in the down side of the loan not being repaid but receive a social return by seeing their funds recycled and used again.

10.9
Taxation

Earlier in the chapter we noted that the government was looking into offering tax incentives for making social investment. Tax and social investment is currently a grey area.

In many ways, tax depends on the type of investment being made. Some investments made will not incur tax, whereas others, due to the nature of the investment model, will or may incur taxation. Some investors who have made social investments have taken the risk that their investment may, in the future, incur a tax charge when the investment is repaid.

In the case of a charitable investor, HMRC could also look at whether a social investment can be classed as non-charitable expenditure. If this is the case, the charity could incur a liability to tax. HMRC will look to test whether a loan or investment is for the benefit of the charity and made on sound commercial terms. The Income and Corporation Taxes Act 1988 contains additional provisions relevant to social investment. The conditions most relevant to social investment are listed here.

- The loan is made to another charity for charitable purposes only.
- The loan is made to the beneficiary of the charity and is made in the course of carrying out the purposes of the charity.

- The loan is made for the benefit of the charity and is not for the avoidance of tax.

HMRC has confirmed that generally social investments made by a charity acting within its objectives would be qualifying expenditure. However, for both charitable investors and others this is a technical area and, as discussed in Chapter 8, the authors recommend that tax advice be taken when considering making any social investment.

10.10
Social enterprise

Social enterprise is often linked to social investment. Social enterprise is currently going through a 'honeymoon period'. As with social investment, it remains to be seen whether the claims of its supporters will see it emerge as a 'new way to do business'.

Charities that trade have been running social enterprises for hundreds of years. This section looks at social enterprise from the perspective of a charity wishing to move on from a subsidiary trading company to setting up a separate legal entity engaging in a form of social business.

We explore briefly the legal and tax implications before looking at capital investment appraisal methods to evaluate whether to invest in a separate social enterprise.

10.11
Legal structures and tax issues

The concept of a trading subsidiary for a charity is well known and well established, and has been covered previously. However, a social enterprise can take on a variety of legal forms, some of which have been created in the last few years. The issues of how to capitalise and finance a separate entity are also the same as for any trading venture that a charity wishes to set up but the focus on profit and paying back 'equity holders' provides some additional complexities.

As well as the regular company limited by shares and guarantee and the CIO (charitable incorporated organisation), a legal form of constitution that has seen year-on-year growth of 20 per cent is the CIC (Community Interest Company). These are limited companies with special additional features and have been specifically created for social enterprises. They can be limited by guarantee or shares. They must be conducted for the community benefit but the test is far less onerous than the public benefit requirement for a charity. The other special features are an 'asset lock' and the concept of limited return. It should be noted that a CIC cannot have a political purpose and cannot be a charity. There is a separate CIC regulator.

The asset lock is designed to deal with the issue of equity involvement and provide a cap on what capital and dividends can be taken out of the CIC while retaining assets for the community benefit. Rules about the asset lock are currently in place but these are under review and, as with all legal structuring, professional advice should be taken.

As an alternative to a CIC, there is also the possibility of registering a social enterprise as an industrial and provident society. These can be created as either a 'cooperative', where the benefit is principally to the members, or as a community benefit model, where the business is created for the benefit of the community. It should be noted that it is also possible to get charitable status, as well as an asset lock applying.

In relation to taxation, social enterprises are not charities and currently do not have the same exemptions, however, there is an on-going consultation on a proposal to grant tax reliefs.

10.12
Financial appraisal

There are a variety of business forms a social enterprise can take, which all require investment – whether a loan from a bank, internal investment from the charity or applying for finance through a social bond. Irrespective of which source of finance is sought, a business plan needs to be prepared. The format of the business plan is virtually identical to a business plan for a bank loan and should cover the following areas.

1. Executive summary
2. Background of organisation
3. Management/governance – trading subsidiary or CIC
4. Services to be offered
5. The market (competition)
6. Method of operation
7. Marketing plan
8. Implementation/timetable
9. Finance
10. Future prospects

This section looks at point 9 – finance. A cash flow budget should always be prepared, which will show anticipated cash in and cash out (this important but relatively simple statement has been covered – see Chapter 3). Understanding financial analysis and viability including risk (also covered – see Chapter 5) is also important. Forecast profit and loss accounts and balance sheets will need to be prepared for up to five years ahead. This will require considerable input using a variety of forecasting techniques based on service pricing (point 5), operational costs (point 5) and market analysis (point 7). One key aspect, particularly if a charity is considering investing its own funds in a new enterprise, is to understand the cost of capital in how to appraise a business opportunity.

Financial analysis, viability and risk

Investment appraisal techniques, such as payback methods and the use of discounted cash flow, are commonly used in the private sector and can be directly transferred to appraise whether to invest in a social enterprise. Clearly, such techniques cannot be used in isolation from other issues, such as governance, ethical considerations and social objectives; however, the bottom line is to make at least a return on capital invested, if not a profit, so quantitative appraisal techniques are vital in aiding decision making. The following sections explore simple payback method, average rate of return method and the effects of inflation.

Payback method
Payback method takes the perspective that the commitment of funds to a project involves two things: the sacrificing of funds to other uses for the duration of the project and the risk that the money committed may be permanently lost. The principal determinant of payback is 'time' and how long management is willing to commit to that project before the initial investment is returned.

For example, a charity is considering investing in a social enterprise, which will cost £100,000. The charity believes the enterprise will make the following Gift Aid back to the charity:

Year	Gift Aid £
1	0
2	15,000
3	25,000
4	35,000
5	50,000
6	60,000

The trustees have a policy that they will approve investment proposals if initial cost is repaid within four years. Should the project proceed?

Answer:

Year	Cumulative return £
1	0
2	15,000
3	40,000
4	75,000
5	125,000
6	185,000

By year 5 the enterprise more than repays the development investment and is making a positive return to the charity. However, it fails to meet the trustees' policy of payback in four years and should either not proceed or the trustees should be asked to reconsider their decision. A social enterprise is similar to a venture capital start company and may well take many more years than normal charity projects to show a positive return.

The payback method has the advantage that it is easy to understand, simple to apply and promotes a prudent approach to decision making, which is particularly important to trustees. The principal disadvantages are that it could reject a potentially lucrative project just because the initial outlay is high relative to the timed return. These disadvantages could prove damaging, for example, by the sixth year the charity would have seen a return in total over the six years of £185,000.

Average rate of return

To resolve the limitations of the payback technique, this method recognises profitability and that it must relate to the amount of capital invested and to the period for which it is required. This requires an organisation to determine a cost of capital from which they will evaluate a project. For trustees seeking to tie up medium-term funds (say five years), a useful cost of capital would be the return on a government five-year stock or long-term cash. Let us assume this is currently 2 per cent. Using the above example the method to calculate this is as follows.

Determine the total cash inflow given by the project:	
In our example this is:	£125,000
Then deduct the original investment:	£100,000
Leaving:	£25,000

This is the amount the project earns over the five years of its life and is therefore equivalent to:

£25,000/5 = £5,000 per annum.

The amount invested in the enterprise was initially £100,000. To calculate the return:

£5000/100,000 x 100 = 5%

This exceeds the current return from the traditional 'risk-free' investment. The project has both repaid the initial cost during the period and made a profit. However, there are no guarantees that you will get your money back.

The disadvantage of the average rate of return method is that it does not allow for the time value of money and the issue of inflation.

Discounted cash flow (DCF)

This is a technique that takes into account issues concerning the time value of money and the problem of inflation (£1 today will be worth less than £1 in a year's time), the total return and the timing of cash flows to when investment will be returned. Recognising the time value of money is done by using discount tables: (available at: www.financingcp. org/docs/CP3_NPVTable.pdf), which set the factor to be used for any interest rate from 1 per cent upwards and from one year onwards. The following example illustrates this using the 5 per cent rate of return wanted:

The present value at year 5 is £103,210, which is £3,210 more than the £100,000 requested, and at year 6 substantially more. At year 4 the trustees' original time forecast the project should not go ahead at 5 per cent return. Leaving the money in a 'safe' investment at 2 per cent is worse, as it would lose money because of inflation, which is running at higher than 2 per cent.

The other issue to consider is the investment risk and return. Currently the social enterprise is offering an additional 3 per cent return – is it worth the risk? The conceptual superiority of DCF means that risk factors can also be factored into any equation and project appraisal.

Year	Cash inflow £	Discount factor 5% from table	Present value £
1	0	0.952	0
2	15,000	0.907	13,605
3	25,000	0.864	21,600
4	35,000	0.823	28,805
5	50,000	0.784	39,200
Total present value of project			103,210
6	60,000	0.746	44,760

Exercise

The trustees of a charity are considering offering a community transport scheme through a separate CIC in a rural area where there is limited public transport. Two business plans have been prepared based on an investment of £80,000. The first plan involves tickets being sold through vouchers to be reclaimed from the local authority. The second plan is based purely on cash but there is the possibility that the local authority may decide to offer their own transport scheme at some point, which would mean that revenues would dramatically fall.

Plan 1	
Year	Income £
1	15,000
2	25,000
3	30,000
4	40,000
5	40,000

Plan 2	
Year	Income £
1	40,000
2	40,000
3	30,000
4	25,000
5	5,000

In option 1, the respective cash flows show time-delayed payments by the local authority until fully running. In option 2, the decline in income makes the assumption that a local authority competitor enters the market.

Assess the merits of each scheme and other factors to consider, using a rate of 7 per cent for:

1. payback method

2. average rate of return

3. DCF.

Answer

1. Payback method

Year	Scheme 1 Amount repaid £	Scheme 2 Amount repaid £
1	15,000	40,000
2	40,000	80,000
3	70,000	
4	110,000	

The second scheme repays the investment in two years; the first scheme does not do so until year 4.

2. Average rate of return

	Scheme 1 £	Scheme 2 £
Total cash inflow	150,000	140,000
Investment	80,000	80,000
Profit	70,000	60,000
Divided by life of project – 5 years	14,000	12,000
Rate of return	17.5%	15%

Both schemes produce a very positive rate of return.

3. DCF

Scheme 1			
Year	Cash inflow £	Discount factor 7%	Present value £
1	15,000	0.935	14,025
2	25,000	0.873	21,825
3	30,000	0.816	24,480
4	40,000	0.763	30,520
5	40,000	0.713	28,520
Total present value of scheme 1			119,370

Scheme 2			
Year	Cash inflow £	Discount factor 7%	Present value £
1	40,000	0.935	37,400
2	40,000	0.873	34,920
3	30,000	0.816	24,480
4	25,000	0.763	19,075
5	5,000	0.713	3,565
Total present value of scheme 2			119,440

Summary

Although on the average rate of return and in total cash the first scheme makes a better return, the second scheme is less risky with a shorter payback. Under DCF Scheme 2 also has a slightly better net present value. A charity would normally go for scheme 1 and a commercial organisation for scheme 2. The question is how social versus enterprise would the board wish to be and does the return adequately compensate for the risk to be taken?

10.13
Conclusion

It is difficult to offer a conclusion on a topic that is still in its early stages of development. This chapter has demonstrated that, although the concept of social investment and legal forms for social enterprise are relatively new, the concepts and practices are, for the most part, relatively traditional.

The growing importance of social investment is reflected in the Charities SORP consultation process, which dedicates an entire module to its treatment.

It will be interesting to watch how the sector develops. Social investment may, in the long term, bring much-needed financing into the charitable and social enterprise area, but it may also be a case of the old parable of 'the emperor's new clothes'.

Further reading and resources

There are some excellent books on different aspects of voluntary sector finance. However, all editions that cover accounting matters will need to be updated for Charities SORP 2015.

Accounting and investment firms have charity mailing lists that provide up-to-date briefings on accounting, regular newsletters and updates on relevant issues, such as the budget, and how they affect charities.

Two academic journals cover charity finance issues:

1. *Financial Accountability and Management*

2. *Public Money, CIPFA.*

Three commercial magazines cover charity financial issues online and in print:

1. *Charity Finance*

2. *Charity Times*

3. *Third Sector.*

Most resources are now online – the following websites provide free and paid-for publications relevant to the sector.

- Charity Commission: www.charity-commission.gov.uk
- NCVO: www.ncvo.org.uk
- HM Revenue and Customs: www.hmrc.gov.uk/charities
- VAT (frequently asked questions, guides from customs and excise with useful links): www.hmrc.gov.uk/vat/index.htm
- Charity Finance Group: www.cfg.org.uk
- The Honorary Treasurers Forum: www.honorarytreasurers.org.uk
- KnowHow NonProfit: www.knowhownonprofit.org
- Directory of Social Change: www.dsc.org.uk
- Bond: for international development: www.bond.org.uk
- Social Enterprise UK: www.socialenterprise.org.uk
- Association of Chief Executives of Voluntary Organisations (ACEVO): www.acevo.org.uk

- Association of Charitable Foundations (ACF): www.acf.org.uk
- The Association of Charitable Organisations (ACO): www.aco.uk.net
- Institute of Fundraising: www.institute-of-fundraising.org.uk
- Centre for Charity Effectiveness, at Cass Business School: www.cass.city.ac.uk/research-and-faculty/centres/cass-centre-for-charity-effectiveness
- New Philanthropy Capital (NPC): www.thinknpc.org
- Institute of Chartered Accountants: Scotland: www.icas.org.uk
- Institute of Chartered Accountants: England and Wales: www.icaew.com
- Institute of Chartered Accountants: Ireland: www.charteredaccountants.ie
- Chartered Institute of Public Finance and Accountancy (CIPFA): www.cipfa.org
- Association of Chartered Certified Accountants (ACCA): www.accaglobal.co.uk
- Chartered Institute of Management Accountants (CIMA): www.cimaglobal.com

For more information on NCVO publications visit www.ncvo.org.uk.

Glossary

Accounting systems
The series of tasks and records of an organisation that process transactions are processed as a means of maintaining financial records.

Activity classification of costs
The aggregation of costs incurred in pursuit of a defined activity (such as the provision of services to elderly people or counselling) and is achieved by adding together all the costs (salaries, rents, depreciation etc) relating to that specific activity.

Annual report and accounts
A set of statements that may comprise the trustees' report and the charity's financial statements.

Audit threshold
The threshold (which may include income, expenditure and asset limits) above which, a charity will be required to have a statutory audit.

Balanced score card
A management method that seeks to find a balance between financial results, customer satisfaction, process performance and competence level.

Branches
Branches (also known as supporters' groups, friends' groups, members' groups etc) are entities or administrative bodies set up, for example, to conduct a particular aspect of the activities of the reporting charity, or to conduct the activities of the reporting charity in a particular geographical area. They may or may not be legal entities that are separate from the reporting charity.

Breakeven point
The level of activity at which there is neither a surplus nor a deficit: total income equates to total cost.

Budget
A quantitative statement, for a defined period of time, which may include planned income, expenses, assets, liabilities and cash flows. A budget provides a focus for the organisation, helps the coordination of activities and facilitates control.

Budget forecast
A prediction of future income and expenditure or receipts and payments for the purpose of preparing budgets.

Budget profiling
The assignment of annual income and expenditure figures to relevant months in the year when the income or expenditure is likely to be receivable or incurred.

Budget variances
The difference, for each expense or income element in a budget, between the budgeted amount and the actual expense or income.

Budget worksheets
Standard templates used for the preparation, update and consolidation of budgets, often produced using a spreadsheet package.

Budgetary control
The establishment of budgets relating the responsibility of individuals or departments to the requirements of a financial policy, and the continuous comparison of actual with budgeted results.

Charity
Any institution established for purposes that are exclusively charitable.

Charity bond
A simple, fixed-income investment product that is similar in structure to any standard corporate or government bond where the borrower enters into a formal contract with investors to repay a loan at maturity, with interest paid at fixed intervals over the life of the bond. The bond itself can be issued as either secured or unsecured debt. The payment of interest and repayment of capital is not tied to specific social outcomes as it would be for a social impact bond. (Source Triodos Bank)

Charity trustees
People who have general control and management of the administration of a charity, regardless of what they are called (for example, directors or governors).

Conflict of interest policy
A statement that seeks to identify instances when the judgement of trustees of a charity may be unduly influenced by their connections with other persons or bodies.

Controllable costs
Costs that can be influenced by the budget holder.

Cost accounting
The establishment of budgets, standard costs and actual costs of operations, processes, activities or products; and the analysis of variances and social use of funds.

Cost centre
A service location, function or activity for which costs are accumulated.

Costs of generating voluntary income
The costs actually incurred by a charity, or agent, in inducing others to make gifts to it that are voluntary income.

Current liabilities
Liabilities that fall due for payment within one year.

Direct cost
Expenditure that can be identified and specifically measured in respect of a relevant activity.

Emolument
A salary, fee or benefit from employment or office.

Endowment funding
A special type of fund that must normally be retained intact and not spent (some endowments are restricted and permanent, while others are unrestricted and expendable).

Equities
Shares in a company; equity shares normally entitle the holder to a dividend and are traded on an exchange.

Exempt supplies (VAT)
Supplies that do not attract VAT, but where no input tax is repayable.

External environment
Key factors that have their origins outside the voluntary organisation but may affect its activities and the fulfilment of charitable objectives.

Extra-statutory concession
The practice of HMRC of allowing certain minor items to avoid tax, even though they are taxable under a strict interpretation of the law. This is normally done to avoid a multitude of disputes about trivial amounts.

Financial procedures manual
A document outlining the key responsibilities of trustees, management and staff, and the controls in place to regulate financial activity.

Governance
A function of trustee boards or director boards that are concerned with the fulfilment of strategic objectives.

Governance costs
Costs associated with the governance arrangements of the charity that relate to the general running of the charity, as opposed to those costs associated with fundraising or charitable activity. The costs will normally include internal and external audit, legal advice for trustees and costs associated with constitutional and statutory requirements and strategic advice.

Governing document
The instrument that defines the reasons why the charity exists and how it is to conduct its internal affairs; it may be in the form of a written constitution, memorandum and articles of association or deed.

Grant
Any voluntary payment (or other transfer of property) in favour of a person or institution.

Income
Money that the organisation is legally entitled to receive. The accounting records will recognise this by recording an entry as soon as legal entitlement exists. It should be distinguished from receipts, which are recorded when the money is actually received.

Incremental budgeting
A method of budgeting that uses the previous period's results and inflates these by a fixed amount, for example, to account for increase in retail prices.

Indirect costs
Expenditure on labour, materials or services that cannot be directly identified with a specific activity.

Input tax (VAT)
The tax paid by the organisation on goods and services purchased. It is offset against output tax and the balance paid over to, or reclaimed from, HMRC.

Internal audit
An independent appraisal function established with an organisation to examine and evaluate its activities as a service to the organisation. Its object is to help members of the organisation to discharge their responsibilities effectively.

Investment assets
Assets held by a charity for the purpose of deriving income and/or capital growth, for example, property and equity shares.

Investment policy
A statement that defines the objectives for holding investments; it will include details of what type of investments are to be held, in what proportions and the expected returns.

Investment portfolio
A basket of investment assets held collectively with the intention of reducing the risk that would arise if these assets were held separately.

Irrecoverable VAT
The proportion of VAT that is incurred and relates to non-business activities and therefore cannot be reclaimed.

Joint venture
A project undertaken by two or more persons or entities joining together with a view to profit, often in connection with a single operation.

Liquid assets
Cash and other assets readily convertible into cash, for example, short-term investments.

Liquidity
A condition in which assets are held in a cash or near-cash form.

Longitudinal study
Research that follows a selected number of individuals or organisations for an extended period.

Mission
The fundamental principles by which an organisation exists and operates.

Non-profit organisations
Any organisation that has a primary objective not exclusively orientated towards the maximisation of wealth for its owners and/or profit. This need not be a registered charity.

Outcomes
Used in performance measurement. Outcomes or impacts are difficult to identify and measure, but might be considered as the desired end results from the outputs of the organisation. However, it can be difficult to prove that a cause-and-effect relationship exists.

Outputs
Not always measured in money terms, but they represent some delivery, service or result of special interest.

Outsourcing
The buying in from a third party of services or goods that had previously been produced internally. The day-to-day management of the process is also delegated to the third party.

Output tax (VAT)
The VAT due on taxable supplies made by the organisation.

Relevant costs
Costs appropriate to a specific management decision.

Reserves
Income available to be spent at the trustees' discretion in furtherance of the charity's objects, which is not yet spent, committed or designated, in other words – 'free' reserves.

Restricted fund
A fund subject to specific trusts within the objects of the charity (for example, by a letter from the donor at the time of the gift or by the terms of a public appeal). It may be a capital fund that cannot be spent but must be retained for the benefit of the charity or an income fund that must be spent on the specified purpose within a reasonable time.

Revolving loan
A loan fund that relies on organisations repaying loans they have taken out. The loan repayments are then used to make loans on to other organisations. Organisations investing in these loan funds will participate in the down side of the loan not being repaid but receive a social return by seeing their funds recycled and used again.

Shareholder value
The maximisation of economic value for shareholders, as measured by share-price performance and flow of dividends.

Social impact bond
Bonds based on a commitment from government to use a proportion of the savings that result from improved social outcomes to reward non-government investors that fund the early intervention activities. The form of the special purpose vehicle set up to deliver this can vary and can involve a combination of loans and equity.

Stakeholders
Any group of people (either internal to the charity or not) or external organisations that may be affected by the decisions and policies of the charity.

Standard rate of VAT
The main rate of VAT (currently 20 per cent) on the cost of goods or services.

Static budget
The original budget that has been approved by the trustees and is not changed to reflect changes in the underlying assumptions used to prepare the budget or inaccurate forecasts.

Strategic planning
The formulation, evaluation and selection of strategies for the purpose of preparing a long-term plan of action to attain objectives.

Support costs
Costs that, while necessary to deliver an activity, do not themselves produce or constitute the output of the charitable activity. Similarly, costs will be incurred in supporting income generation activities, such as fundraising, and in supporting the governance of the charity.

Taxable person (VAT)
An individual or organisation etc that is, or ought to be, registered for VAT because their taxable supplies are above the current limit.

Tax point (VAT)
The date at which a taxable supply of goods is treated as taking place.

Taxable supplies
Supplies made in the UK that are not specifically exempted.

Treasury management
The handling of all financial matters, the generation of external and internal funds for an organisation and the management of currencies and cash flows.

Trustee board
A collective body of trustees responsible in law for the activities of the charity, whether officially designated as trustees or not.

VAT (value added tax)
A tax collected by HMRC charged on supplies of goods and services.

Vendorism
The practice of charging fees for the provision of services or activities that the organisation exists to supply.

Venturing
Non-related commercial activities with the sole rationale to raise money for the agency.

Virement
The authority to apply savings under one sub-head of a budget to meet excesses on others.

Working capital
The capital available for conducting the day-to-day operations of an organisation; normally, the excess of current assets over current liabilities.

Zero-based budgeting
A method of budgeting that requires each cost element to be specifically justified as though the activities to which the budget relates were being undertaken for the first time. Without approval, the budget allowance is zero.

Zero rate of VAT
A supply that is taxable but the rate is 0 per cent. Relevant VAT on the inputs can be reclaimed.

Notes